We believe in one God,
the Father, the Almighty,
maker of heaven and earth,
of all that is seen and unseen.

NICENE CREED

There is no mystery in heaven or earth
so great as this—a suffering Deity,
an almighty Savior nailed to the Cross.

SAMUEL M. ZWEMER

Human history seems always to be without God.
Yet God's will and working run through everything.
Ultimately His will is done.

CHRISTOPH BLUMHARDT

There is only one question which is really serious,
and that is the question concerning the being
and nature of God. From this all other questions
derive their significance.

EMIL BRUNNER

God himself is present,
not in weakness that permits men to suffer
without hope and perspective,
but in the sovereignty of his love.

KARL BARTH

Other books by Donald G. Bloesch

CENTERS OF CHRISTIAN RENEWAL

THE CHRISTIAN LIFE AND SALVATION

THE CRISIS OF PIETY

THE CHRISTIAN WITNESS IN A SECULAR AGE

CHRISTIAN SPIRITUALITY EAST AND WEST *(coauthor)*

THE REFORM OF THE CHURCH

THE GROUND OF CERTAINTY

SERVANTS OF CHRIST *(editor)*

THE EVANGELICAL RENAISSANCE

WELLSPRINGS OF RENEWAL

LIGHT A FIRE

THE INVADED CHURCH

JESUS IS VICTOR! KARL BARTH'S DOCTRINE OF SALVATION

THE ORTHODOX EVANGELICALS *(coeditor)*

ESSENTIALS OF EVANGELICAL THEOLOGY, VOL. 1: GOD, AUTHORITY, AND SALVATION

ESSENTIALS OF EVANGELICAL THEOLOGY, VOL. 2: LIFE, MINISTRY, AND HOPE

THE STRUGGLE OF PRAYER

FAITH AND ITS COUNTERFEITS

IS THE BIBLE SEXIST?

THE FUTURE OF EVANGELICAL CHRISTIANITY

CRUMBLING FOUNDATIONS

THE BATTLE FOR THE TRINITY

A HERMENEUTICS OF ULTIMACY: PERIL OR PROMISE? *(coauthor)*

FREEDOM FOR OBEDIENCE

THEOLOGICAL NOTEBOOK VOL. 1

THEOLOGICAL NOTEBOOK VOL. 2

A THEOLOGY OF WORD & SPIRIT

HOLY SCRIPTURE

· CHRISTIAN FOUNDATIONS ·

GOD
THE
ALMIGHTY

POWER, WISDOM, HOLINESS, LOVE

DONALD G. BLOESCH

INTERVARSITY PRESS
DOWNERS GROVE, ILLINOIS 60515

InterVarsity Press® is the book-publishing division of InterVarsity Christian Fellowship®, a student movement active on campus at hundreds of universities, colleges and schools of nursing in the United States of America, and a member movement of the International Fellowship of Evangelical Students. For information about local and regional activities, write Public Relations Dept., InterVarsity Christian Fellowship, 6400 Schroeder Rd., P.O. Box 7895, Madison, WI 53707-7895.

Scripture quotations, unless otherwise noted, are from the Revised Standard Version of the Bible, copyright 1946, 1952, 1971 by the Division of Christian Education of the National Council of the Churches of Christ in the U.S.A., and are used by permission.

Cover illustration: Guy Wolek

ISBN 0-8308-1413-2

Printed in the United States of America ∞

Library of Congress Cataloging-in-Publication Data

Bloesch, Donald G., 1928-
    God, the Almighty: power, wisdom, holiness, love/Donald G.
  Bloesch.
        p.   cm.—(Christian foundations)
    Includes bibliographical references and index.
    ISBN 0-8308-1413-2 (cloth: alk. paper)
    1. God—Attributes.   I. Title.   II. Series: Bloesch, Donald G.,
  1928-   Christian foundations.
  BT130.B54   1995
  231'.4—dc20   95-40450
                                                              CIP

17	16	15	14	13	12	11	10	9	8	7	6	5	4	3	2	1
09	08	07	06	05	04	03	02	01	00	99	98	97	96	95		

*Dedicated to the
memory of Karl Barth &
Emil Brunner*

Acknowledgments

I am deeply grateful to my wife Brenda for her painstaking work in editing this manuscript; to Mary Anne Knefel and Susan Ebertz of the University of Dubuque Seminary library for their generous assistance in locating important books; to my former teachers Daniel Day Williams and Bernard E. Meland for introducing me to process philosophy and theology, against which I have sought to forge a viable biblical alternative; to my colleague Arthur C. Cochrane for his devastating critique of existentialism; to Mark Achtemeier of Dubuque Theological Seminary and Winston Persaud of Wartburg Theological Seminary for their perceptive comments on models of the Trinity; to Elmer Colyer of Dubuque Seminary for his assistance in understanding Torrance's view of the Trinity; to William Barrett, an alumnus of Dubuque Seminary and now a United Methodist pastor, for his insightful paper on the doctrine of God in Thomas Aquinas and Karl Barth; and to my nephew David Bloesch for his helpful suggestions regarding illustrations for the Trinity. I also wish to thank James Mark Kushiner for granting me permission to include parts of my article "Salt and Light" (previously published in *Touchstone,* Fall 1992) under the section heading "The Call to Holiness" in chapter six; and the Hope Publishing Company in Carol Stream, Ill. (60188), for allowing me to quote from Brian Wren's celebrated hymn, "Bring Many Names" (copyright 1989).

Abbreviations for Biblical Translations

AAT	An American Translation (Smith–Goodspeed)
GNB	Good News Bible
GNC	God's New Covenant
JB	Jerusalem Bible
KJV	King James Version
LB	Living Bible
NASB	New American Standard Bible
NEB	New English Bible
NIV	New International Version
NJB	New Jerusalem Bible
NKJ	New King James Version
NRSV	New Revised Standard Version
REB	Revised English Bible

(Note: Bible references not otherwise indicated are from the Revised Standard Version.)

Preface

This Christian Foundations series is addressed to the whole church—primarily for the purpose of healing wounds and building bridges. But I also intend to show where bridges cannot be built. Reaching out in love must not be a pretext for sacrificing the integrity of the faith. We must strive to be ecumenical and evangelical at the same time—reaching out to the whole church but remaining solidly anchored in the gospel.

A work of this kind will necessarily have a polemical thrust. I sternly oppose those who would make God culpable for human misery (such as Herman Hoeksema and Ronald Goetz). God is not the creator of sin; sin is the free act of disobedience to God. I also take exception to the finite God of process theology, which portrays God as struggling along with the creature for self-realization. In addition I wish to counter the inveterate tendency in so much traditional theology to make God remote from the human creation. We see this aberration in Arianism, Monarchianism and deism.

We are living in an age bedeviled by a crisis of truth. The historicist, relativist mentality of our times disputes the traditional Christian as well as Hellenistic notion that there is such a thing as absolute truth. We deconstruct rather than construct and thereby end without any sure and certain compass to guide us.

Hand in hand with the crisis of truth is a crisis of faith in which the act of faith is divorced from conceptual knowledge. Faith becomes a leap in the dark rather than a perduring grasp of certainties set forth in Holy Scripture. Faith is more a struggle for certainty than a venture of obedience on the basis of certainty.

My theological stance could be designated as centrist evangelical in the sense of remaining in continuity with the message of Holy Scripture and the wisdom of sacred tradition. Being centrist must not be confused with taking the middle road between fundamentalism and liberalism. It embraces the truth in both camps and negates the untruth in these positions as well. Being a centrist evangelical means building upon the center or core of the faith—the gospel of God's reconciling act in Jesus Christ attested in Holy Scripture and clarified by the fathers and teachers of the faith through the ages. But whereas the fathers and teachers are fallible, the Word of God in Holy Scripture is infallible. Yet this Word is not a propositional formula at human disposal but the reaching out of the hand of God upon the human heart and conscience.

I readily acknowledge foundations of the faith without being a foundationalist in the technical sense. The view of foundationalism is that our basic beliefs—the premises that undergird the way we look at the world—are unalterable, incorrigible and indubitable. But only God's Word is beyond alteration and correction and is absolutely certain, and God's Word can never be identified with our limited interpretations and articulations. The foundation for Christian faith is not a timeless principle but a personal address. It is not a self-evident truth but the personification of truth in Jesus Christ.

I am a foundationalist in the loose rather than the strict sense. While not holding to a priori, self-evident principles that reside in the human mind (as in Cartesianism), I do affirm the intractable reality of the living God, which constitutes the irrevocable foundation. Yet this foundation is outside the purview of human reason and imagination. It is one that we are beginning to know by faith, not one we already possess as the substructure of human knowledge.

Today it is fashionable to distinguish between modern and postmodern, the latter indicating the collapse of the universal norms and self-evident truths associated with the Enlightenment.[1] Postmodernism might be regarded as a new form of Romanticism that stresses the particular over the universal, the imaginative over the theoretical, the mystical over the rational. It can be shown that the seeds of pluralism and relativism characteristic of the current period were already present in the Renaissance and the Enlightenment, that postmodernity is really a new phase of modernity.[2]

I wish to be neither modern nor postmodern nor even premodern, but instead a dialectical critic of modernity and postmodernity.[3] Blithely returning to past positions, such as the consensus of the early church or the creeds and confessions of the Reformation or Counter-Reformation, is a false path that can only further isolate theology from the currents of thought and life in the present. We must take our stand within the modern ethos, since this is our cultural inheritance, but rigorously critique it in the light of the transcendent gospel of God. Our approach should be dialectical in the sense of trying to hold together polar opposites but moving beyond them to the synthesis given by the living Word of God. We should affirm what is just and true in the Enlightenment and Romanticism but negate what is pretentious and idolatrous. We should be prophets to the age in which we live rather than voices of a past age that may well be discredited by history. One should keep in mind that the religious imperialism rampant in seventeenth-century Catholicism and Protestantism paved the way for the not surprisingly severe reaction of the Enlightenment, which stressed peace and tolerance over religious fanaticism. Predictably, this reforming zeal did not prevent the Enlightenment from engendering new fanaticisms, such as the French Revolution.

I regard this particular volume, which is centered on the doctrine of God, as perhaps the most important in this series. Any cursory examination of academic theology today will reveal a mounting controversy over the concept of God. The current emphases are not altogether unbiblical, but they are irremediably imbalanced. God is portrayed as vulnerable (Jürgen Moltmann, Clark Pinnock), as lover (Norman Pittenger, Ronald Goetz), as friend (Alfred North Whitehead, Sallie McFague), as empowerer (Rosemary Radford Ruether). What is lacking in so many instances is a strong affirmation of the holiness and almightiness of God.

God is not simply *with* us and *in* us, but he is also *against* us and *over* us. He is judge as well as savior, master as well as friend, transcendent as well as immanent. Without returning to the equally unsatisfactory portrayal of God as absolute power, I shall try to hold in dialectical tension the polarities that are reflected in God's nature and activity—his majesty as well as his vulnerability, his sovereignty as well as his grace, his wholly otherness as well as his unsurpassable closeness, his holiness as well as his love.

I shall endeavor to state the case for a biblical theism that must be radically differentiated from classical theism (which in its Christian form unites classical and biblical themes), from pantheism (which dissolves the lines of demarcation between God and the world) and from panentheism (which tries to preserve a distinction between God and the world within a higher unity). While atheism and agnosticism continue to be live options for many people today, the contemporary climate has an unmistakable panentheistic and pantheistic hue, and I shall try to counter these misconceptions in particular.

Some who are committed to the faith of Nicaea and Chalcedon might wonder why I do not begin this volume with an excursus on the doctrine of the Trinity. I think the biblical way is to deal first with the mystery of God's self-revelation in Jesus Christ and then find in this revelation allusions to the Trinity. The doctrine of the Trinity did not emerge in the consciousness of the church until the church was able to grasp both the inseparability and necessary distinction between God and Jesus Christ. In contrast to liberal theology, such as we find in Schleiermacher, I do not set out to present a case for the god of ethical monotheism and then insert the Trinity as an appendage. But neither do I begin with an abstract concept of the Trinity and then try to relate this to biblical revelation. My intention is to begin with the living God of biblical faith and then reflect upon this God as a Trinity.

My principal mentors in this particular study are Karl Barth, Emil Brunner and Reinhold Niebuhr. These theologians more than most others have detected the dangers of a too-ready accommodation of biblical faith to Greek ontology and have sought to preserve the unique stance of biblical spirituality. I also acknowledge among my mentors such luminaries of Reformation theology as Martin Luther and John Calvin. I do not accept any of these men uncritically, since my final standard of authority is Holy Scripture, not church tradition.

My foils in this study include Paul Tillich, Alfred North Whitehead, Charles Hartshorne, Henry Nelson Wieman, Schubert Ogden, Bernard Meland, John Cobb and Rosemary Ruether. These scholars illustrate the dawning of a new mysticism, a mysticism of the earth and history, which is to be carefully distinguished from the otherworldly mysticism fostered by Platonism and Neoplatonism. This new stance is less mystical than vitalistic, less idealistic than naturalistic, less monistic than pluralistic. I find in process theology in particular a formidable challenge to the traditional ways of understanding God. I pay tribute to these scholars for prodding me to redefine the Christian doctrine of God in the face of the emergence of a new worldview.

My problems in this study are with Jürgen Moltmann, Wolfhart Pannenberg, Karl Rahner, Augustine and Thomas Aquinas, among others. All these theologians have sought to stand within the tradition of Christian thought and experience and yet maintain a fruitful openness to the philosophies that have shaped the thought-world of their age. Their goal is to be biblical and philosophical at the same time, and this accounts for some of the ambiguities in their positions. Nevertheless, I confess to having benefited from their profound insights on this critical issue in the church.

I also have difficulties with so-called progressive evangelicals like Clark Pinnock, John Sanders and Richard Rice, with whom I share many of the same concerns. I am at one with them in trying to disengage biblical insights from the ontological categories of Hellenism. These scholars are challenging because they present a view of God's relationship to the world that breaks decisively with traditional Christian theism, appealing both to the Bible and to practical human wisdom and experience. They are disturbing because they seem to be accommodating the faith to the ethos of modernity with its emphasis on human responsibility, creativity, democratic consensus and an open future. Their "free will theism" appears at times to be perilously close to process theism, but their God is clearly superior in power to the process god and resonates more deeply with biblical themes.[4]

My friends in this study include Søren Kierkegaard, P. T. Forsyth, Anders Nygren, Hans Urs von Balthasar, Eberhard Jüngel and Thomas Torrance. I also discern marked affinities with Athanasius and Irenaeus. A theologian like Augustine is both a friend and a problem in that his overtly biblical stance is counterbalanced by a profound indebtedness to Platonism and Neoplatonism, which from my point of view stand in diametrical opposition to the insights and affirmations of biblical faith.

Finally I wish to acknowledge my gratitude to former teachers who were decisive influences in my theological pilgrimage: Daniel Day Williams, Bernard Meland, Daniel Jenkins, James Hastings Nichols, J. Coert Rylaarsdam, Wilhelm Pauck, Jaroslav Pelikan and Charles Hartshorne. I must, of course, include Karl Barth, whose seminars I attended on my first sabbatical from Dubuque Theological Seminary (1963–64), and Arthur C. Cochrane, my esteemed colleague in theology at Dubuque for many years. I have learned from all these men, including those in the process camp. Their patience and tolerance in dealing with a student who frequently took issue with their presuppositions and conclusions will always be appreciated. I have had the privilege of studying under some great minds, thanks to the providence of a God of infinite power and profound loving-kindness. My quest for truth has taken me in a different direction from some of my teachers, but I have benefited positively as well as negatively from their instruction. My doctoral thesis at the University of Chicago was on the theology of Reinhold Niebuhr, and even here I had some difficulty—more with his apologetic method than with his theological conclusions (though differences also emerged in this area). What I appreciated in Niebuhr was his acute discernment that the personal and dramatic categories of biblical faith could not be neatly subsumed under some overarching ontology without doing an injustice to the message of faith. This note will reappear throughout this volume.

·ONE·

INTR○DUCTI○N

We cannot imagine the power of the Almighty,
and yet he is so just and merciful that he does not destroy us.

J O B   3 7 : 2 3   L B

Our God comes and does not keep silence,
before him is a devouring fire, and a mighty tempest all around him.

P S A L M   5 0 : 3   N R S V

God is greater than his laws. He is not tied up by them.
He can act independent of them.

H E N R Y   W A R D   B E E C H E R

That God is love is certainly universally true,
but it is not necessary truth, for He does not have to love us,
nor does He owe it to Himself or to us to love us.

T H O M A S   F .   T O R R A N C E

I t is becoming increasingly clear that a palpably different understanding of God and his relationship to the world is steadily pressing
itself upon the modern consciousness. A new immanentalism is
displacing the transcendentalism that has hitherto characterized both
Catholic and Protestant theology. The emphasis today is not on the
almightiness of God but on his vulnerability. Attention is given to God's
empathy with the world rather than his majesty, his pathos rather than
his infinite beatitude. The idea of a suffering God is supplanting the idea
of an impassible God, vigorously defended in Christian tradition. God is
no longer the infinite supreme being beyond world history but now "the
Infinite in the finite" (Schleiermacher).[1] God is no longer a static Infinite
but now a dynamic Infinite that "emerges" out of the void but also
"rushes in" to fill the void (Sri Aurobindo).[2] God is no longer some

"cosmic person out there" but the mystery of the cosmic process itself.[3]

There is a growing tendency to downplay the personal dimension of God and to reconceive God as an impersonal life force or a suprapersonal ground of being. The vitalist philosopher Henri Bergson envisaged God as "unceasing life, action, freedom."[4] For Hegel, who has a wide influence over contemporary theology, God is an Eternal Idea that unfolds itself in history rather than an almighty King who rules over history. In his view God is not sovereign Creator but eternal creativity. For Spinoza nothing is external to Absolute Being: all is included in the Absolute.

Jürgen Moltmann, who freely acknowledges his indebtedness to Hegel, is critical of classical monotheism, which portrays God as a dictatorial monarch. His stress is on the inseparability of God and creation rather than on God's transcendence over creation. God is not an almighty despot but an all-encompassing Fatherly-Motherly Spirit that upholds us and nurtures us.[5] "What he *is* is not almighty power; what he *is* is love."[6]

Both Moltmann and Wolfhart Pannenberg have been associated with "the theology of hope," which locates transcendence in the future. Transcendence is no longer a spatial but a temporal metaphor connoting the *telos* of history. God becomes the "power of the future" or the "unassuredness of the future." Our hope is not in a transcendent realm beyond history but in the undisclosed possibilities in the unfolding of history.

Process theology propounds the idea of a finite God, who is striving to realize his full potentialities in conjunction with our striving. It is said that God is actually finite but potentially infinite. God is not transcendent over the cosmos but "the supreme Creative and Receptive Spirit of the cosmos" (Hartshorne).[7] Or God is portrayed as "the sensitive Nature" within nature (Bernard Meland). While most process theologians acknowledge personal traits in God, they do not really see God as a person but as an all-embracing superconsciousness. For Henry Nelson Wieman, "If God is . . . creativity, God cannot be a person. Creativity is ontologically prior to personality."[8]

Process thought veers dangerously close to pantheism in which the world process is virtually equated with deity. According to Teilhard de Chardin, "Since God cannot be conceived except as monopolising in himself the totality of being—then either the world is no more than appearance—or else it is in itself a part, an aspect, or a phase of God."[9]

For the most part, process theologians prefer to describe their position as panentheistic rather than pantheistic, since God is not identical with the world but inseparable from it. God is the creative force that moves the world to higher possibilities rather than the sum total of all existents. God is in the world, and the world is in God. It is sometimes said that the world is the body of God and God is the soul of the world (Hartshorne).[10] We have only internal relations with God, not external.[11]

The immanence of God is a dominant motif in the Minjung theology in Korea, which depicts God as "the immanent historical force of the process of humanization."[12] God is not the sovereign creator of the world but the agent of creative change that spurs the world on to a higher degree of justice and equality.

In New Age theology God becomes "a pulsating, inexhaustible cosmic energy," a supraconsciousness that enfolds all things.[13] For Jay McDaniel, "Reality is a verb rather than a noun, a flux rather than a stasis, a process of becoming rather than a state of being."[14] He refers to the mystery of being as a "divine eros" and a "cosmic river."[15] Similarly Matthew Fox speaks of God as "a great underground river" that animates and revitalizes nature.[16] Meinrad Craighead, who reflects both New Age and feminist motifs, calls for a religion "connected to the metamorphoses of nature: the pure potential of water, the transformative power of blood, the seasonal rhythms of the earth, the cycles of lunar dark and light."[17]

In his earlier phase Hans Küng was ready to acknowledge the infinite qualitative gulf between God and creation. The true God "does not belong simply to the world, he is not part of the world: neither as the natural ground of the world nor as world force or world law. He is not merely form, figure and order of reality. He is and remains the wholly

Other."[18] Küng later gravitated toward a panentheistic conception in which God and the world, though distinct, exist in an inseparable unity.[19]

Like Küng, Paul Tillich was anxious to distance himself from a super-naturalism that separates God and finite existence. He affirmed a "God above God," who transcends the polarity of being and nonbeing, infinity and finitude, actuality and potentiality. This is also a God beyond the personal, though it includes the personal within itself. God is not a being over against the world but being–itself, the infinite ground of the world. God is not an infinite person but "creative life" that vitalizes and actu-alizes nature and history. Tillich belongs to the tradition of vitalistic, voluntaristic philosophy represented by Schelling and Nietzsche in which "will is original being."[20] "Being is not a thing; it is not a person; it is will."[21] Tillich also displays a marked affinity to Neoplatonism, which depicts God as the abysmal reality beyond essence and existence.[22] God is not externally related to the world but only internally. Tillich has described his position as "eschatological panentheism" and "ecstatic naturalism."

The new currents of theology (especially process, feminist and lib-erationist) are making a noticeable impact on liturgy and hymnody in the church. The so-called inclusive language hymnals in the main-line denominations carry a significant number of hymns by Brian Wren, for whom God is an essentially nameless being whose mysterious work-ing can nevertheless be illumined by metaphors drawn from human experience. In his hymn "Bring Many Names," after celebrating "strong mother God," "warm father God" and "old, aching God," the author continues:

    Young, growing God, eager, on the move
    saying no to falsehood and unkindness,
    crying out for justice, giving all you have.[23]

God is no longer the majestic and Holy One who inspires awe and worship but the heroic God, the pathfinder and innovator, who elicits both our sympathy and admiration, challenging us to work with him/her in creating a more humane society.[24]

Questionable Alternatives

Much of the reinterpretation of the doctrine of God can be traced to a rising reaction against classical theism—the legacy of Hellenism that has left an indelible imprint on Christian theology. Here God is depicted as immutable, self-contained, all-sufficient, impassible, supremely detached from the world of pain and suffering. How can this kind of God be reconciled with the biblical God who earnestly cares for his people— even to the extent of taking their pain and guilt upon himself in the incarnation and atoning death of his Son? This God is personal but not in the sense that there are reciprocal relations between God and the human creature. Emil Brunner observes, "The thought-of person—say, the idea of God in theistic metaphysics—is not truly personal, because it does not assert itself over against me but is immanent in my thoughts."[25] Though questionable in the light of the total biblical witness, classical theism nevertheless has its defenders and is still a viable theological option today.[26]

Even more suspect from a biblical perspective is pantheism; here God is depicted as the all-embracing reality of which the phenomenal world is only an appearance or manifestation. Pantheism sometimes takes the form of absolute idealism in which the final reality that permeates everything else is mind.[27] Pantheism is a form of monism that conceives of reality as a unified whole. The Renaissance philosopher Giordano Bruno can be considered a pantheist, for he saw God and the infinite universe as the same thing but viewed from two different perspectives. In the seventeenth century Benedict de Spinoza envisioned the world as the necessary expression of God's nature. In our day Grace Jantzen, who espouses a kind of nature mysticism, is willing to identify herself as a pantheist in the broad sense of this word.[28]

Many theologians in the current period are attracted to panentheism, which portrays God and the world as mutually dependent, though still distinct. In Moltmann's view, while monotheism is associated with patriarchy and pantheism with matriarchy, panentheism is correlative with androgyny.[29] Panentheism denies the essential independence of God—

that God exists in himself as a supreme being apart from the world. As biblical Christians we must affirm that God has no fundamental need for the world, that his act of creating the world is gratuitous, not a metaphysical or rational necessity. I have considerable difficulty with Moltmann's asseveration that God really needs "those whom in the suffering of his love he loves unendingly."[30] In panentheism the absoluteness of God is his absolute relatedness to the world. The absolute becomes "the totally relative" (Hartshorne).

Still another unsatisfactory position is deism, which acknowledges God as supreme but totally detached from the world of history and suffering. He has created the world but allows it to operate by its own laws. According to René Descartes, who has aptly been called the father of the Enlightenment, God "after creating the world and setting it in motion according to the laws of geometry and mechanics . . . does not interfere with the mechanical clockwork of the universe."[31] Important representatives of deism in the seventeenth and eighteenth centuries were Lord Herbert of Cherbury, Pierre Charron, John Toland, Samuel Clarke and Voltaire. Deism can be regarded as an aberrant form of classical theism that stresses God's aseity (the idea that God exists from himself) but not his all-surpassing love and infinite tender care. Against this position those of us who identify ourselves as biblical theists contend that God is not only a benevolent Creator and Ruler but also a compassionate Redeemer. He is not only a providential Provider but also Savior and Lord.

Agnosticism is yet another temptation that must be combated. This position is closely associated with the mystical tradition, which portrays God as beyond the rational and the sensible, and the experience of God as ineffable.[32] Eckhart spoke for many mystics when he said, "God who is without name—he has no name—is ineffable; and the soul in its ground is likewise ineffable; just as ineffable as he is."[33] We can be dimly aware of some higher power or force in the universe, but we cannot grasp the nature of this reality. Emerson put it well: "The baffled intellect must still kneel before this cause, which refuses to be named—ineffable cause."[34] The God that cannot be named can only be described by metaphors that elude rational comprehension, such as "the Divine Darkness" and "the Silent Darkness." Agnosticism is also reflected in the critical philosophy of Immanuel Kant, who contended that God cannot be rationally known, but we should act as if he existed in order to give moral meaning to our lives.

Finally, the biblical Christian should resist the temptation of dualism, which draws a bifurcation between God and material reality. In addition to "being" Plato postulated "nonbeing"—a preexistent reality and power out of which God forms the world. For the Gnostics, spiritual reality is entangled in the web of material reality, and the human goal is to discover a point of identity with the spiritual. A dualistic mentality was also evident in Descartes, who held that reality is divided between thought and extension. In the biblical view God or spiritual reality does not preexist with material reality, but the latter is contingent on God's free decision. The world is real, but it is temporal and provisional. Only the living God is unconditionally real.

Against pantheism and panentheism, biblical faith insists that God is unlimited in his power, wisdom and love but not in his being. He has his own time and space. He is a person—not a cosmic energy or all-pervasive presence. The living God is not continuous with nature and humanity but discontinuous. Between God and humanity there is an infinite qualitative difference (Kierkegaard). God upholds and directs the human creation but must never be confused with any part of this creation, even with the highest part. This is why God can validly be referred to as "the Absolutely Different" (Kierkegaard) and "the Wholly Other" (Barth), though these designations become misleading if they are taken only by themselves.

In the early mid-twentieth century the theology of crisis (Barth, Brunner) recovered the sense of the utter transcendence of the living God over his earthly and human creation, though its impact was considerably blunted with the rise of neoliberalism (Bultmann, Tillich, Wieman), which began to dominate the theological world already in the

1950s. Emil Brunner aptly voiced the mood of crisis theology: "Only He who stands free and unhindered above the law of the world, and above the law of thought, is in truth Creator and Lord; and the proof of this His freedom above the law of the world and above the law of thought is His revelation, the 'offence' for thought."[35]

Against classical theism and deism, biblical faith insists that God is life as well as being, that God is free to act in history and does not simply tower above history. God is indeed utterly transcendent, but he is also radically immanent. His immanence is an act of his freedom, not a quality of his being. Just as he freely relates to his creation, so he is also free to withdraw himself from his creation. The God of the Bible is both the Wholly Other and the Infinitely Near. He is both God transcendent and God *with* us and *for* us. God is never immanent without being essentially transcendent, just as he does not remain transcendent without making himself for our sakes immanent.

The God of the Bible does not grow (as in the process view), but he is always in movement. God does not merely exist: he comes. He does not simply think: he acts. The psalmist declares, "The God who loves me is coming, God will show me my enemies defeated" (Ps 59:10 JB). God is not static essence but being in action. He is not a suprapersonal ground of being, nor is he personalized becoming; instead he is being in person who lives and exists by his own power and who freely relates to all contingent beings.

In classical thought God's relation to the world is best described as *detachment*. In modern thought it is conceived of in terms of *identity*. In authentically Christian thought the key word is *identification*: God freely identifies himself with the travail and pain of his human creation. God does not need the world, but he creates the world out of his bountiful grace and remains with the world in its struggle for fulfillment and happiness.

God is other, but he does not remain other. He is powerful, but he is free to withhold as well as to display his power. God is best described not as the Absolutely Other (as in mysticism and existentialism) nor as the Creative Force (as in process thought and New Age religion) but as the majestic Lord and loving Savior (as in biblical religion). While there is an unmistakable masculine cast to biblical religion because of the stress on God's aggressive initiative in creation and redemption, the feminine dimension is by no means neglected but assimilated into the outgoing movement of God.

The Gender Issue

The question of the gender of God is a focal point in contemporary discussion. Feminist and liberationist theologians have challenged the supposed patriarchal bias of traditional theology, asking whether God is not better conceived in androgynous and feminine terms. According to Moltmann, God should be understood no longer along unisexual and patriarchal lines but "bisexually or transexually" (that is, embracing or transcending aspects of both sexes).[36] The kingdom of God is "the kingdom of fatherly and motherly compassion," not "the kingdom of dominating majesty and slavish subjection."[37] Anna Case-Winters sees the womb of the goddess as "a promising image for the God-world relation and for divine power."[38] Hartshorne disavowed the traditional portrayal of God as "all-creative, all-determining Cause . . . influenced by nothing. . . . Much more appropriate is the idea of a mother, influencing, but sympathetic to and hence influenced by, her child and delighting in its growing creativity and freedom."[39] New Age philosopher and mythologist Joseph Campbell called for a return to a mysticism of nature: "You get a totally different way of living according to whether your myth presents nature as fallen or whether nature is itself a manifestation of divinity, and the spirit is the revelation of the divinity that is inherent in nature."[40]

In striking contrast to the deities upheld by the fertility cults of the ancient Mideast, the God of the Bible infinitely transcends human sexuality and gender. And yet since God fashioned man and woman in his own image, we must surmise that gender is not foreign to his nature. His actions create the impression of gender and are so described in the

Bible. He is the ground of both the masculine and the feminine, yet he chooses to relate to us in the form of the masculine—as Lord, Father, Son and so on. God is described in feminine imagery as well, but the masculine is always dominant, and God is never addressed as "Mother."[41] The God of the Bible was often engaged in battle with the ancient religion of the goddess; yet this God is not identical with the Sky Father of primitive religion either. The true, living God infinitely transcends the polarity of the Sky Father and the Earth Mother. He is not simply "above" and "beneath" but "over," "in," "through" and "around." He is essentially above us and outside us, but he relates to us where we are—in our earthly pilgrimage through this valley of tears (cf. Ps 23:4).

Evangelical theology will declare its profound misgivings concerning nature mysticism and goddess religion, first because this kind of faith orientation subverts the discontinuity between God and nature, and second because it reduces God to an impersonal life force or creative process within nature. The true God is not an impersonal force but an all-powerful and all-discerning being. He is here not in the sense of a vague omnipresence but in the sense of a compelling presence that presses for dialogue with the human creature.

In the contemporary quest for inclusive language about God, it is often forgotten that the true God is both inclusive and exclusive of humanity. He includes the whole of humankind in his plan of redemption, but he excludes humans as co-redeemers and co-gods (cf. Gen 3:5; Ex 20:3). Every human being is made in his image and therefore included in his overall vision and purpose. But our origin is in time, not eternity, and therefore an infinite abyss separates us from God. We are only creatures, whereas God alone is Creator; we are only finite, whereas God alone is infinite.

God will remain "He" because he is personal, and the substitution of the noun "God" for the personal pronoun invariably ends in an impersonal God. This "He" assuredly does not mean that God is male but that God relates to us primarily in the masculine mode, as Father and Lord. There are some who refer to Jesus as "He" but to Christ and God as "it."

This betrays a creeping Nestorianism in which the unity between Jesus and God is dissolved. A deist could speak of "Godself" rather than "God himself" because the God of deism totally transcends gender and therefore personal specificity. A mystic of the Neoplatonic variety would be reluctant even to use the expression "Godself" because God infinitely transcends personhood, which connotes individuation. An evangelical Christian will support the use of "God himself" and similar expressions because the God of the Bible is supremely personal and therefore encompasses rather than nullifies gender.

The Theological Task

In the current theological milieu the theologian is often portrayed as an artist who mediates between the natural and the supernatural, the phenomenal and the transcendental, the real and the ideal. For Gordon Kaufman theology is no longer a reinterpretation of an authoritative scripture and tradition but an "imaginative construction" of a picture of God that facilitates the liberation of people from oppression.[42] John Thiel sees "individual creativity" playing some role in all "acts of theological conception and expression."[43] Creative imagination becomes a point of contact with divine revelation (Garrett Green), thereby taking precedence over logical deduction or rational reflection.[44]

In contrast to this neo-romantic stance, I regard the theologian as primarily a *witness* to God's mighty deeds in a past history, the history mirrored in Holy Scripture. Our task is not to rename or reenvision the divine mystery but to elucidate it and to reaffirm it. Theology is neither the systematizing of divinely revealed concepts (as in scholastic orthodoxy) nor the clarification of states of inner consciousness (as in romanticist liberalism) but the explication of the mystery of God's self-revelation in Jesus Christ. Faithful reasoning, moreover, never exhausts this mystery but enhances it.

Theology will recover its integrity only when it bows before the reality of God's self-revelation in Jesus Christ communicated to us by the Spirit through Holy Scripture and the ongoing commentary on Scripture in the church. Theology is not "reflection on the praxis of the people of God"[45] but reflection on the mystery of God's self-revelation to his people. Since Holy Scripture is the primary source and witness of this revelation, Scripture will be the fundamental guide and norm in any theology that claims to be faithful to the message of the apostolic church and the Protestant Reformation.

In place of both a constructive theology (as in Kaufman) and a descriptive theology (as in Lindbeck), I propose an expositional theology—one that expounds the abiding truth of God's Word in Holy Scripture and then relates it to the contemporary situation. This endeavor will include a polemical and apologetic dimension, but it will at the same time acknowledge that God is the final persuader as well as the elector. We by ourselves can persuade others of the cogency of the biblical worldview, but of ourselves we have no power to convince the outsider of the truth of the gospel. Only God himself can do this, and he will do this sometimes despite and over against our evangelistic strategy and apologetic ingenuity.

In contrast to those in the theological world who are intimidated by the growing awareness of pluralism in our society, I contend that we must not rest content with anything short of conversion to the Lord Jesus Christ and regeneration by his Spirit. Yielding to the pressures of living in a pluralistic and relativistic milieu, Schubert Ogden is willing to settle for demonstrating the relative adequacy of Christian core beliefs, cautioning that "we must scrupulously avoid even a hint of dogmatism in our attempts to formulate existential truth."[46] I would press for an even greater humility—recognizing that the task of communicating the truth of the gospel is impossible for men and women in any period of history but that God may send his Spirit into our feeble attempts to render an intelligible witness and that outsiders—including those hardened in their antipathy to all truth and goodness—may actually come to experience the redeeming power of God's mercy and be made disciples of Christ, the living Lord and Savior. Our hope must rest not on apologetic expertise, not on artistic visualization of the mysteries of faith, not even on evangelistic technique, but on the outpouring of the Spirit of God who has promised to remain faithful to the people of God in their witness by word and deed to the fact of redemption through the atoning sacrifice of Christ on the cross. It is not we who win the world to Christ, but we can be ambassadors and heralds of the One who alone overcomes the principalities and powers, who may deign to use us but who basically does not need us. He may allow us to bear witness to the inbreaking of his kingdom, but he himself will usher in the kingdom in his own way and time and will secure it in the face of its many adversaries.

In our haste to return to the God of biblical revelation we must not make the mistake of severing theological vision from ontological conceptuality as does Jean-Luc Marion, who supports a postmodern deconstruction of the metaphysics of being for the purpose of retrieving the true God who manifests himself as "the icon of love" and "the icon of the invisible."[47] God, he says, is to be thought of no longer as the highest being or even being-itself but as unconditional love. Yet revelation can and does employ the philosophic language of Hellenism as well as the poetic, dramatic language of Hebraism in order to reach the intelligentsia of every age. Revelation indeed consists of personal encounter, but we cannot make sense of this encounter without relating it to the metaphysical themes that have engrossed philosophers through the ages.[48] God is not dependent on the language of being for his existence, but he freely utilizes this language in order to reach the minds of serious Christians who rightly seek to reflect upon their faith for the purpose of both deeper understanding and evangelistic outreach.

The task of theology is to articulate the message of faith in the conceptuality of the age while at the same time bringing this conceptuality under the searing critique of divine revelation. In the process, cultural concepts and images are transformed as they become bearers of transcendent meaning. The language of ontology can never take the place of the parabolic language of Zion, the unique vessel of God's self-revelation in salvation history, but it can serve to elucidate the biblical witness through the gracious condescension of the Spirit. In and of itself the finite is not capable of receiving the infinite, but the infinite can penetrate the finite.[49] The finite can become a prism through which the living God shines the light of his countenance upon us and grants us a new horizon of meaning. The Bible itself is such a prism, but cultural concepts when united with the biblical message to form part of the church's proclamation can also be a means that the Spirit uses to exalt Jesus Christ in the world.

• T W O •

THEOLOGY'S ATTEMPT to DEFINE GOD

It is difficult to conceive of God, but to define Him in words
is an impossibility.
GREGORY OF NAZIANZUS

The philosophers' God is . . . always spoken about as an "it,"
a hypothesis to explain the universe.
WILLIAM HORDERN

How can we find anew the power
to name God in a mystical-prophetic way? That is theology's
central postmodern question.
DAVID TRACY

God defines himself when he identifies himself with the dead Jesus.
EBERHARD JÜNGEL

I n the awesome attempt to define God, theology must do more than simply repeat the mainly figurative language of the biblical narrative. It must also draw upon the conceptual language of philosophy in order to illuminate the mystery of the God who revealed himself in biblical history and most of all in Jesus Christ. The Bible is not a treatise on metaphysics, but its affirmations have ineradicable metaphysical implications. It does not present us with a full-blown ontology, but its depictions of God have an unmistakable ontological cast.

In drawing upon philosophy in order to serve the mandate of faith to understand its object, theology must beware of aligning the faith too closely with any one philosophical system. The God that theology upholds is not comprehensible to the human mind. Although on the basis of God's self-revelation in Christ we can know something about this God, a residue of mystery remains—even for faith. The God of the Bible cannot be described in univocal language, only by means of analogy, metaphor and simile. By its very nature philosophy tends toward logical precision and rational elucidation. It seeks to know the ultimate in the sense of rational comprehension, whereas theology's goal is to serve the ultimate. Yet in order to fulfill this task, theology too must try to understand, even while recognizing that its formulations will always be open-ended and incomplete.

Theology is free to use philosophical terminology in order to elucidate biblical meanings, but it must not become bound to this terminology. Philosophical concepts can serve the gospel but must not be allowed to force the gospel into a conceptual mold. The God of philosophy is a metaphysical first principle. The God of the Bible is the supreme metaphysician. The God of philosophy is capable of being thought and thereby mastered. The God of theology remains hidden and inscrutable until he makes himself known.

The tradition of Catholic and Protestant scholasticism generally sees philosophy as a preamble to theology. Philosophy furnishes a rational foundation on which to build a superstructure with the aid of divine revelation. We begin with a general concept of being or goodness and then attribute to God the fullness of being. God becomes the *ens perfectissimum* ("the most perfect being") or the *ens realissimum* ("the most real being"). But the God of the Bible is not simply the perfection of being or the principle of being but being-in-person.[1] Nor is he a personified being but the dynamic of an eternity who embodies being. He is "not a static perfection but the absolutely unlimited Act and Energy" (Mascall).[2] He is not simply the supreme being *(ens)* but the act of being *(esse),* "the very act of being which is prior to all beings" (Macquarrie).[3] He is the being who in the reality of his person realizes and unites the fullness of all being in himself (Barth).[4]

In the scholastic tradition God is sometimes described as *ens causa sui* ("the cause of its own being"). Yet this concept can be misleading because God does not simply produce himself: God gives himself—to himself and to the world that he has created. According to Barth, "If we say that God is *a se,* we do not mean that God creates, produces, and causes himself, but that . . . he is the one who already has and is in himself everything."[5] For Arthur Cochrane, "What God creates and causes is not himself, but a reality distinct from himself."[6]

Philosophical theology has also defined God as *actus purus,* a concept derived from Aristotle to denote the final perfection of completely realized form, the fulfillment of all possibility. The truth in this notion is that "in God there is no mere potentiality or receptivity, or need, but that God is the pure activity who posits, creates, gives."[7] But if pressed too far this concept serves to obscure the biblical affirmation that God is not pure unceasing activity but a person who acts in freedom. This is why we must add *et singularis* to *actus purus:* God is a particular being and not simply the principle of activity.[8]

Barth was profoundly aware that human reason cannot successfully combine the concepts of God's aseity and personality. When we attribute personality to God, God's aseity is compromised and the lordship of God is limited and subverted. This is because personality entails individuality, and individuality connotes limitation.[9] We can hold the two concepts together only by faith in God's self-revelation in which God reveals himself as both sovereign freedom and a person who loves. We need to recognize that "our concept of aseity breaks down when it is applied to God, so that with our word we cannot speak *the* Word. We can only speak two words if we are to describe the nature of God as it is. We can only say 'I am' and 'the Lord'—personality and aseity. These two words are one word as God's Word."[10]

The God of revelation is neither a transcendental idea or ideal (as in idealism) nor an object "out there" accessible to sense perception (as in realism). Instead, he is a living subject who includes the whole of the objective world in his comprehensive vision. He is not a being alongside other beings but the infinite being who is himself the source and ground of all finite beings. He is not simply the power of being or the presence of spirit in being (as in idealism) but the infinite lord and judge of all being.

Some philosophical concepts have proved demonstrably fruitful in safeguarding the mystery of God's self-revelation in Jesus Christ and in Holy Scripture. One of these is *Deus non est in genere* (propounded by Thomas Aquinas among others). The meaning is that the true God does not belong to a genus or general category such as being, process, personality, agency and so on. On the contrary, we come to know what true being and also true personhood are by God's gracious act of disclosing himself as the living Spirit who eternally is and who eternally becomes. God is to be understood first of all not in terms of an abstract concept of being or process; instead, these philosophical concepts are to be interpreted in terms of God's self-revelation in Christ.

We must also affirm the motto of the church fathers: *Deus semper maior* ("God is always greater"). No matter how sublime our depictions of the majesty of God, no human formulation or insight can encompass deity. God always exceeds the limits of our conceptualizing and imagining. Once we identify our concepts with the divine reality itself, we sink into the quicksand of idolatry, for God is neither a graven nor a conceptual image. Yet our concepts and images are necessary and useful so long as they are treated as signs that point beyond themselves to the transformative divine reality that is both hidden and revealed in Jesus Christ.

Can theology avail itself of the principles of logic in clarifying the biblical vision of a God who acts in history? It is sometimes alleged that even God is bound to the law of noncontradiction. But God is not bound to anything external to his being, though he is true to himself, to what he has revealed and promised. He cannot contradict himself, but this does not mean that he cannot overturn or shatter principles of human logic. Indeed, as Kierkegaard reminds us, he reveals himself as the Absolute Paradox, God in man, eternity in time—a paradox that human reason cannot fathom, though there is no paradox in God himself.[11] One may say that God is the ground and source of logical principles, but God's logic transcends human logic just as his being transcends human being. God is not subject to the law of noncontradiction as a principle of human discourse, but this law is subject to the will of God, who sanctions it as reflective of his own nature. Thomas Aquinas was inclined not only to limit God's acts to what is not incompatible with his being but also to limit them as to what does not contradict logical coherence. Yet Thomas also denied univocal predication for God and insisted that even in analogical predication what we do not know exceeds by far what we are able to glean even from the resources of faith and tradition.[12]

Barth perceived that in their penchant for philosophical appellations for God, both medieval scholastic theology and Protestant orthodoxy rendered God impersonal, though this was not their intention.[13] To describe God as the most perfect being and to identify his attributes primarily as aseity, immensity, simplicity, immutability, omnipotence and so on is to lose sight of the biblical witness that the true God is one who acts in history, who addresses humanity in its brokenness and despair, who enters into human pain and suffering. The immobile and self-sufficient God of the Hellenistic philosophical tradition is a far cry from the God who loves and judges, who gives grace and withholds grace, who agonizes over human sin and seeks to rescue the human creature from sin. We can and must avail ourselves of philosophical concepts, but we must not let these concepts rule our thinking. We must always be prepared to modify them and perhaps set them aside as new light breaks forth from God's holy Word. As theologians we should not use biblical images to illustrate and support a philosophical vision, but we may use philosophical concepts to clarify the biblical vision.

Eberhard Jüngel, who draws heavily on Barthian theology, proposes that "we human beings must learn to understand ourselves as relational beings instead of as subjects in the center of things. We must learn to conceive of being as a *being-together* instead of as substance."[14] God must be reconceived as being in community; the Trinity is "a community of mutual otherness."[15] This makes it possible to envisage God as One who gives of himself and shares with his creation as opposed to a God who is engrossed in the enjoyment of his own perfection (as in Aristotle).

Neither theologians nor philosophers can define God, but God can and does define himself. He truly reveals his will and purpose to those with the eyes to see and the ears to hear. We cannot name God, but God names himself in the trinitarian unfolding of his revelation in Holy Scripture. Yet even in his revelation God remains partially hidden *(Deus absconditus)*. For God to cause his light to shine on us directly would be to overwhelm us. God reveals only what is adequate for our salvation and vocation as his ambassadors and heralds. God remains mystery even in his revelation, but meaning shines through this mystery as we ponder it in the recollection of faith and strive to live according to it by faith working through love (Gal 5:6).

Act and Being

The living God of the Bible is not static being but act in being. He is not immobile but free to interact with his creation. God is in movement but not in development. He acts, but he does not become other than he is. One could perhaps say that God is the unity of potentiality and actuality in the dynamism of an unceasing becoming, but God remains eternal being even as he freely relates to himself and to his creatures. Every possibility that will be realized in the world is already realized in the mind of God, but he unceasingly gives these possibilities concrete existence in the realm of temporality.

Christian faith transcends the polarity of essentialism and actualism. In the Platonic tradition essentialism means to affirm the reality of eternally immutable abstract forms. In the actualism that has its genesis in the pre-Socratic philosopher Heraclitus, ultimate reality is becoming, which means that everything is in the process of change.[16] For Aristotle the essence of things is what they are in their final completed state. God is pure actuality without potentiality, realized perfection rather than the perfect One who is constantly realizing his purposes anew in the world. According to Barth, essence does not precede action, but God's action cannot be severed from what he is in himself. God's own inner history is a history of action. He is not pure essence—unmoved and unmoving. Barth does not begin with the polarity of being and becoming but with the being of God in act. Against philosophical actualism, Christian faith does not view God's being *as* his act but instead affirms God's being *in* his act.

God does not tower above the world of temporality and materiality in sublime detachment. Instead, God interacts with his creation, seeking to bring it toward its divinely appointed goal. Yet we must refrain from going the way of Hegel, who conceived of God "only in his divine action, revelation, creation, reconciliation [and] redemption," holding that God becomes "a graven image as soon as he becomes identified with one single moment, made absolute, of this activity."[17] The Christian faith affirms that God is God apart from his action of creation, reconciliation and redemption and that God becomes man at one single point in human history, even though our senses can apprehend only the sign of this reality, not the reality itself. Yet biblical Christianity also maintains that God even in himself is act as well as being, that his being is dynamic, not static. God interacts with himself before he acts upon the world. God's being is in his action, even though we must not say that God is obliged to act in a particular way. God does not become a living God by going out of himself (as in Hegel); his creation and redemption demonstrate that he already is a living God.

Thomas Torrance gives cogent articulation to the inseparability of God's action and being:

That God's *energeia*, or Act, inheres in his Being, means that God's Being is in his Act and his Act is in his Being. He is not Being which also acts, but Being which acts precisely as Being, for his Being is intrinsically active, dynamic Being. Hence, there can be no thought of knowing God in his Being stripped of his Act, behind the back of his Act, or apart from his active Reality as God, for there is no such god.[18]

The voluntarist philosopher Fichte separated the principle of being from that of act and thereby could not avoid a God that was impersonal. "Speaking in a purely philosophical manner one would have to say of God: He is . . . not a being but a *pure activity,* the life and principle of a supersensible world-order."[19] Fichte called God "creative life," "dynamic creative Reason," "sublime and living Will" and also "infinite Will." Against Fichte I maintain that God is not simply life or act but the One who lives and acts. He is not an impersonal will to actualization but the living Lord who freely wills to actualize his purposes for the good of his creation.

Paul Tillich regarded it as a mistake to view God as pure actuality, for this would connote lifelessness.[20] Instead, drawing upon Boehme and Schelling, Tillich posited a contingency or primordial creativity in God that accounts for the dynamic character of his being. God is being-itself who unceasingly overcomes the nonbeing that he contains within himself. In contradistinction to Tillich I contend that God is a being who acts, not being-itself (though he could be called this symbolically). God is not love itself (as Tillich also implies) but a being who loves. God does not contain an anarchic freedom within himself that must be overcome, but God freely expresses his eternal will in acts of self-giving love. God is not suprapersonal (as in Tillich) but personal in the proper and original sense. He is person par excellence, and our personhood derives from his.

I concur with Jüngel, who cautions that we should not speak of a God who becomes but of a God whose being is dynamic, not static. "Becoming" indicates the manner in which God exists.[21] God is a personal being who is ever active, a being who constantly intercedes and intervenes, a God who pursues fallen human beings into the darkness. God is not the world, and yet the world is included in his vision and exists under his direction and control. God does not reside in the depths of nature, but he is constantly active in shaping both nature and history according to his purposes.

Essence and Existence

In Hellenistic tradition, essence indicates the inherent, unchanging nature of a thing or class of things. It is the true substance of the object under consideration as opposed to what is accidental, phenomenal or illusory. It is the spiritual reality that lies behind the material phenomenon (Plato). Existence, on the other hand, suggests contingency, temporality and materiality. This is why Plato could say that God is beyond existence.[22] For Plotinus and the Neoplatonists, ultimate reality, which they called "the One," lies beyond being and reason, even beyond the Good.[23] Origen endorsed the Platonic position that God is "above mind and being," though in practice he described God as having a simple intellectual nature.[24] Similarly Tillich spoke of God transcending both essence and existence. This is "the God above God," the God who transcends the polarity of infinity and finitude.[25]

Biblical faith, by contrast, does not shrink from viewing God as an existent being (Heb 11:6), though he exists not in the way the creature exists—as dependent and contingent—but as independent and unconditioned. He exists by his own power and is the cause of his own being (meaning that the mystery of his being resides in himself, not that he must create his own being). Having no need of any other power or reality, he is the uncaused ground and source of all finite being. As Jüngel succinctly puts it, "*God comes from God.* Nothing other than God himself can be regarded as God's origin. Neither being, nor nothingness. God is his own origin. God lives, and he lives totally out of himself."[26] For Thomas Aquinas, and I agree, essence and existence are one in God. God's essence is his existence.

Descartes (1596–1650) broke with Aristotelian tradition when he defined God in terms of God's self-causing all-powerfulness rather than the self-contemplation of his own infinite being.[27] For Descartes the essence of God is to create, not to be (as in Thomas). A more biblical perspective would affirm that the essence of God is neither to be nor to create but to coexist in love. God is not a solitary being, detached and remote from the world of human discourse and activity, but a trinitarian fellowship of love. Because he experiences love within himself he can relate in love to his creation. He is not simply Creator but Father to those whom he adopts into his kingdom. He is not simply the sustainer of the world but the suffering servant who redeems the world (Is 53).

God revealed himself as the "I am who I am" (Ex 3:13-14), but the medieval scholastic translation of this as "the One who is" is not wholly adequate and can be misleading. God is not simply the principle of being, nor even an eternal being, but a fellowship of mutual relatedness who remains the same even in his changing modes of action. Even as "I will be who I will be" (another possible translation), he remains the great "I am." He is the infinite One who encompasses finitude (limitation) within himself, the eternal one who is at the same time the source and wellspring of temporality. He is simultaneously ever at rest and ever at work (Augustine).[28]

Essence and Attributes

In scholastic theology (both Catholic and Protestant) a distinction is generally made between God's essence and God's attributes, the former referring to the abiding or core feature of God's being and nature. Yet these theologians were also emphatic that there can be no hard and fast lines between divine essence and the divine attributes, since the latter are simply the expression or manifestation of the former. In summarizing the Reformed position Heinrich Heppe contends that "the divine attributes are not something different from the nature and existence of God, so that the latter may be thought of as distinct from the former. . . . Rather the attributes of God are the divine nature itself in its relation to the world."[29] Indeed, "No elements in God are distinguished essentially. All the things in God are one indivisible and most single essence."[30] According to the Reformed theologian Polanus: "God's essential attributes are *really His very essence*; and they do not actually differ from God's essence or from each other."[31] In Lutheran orthodoxy the attributes are not "something supplementary to the essence of God," but in them "we describe the divine essence only according to its special features, because we cannot otherwise conceive of it."[32]

Arthur Cochrane notes that the concept of attribute has a nominalistic ring, suggesting something external, added to the nature of God.[33] He thinks it more appropriate to speak of the properties of God—that which belongs to God. Barth used the term "perfections" of God, which is also found in Protestant orthodoxy. For Barth God not only has perfections: he is his perfections. If we continue to speak of essence and attributes, we must insist that the essence of God is reflected in his attributes; the attributes, on the other hand, are manifestations of his essence. The God of the Bible is not monochrome. He radiates his splendor in myriad ways.

Liberal theology made the mistake of reducing the divine attributes to modes of human consciousness. For Schleiermacher the attributes of God do not describe the inner being of God but instead refer to our feeling of dependence in relation to him.[34] Omnipotence, for example, was said to describe not God in himself but the human experience of God as he relates himself to us.

While all the perfections of God are simply variants of the mystery of his being, we can certainly point to some as more illustrative of his nature and work than others. Without minimizing or denying any of his perfections, we should recognize that there is biblical warrant for speaking of his essential attributes or perfections as holiness, love, wisdom, power and glory. Yet these are not to be separated but to be celebrated in their indivisible unity. God's power is in the service of his holiness and love. He exercises his power by means of his wisdom and for the purpose of manifesting his glory.

The older Reformed theology distinguished between the communicable and incommunicable attributes of God. According to the Leiden Synopsis the former are life, wisdom, will and power and the latter simplicity, infinity, eternity and immensity.[35] For the Reformed theologian J. H. Heidegger the communicable attributes are life, intellect, will, goodness, justice, liberty, power and beatitude; the incommunicable include his independence, simplicity, infinity and immutability. His eternity and immensity are classed under infinity.[36]

Distinctions were also made between the metaphysical and moral attributes (infinity and eternity being examples of the first and holiness and love of the second) and the positive and negative attributes. The positive attributes are arrived at by the way of affirmation *(via eminentiae)* and the negative by the way of negation *(via negationis)*. In Lutheran theology the negative attributes are "unity, simplicity, immutability, infinity, immensity [and] eternity." The positive are "life, knowledge, wisdom, holiness, justice, truth, power, goodness, perfection."[37]

Barth divided the perfections of God under freedom and love. The perfections of divine loving are grace and holiness, mercy and righteousness, patience and wisdom. Those that relate to divine freedom are unity and omnipresence, immutability and omnipotence, eternity and glory. Like the scholastic theologians Barth was adamant that these perfections must not be separated but held together in the mystery of an underlying unity and harmony. God loves in his freedom, and in his freedom he chooses to love. He is patient in his wisdom, and in his wisdom he exercises patience. He is merciful in his holiness, and as a holy God he manifests grace.

In our delineation of the attributes or perfections of God, we must guard against singling out any of them as giving an exhaustive definition of who God is. If we say that God is exhaustively love, we are then neglecting his holiness and righteousness. A love reductionism can be detected in Nygren,[38] Jüngel[39] and to a lesser degree in Ritschl. According to Ritschl the idea of the wrath of God and of the holiness of God (as distinct from his righteousness) implies the negation of God's love and reflects the legacy of Old Testament legal religion.[40] On the other hand, it is possible to magnify the holiness and majesty of God to such a degree that his love is relegated to secondary significance. It is interesting to note that the Westminster Shorter Catechism defines God as "a Spirit, infinite, eternal, and unchangeable, in his being, wisdom, power, holiness, justice, goodness and truth."[41] Cochrane makes this astute comment: "Because orthodoxy had been dominated by the idea of God's sovereignty conceived as absolute power, knowing and willing, we find here no mention of the love of God, nor of his mercy and grace."[42]

We must also be alert to the temptation of trying to get beyond the attributes to an unchanging essence that is unfathomable and ineffable. In the writings of the first-century Jewish mystical philosopher Philo, "God's unchangeableness and disengagement were pushed so far that God was conceived to be entirely without attributes—pure being."[43] God could therefore be described only in negative terms, and the experience of God was practically devoid of noetic content. No wonder Hellenistic philosophers regarded as absurd the Christian claim that God revealed himself as unbounded love by entering into human affliction in a particular time in history.

In this same mystical tradition an attempt was made to get beyond the revealed names of God to a God who is essentially nameless, qualitatively beyond all anthropomorphism. I here agree fully with Carl Henry: "The Name and the intelligibility of revelation stand or fall together; they are not antithetical emphases. The reality of Yahweh as the living God does not in any sense depend upon an anti-intellective religious theory that blurs the Name in superrational mysticism."[44]

On the current scene there is a move to disavow the personal name for God—Father, Son and Holy Spirit—as too constrictive, and to substitute depictions that render God suprapersonal, such as the Abyss of Silence, the infinite ground and depth of all being, the Directive of History, and the all-pervasive Eternal Spirit. The Greek Orthodox theologian Thomas Hopko presents a convincing case that this kind of emphasis contradicts the intentions of the church fathers, for whom God is essentially beyond being but not "hypostatically beyond Father, Son and Holy Spirit. For God is supraessential and even nonessential. But God is not suprahypostatic or nonhypostatic, suprapersonal or nonpersonal."[45] Even those who were more mystically inclined continued to celebrate the God who reveals himself as Father, Son and Spirit, although in their philosophical speculation they wished to affirm a God beyond essence or being.

God and Necessity

Biblical faith is clear that the living God is not bound by any necessity save that of his love, which is the core of his nature. He does not need to create the world in order to overcome his supposed loneliness, for he is a community of persons within himself and derives the satisfaction of intimate fellowship from within himself as a Trinity of persons. Nor does he need to create the world because of a superabundance of energy that must have an outlet. The only reason for the creation is that he wills to share his love, but he is under no compulsion to do so. He loves humanity for the sake of humanity, not for the sake of his own enrichment, for he is already the summation of all value.[46] Moreover, his love is not the love that seeks its own fulfillment but the love that gives of itself sacrificially—the love that does not seek its own (cf. 1 Cor 10:24; 13:5 KJV).

In his groundbreaking book *The Great Chain of Being,* now a philosophical classic, Arthur Lovejoy traces what he calls "the principle of plenitude" in the history of Western thought.[47] This principle, which originated with Plato, is that the Good must diffuse itself if it is in fact divine, and this means that every conceptual possibility must be actualized, thus accounting for the fullness and complexity of the universe. God must create in order to be God, and in the Platonic and Neoplatonic traditions this creation was envisioned as an emanation that proceeds out of the being of God necessarily. God is like a fountain that must overflow or a waterfall that must descend from the sublime heights of eternity. According to Lovejoy, Plato really had two gods: the self-sufficient Absolute outside time and the Self-Transcending Fecundity that gave rise to time.[48] In Neoplatonism God not only goes out of himself as light shines into the darkness but also returns to himself as light floods back to its source. For Spinoza, who belongs to this tradition, the existence of the world is a metaphysical necessity, for it is the logical predicate of the God who is its eternal ground. Likewise in Hegel the universe is not an act of the sovereign freedom of God but is necessary to the very being of God. It signifies the unfolding of the Absolute in history and the return of the Absolute to itself. In seeking to counter Neoplatonic determinism Thomas Aquinas denied an absolute rational necessity for all things. God chooses the good not as necessary to his own goodness but as "becoming to its own goodness."[49] (Lovejoy questions whether Thomas really succeeded in breaking with the principle of plenitude.)[50] Similarly, in distinguishing his position from that of Spinoza, Leibniz held that the world is created not by a metaphysical necessity but by a moral necessity.[51] But even here it is questionable whether he successfully avoided determinism. Lovejoy points out that in this whole tradition love is understood in terms of its generative or creative power rather than its redemptive motivation. Love becomes the overflowing power of God, power that is absolute and irresistible because it proceeds necessarily from the very being of God.

In process philosophy the world is no longer a closed continuum that is the logical or inevitable expression of a divine determination but now an open universe filled with infinite possibilities that have yet to be realized. God is not the principle of plenitude but the principle of limitation (Whitehead). God chooses between disparate values and leaves some possibilities unrealized. God is no longer "Absolute Rationality" but "the Ultimate Irrationality" (Whitehead),[52] since the chain of rational determinism is broken. But the conclusion that process philosophers do not hesitate to draw is that the world is partly or wholly a matter of chance. Indeterminacy rather than fate characterizes human existence. By our free will we shape our own destiny and thereby affect the destiny of others. We are called not to resign to the order of things but to advance into novelty (Whitehead). The universe is not a great chain of being that is already completed in the mind of God but an unfinished project of emergent evolution. For William James the world process is a gamble that involves enormous risks, for it contains the element of the unpredictable and irrational. God is our partner in constructing the universe.[53]

In the biblical or evangelical view, God is neither Absolute Power (in the sense that his power is unrestricted) nor a Life Force within the universe that needs to be harnessed for the sake of divine and human fulfillment. Rather he is the living Lord who creates the universe as an act of grace and rules the universe for the sake of bringing it redemption from the evil that has intruded into it through demonic and human sin. God directs the universe as its providential governor and guide, and his providence is radically different from the Fate of classical spirituality as well as from the Chance of modern spirituality. He chooses to work out his purposes in and through human freedom, but he will finally bring in his kingdom in his own way and time. We as human creatures are neither co-creators nor co-redeemers with God, but we can witness to the wonder of his creation and the glory of his redemption through our words and deeds. We cannot produce or merit his grace, but we can herald it and demonstrate it through our life and work.

The God who creates and redeems by necessity is not the God of the Bible, who creates and redeems gratuitously. God does not create "because of a superabundance which has to find an outlet, as it were, and if it did not overflow in the creation of a world would be imperfection, discord or suffering."[54] God creates out of the freedom of his love, not because he must create but because he inexplicably wills to bestow life on a world whose doom and destruction he already foresees.

In contradistinction to the god of Greek philosophy, the personal God of biblical religion has a heart. "He can feel and be affected. . . . He cannot be moved from outside by an extraneous power. But this does not mean that He is not capable of moving Himself." No, God is "moved and stirred" by his own "free power" to relieve our distress.[55]

There is no necessity or justice to which God must conform. He is his own necessity, and he wills justice because it is his nature to do so. God is not "the One who loves necessarily" but "the One who loves in freedom."[56] The biblical Christian would not say with the philosopher Nicolas Malebranche that "God necessarily loves that which is supremely and infinitely lovable, His own substance, the infinite good."[57] This is still eros love, the love that is attracted to what has greatest value. God does love himself, but he does so with agape, for as a fellowship of persons he can experience self-giving love.

God is free to be himself and to go out of himself.[58] He is free to remain in the impassible glory of his trinitarian life, and he is free to take suffering and pain upon himself by giving life to a new creation. He is not the "Unmoved Mover" (Aristotle); he allows himself to be moved by the cries and anguish of his people. Yet there is no metaphysical necessity that drives him out of himself to answer human need but simply the boundlessness of his compassion, which is incomparable and incomprehensible.

The Reformed theologian Adrio König acknowledges that God indeed has "a need for fellowship, and in *this* sense an inward drive towards community. But it is his own, freely self-imposed need, that was not thrust on him from without, and it is a need which belongs to his being, and is satisfied by his being, in his trinitarian fellowship, and for the satisfaction of which he was not obliged to turn to anything outside of himself."[59]

For Plato and Plotinus the essence of ultimate reality, which we may call "God," is infinite fecundity. For Duns Scotus the essence of God consists in the infinity of his being. For William of Occam God's essence consists in the power of his will. From my theological perspective the essence of God consists in the holiness of his love.

Rationalism and Mysticism

In delineating a doctrine of God, we must avoid both the Scylla of rationalism and the Charybdis of mysticism. Rationalism reduces God to the axioms of logic; mysticism presents a God who is absolute mystery, before which we can only stand in awe and wonder. For the Christian mystic Dionysius the Pseudo-Areopagite, God is unapproachable and incommunicable. In rationalism God is fully intelligible and comprehensible. His logic is the same as ours, and this is why he can be described univocally. God is envisioned as pure thought (Aristotle), and the incarnation is described as logic becoming incarnate (Gordon Clark). In mysticism one can talk about God only in metaphors and similes. He remains basically unknowable, though he can be experienced. Whereas rationalism has been associated in Christian tradition with rational theism, pantheism and panentheism, a thoroughgoing mysticism finally ends in agnosticism, though a great number of Christian mystics have been panentheists and some even pantheists.

Rationalism in the form of rational theism rests on the antithesis between subject and object, and so reduces God to an object in our understanding or in our experience. Mysticism seeks to transcend the subject–object antithesis in order to attain an underlying unity in which God is discovered as the ground or core of the self. Christian faith does not overturn the subject–object polarity but sees it in a new perspective—as an encounter between the living God who stands outside us and the believing subject who knows only as being known by God (cf. 1 Cor 8:3; Gal 4:9).

My own position on this question can be clarified by comparing it with some others. For Descartes the human person is the subject and God is the object. For Emil Brunner the human person and God are both subjects. For Barth God is subject and the human person is object. For the mystics the subject–object relationship is transcended by the loss of subjectivity and objectivity in an undifferentiated unity. In my position (which is also found in Barth) God makes himself an object to our understanding even while meeting us as a subject in the divine–human encounter. The subject–object relationship must not be dissolved (as in idealism) nor entirely transcended (as in mysticism); instead, it must be transformed and redirected (as in biblical personalism).

Rationalism defines God as exhaustively rational so that God becomes an absolute principle, the principle of being or an all-knowing Intellect. In Christian faith God is the Holy One, who includes rationality but also transcends it. He is not simply an all-comprehending Reason but infinite power and majesty. That is why the proper response to this God is awe and wonder (Is 6), not dispassionate reflection. In the older scholasticism God is absolute rationality. In Neoplatonic mysticism God is the abysmal One beyond rationality. In neo-mysticism God is the ultimate irrationality. In the catholic evangelicalism I espouse, God is the eminently rational actuality, the unity of dynamic will and supreme wisdom.

In the tradition of philosophical idealism it is fashionable to differentiate spirit from nature; God who becomes pure spirit is thereby effectively removed from nature. Arthur Cochrane expresses well my own sentiments:

> Whoever describes God as the absolute or infinite spirit, and by this absolute means nature purified, should ask whether he has not exchanged the reality of God for the reality of the spirit world. Scripture speaks not only of God as a Spirit but of his nature as well—of his wrath and mercy, and of his face, arms, hands, and feet. Surely not all of these are to be understood symbolically, nor are the Trinitarian definitions of God as Father, Son, and Holy Spirit to be taken as unreal, as if the real were a pure spirit or being–itself.[60]

With Barth and Cochrane I affirm that God exists in the unity of his nature and his Spirit. The so-called pure spirit of idealistic and mystical philosophy is most likely the hypostasis of our own created spirit.[61] Whenever we seek to find God in a spiritual realm beyond nature we are in the domain of Platonism and Neoplatonism, not of Christian faith. Christian faith does indeed assert that God is Spirit, but this deity descends into the realm of nature and history incarnating himself in human flesh. The resurrection from the dead does not mean an elevation above the material but the union of the material and spiritual in a holy community on a transfigured earth. The Christian vision is not a disembodied spiritual unity with God but the glorification and transfiguration of human flesh.

The God of the Bible is both the *Deus revelatus* ("the revealed God") and the *Deus absconditus* ("the hidden God"). In pure mysticism he is the latter only, and in evangelical rationalism he is exclusively the former. God is, of course, hidden outside his revelation in Jesus Christ, but he remains hidden even in his revelation. We can truly know but only partially. We can begin to understand, but we cannot comprehend.

When we encounter God we encounter mystery, but meaning shines through mystery.

The rationalist mentality assumes that we can reach divine reality by reasoning. A certain kind of agnosticism denies the possibility of a theoretical knowledge of God but advocates acting as if God existed in order to give our lives moral meaning (Kant). Irrationalism asserts that God is totally veiled to human cognition and our only recourse is a blind leap in the dark. Against rationalism theology insists that it is not reason but divine grace that brings us into contact with ultimate reality. Against irrationalism theology contends that it is sin, not reason, that is the primary obstacle to true understanding. Against agnosticism theology maintains that we can truly know, though not on the basis of either reason or mystical experience but on the basis of God's self-revelation in Jesus Christ supremely attested in Holy Scripture.

The God of the Bible is incomparable but not unthinkable. He is incomprehensible but not unintelligible. We can describe his being and acts by way of analogy but not literally or directly. We do not begin our analogical depictions of God by examining human attributes and experiences, but we begin with God's self-revelation and then seek to find reflections of God's being and workings in our experiences. This is the way not of an analogy of being *(analogia entis)*, in which we begin with created being and then proceed to the uncreated, but of an analogy of faith *(analogia fidei)*, in which we begin with an acknowledgment of God's self-revelation in the Jesus Christ of history.

God infinitely transcends the human creation, and yet God embodies humanity within himself. He stands infinitely beyond materiality, but he has his own divine nature, his own supernatural body. The Bible does not hesitate to speak of the "ears," "eyes," "hands" and even "back" of God, though we are not to understand these depictions as literal or univocal designations. The God of the Bible is not anthropomorphic, but he is probably closer to the manlike gods of primitive religion than to the more refined spiritual conceptions of deity in mysticism and idealism.

Supernaturalism and Naturalism

Classical theism generally portrays God as the highest being or the fundamental substance of the universe. The supernatural is seen as the preeminence of the natural or the summit of the scale of being. Nature is the substratum, and the heavenly realm is the pinnacle of existence. In Thomistic philosophy nature is the preamble to grace, and grace is the completion of nature. Nature is the lower story and supernature the upper story of cosmic reality. Miracles are explained as the intrusion of supernature into nature.

Paul Tillich criticized this view of things on the basis that it undercuts the essential transcendence of God.[62] For Tillich supernaturalism as a supraworld is dangerous when taken literally because it makes the infinite finite and the eternal temporal. He preferred to speak of infinity as the ground and depth of the finite rather than a separate realm above the finite. The question is, however, whether he succeeded in affirming the total transcendence of God over nature and history, since infinity becomes finitude transcending itself. He actually substituted an "ecstatic naturalism" for classical supernaturalism.

Tillich was right that infinity is not simply a higher or the highest gradation of the finite, but he was wrong to deny the reality of a higher world beyond the finite. The supernatural is not simply an extension of the natural but the ground and basis of the natural. Nature was created by God ex nihilo, and this means that there will forever be an infinite distance between God and his creation. God is not inseparable from nature as its ground and depth, nor does God tower above nature in sublime detachment (as in Hellenistic philosophy); rather God creates nature and unceasingly relates himself to nature as its providential governor and guide. Similarly God initiates human history and continually interacts with humanity in the midst of its historical experience as he seeks to work out his purposes in history.

In the older supernaturalism the distinction between God and the world was equivalent to the distinction between eternity and time. God was envisaged as a timeless Absolute outside nature and history. Kierkegaard illustrated this position when he declared: "It is the perfection of the Eternal to have no history and, of all that is, the Eternal alone has absolutely no history."[63] Yet Kierkegaard took pains to distance himself from the legacy of Hellenism by maintaining that the changelessness of God is not the "chilling indifference" or "devastating loftiness" of a self-sufficient Absolute but the perpetual concern of the living God of the Bible who hears and answers prayer.[64]

Barth is helpful in this area, as in many others, by seeking to correct Christian tradition in the light of a fresh understanding of the biblical witness. We must avoid saying that God is timeless or spaceless, for this reduces God to a force or power that upholds the universe as its ground rather than a personal being who enters into real relationships with the human creature. God is able to create and relate to creatures in historical time and space because he has his own ontological time and space. The God who dwells properly and originally in the fellowship of the Godhead dwells symbolically and sacramentally in the universe that he has created.[65] If God were absolutely nonspatial, he would then be lifeless and loveless, for fellowship involves spatiality and temporality.

Barth identified God with the Eternal One who creates time but who paradoxically has time within himself. Eternity is not time as we experience it, for "Eternity is just the duration which is lacking to time. . . . It has and is simultaneity."[66] For Barth God is both timeless and temporal. "He is timeless in that the defects of our time, its fleetingness and its separations, are alien to Him and disappear. . . . He is temporal in that our time with its defects is not so alien to Him that He cannot take it to Himself."[67] The reality that is God's time is the basis of all time.[68]

Just as the eternity of God includes time, so the ontology of God includes being. "God is both the prototype and foreordination of all being, and therefore also the prototype and foreordination of time."[69] God is not simply the highest being but the Lord of being, the Eternal One who includes being within himself and who produces being. Barth gave priority to eternity over being: "Eternity is before and after, above and below being. Being does not include eternity, but eternity includes being."[70]

Just as Barth related eternity to time and being to becoming, so he perceived an inseparable relationship between infinity and finitude. God is not "absolute infinity," as the older theologians understood it, because this would then exclude the possibility of fellowship with God within the structures of finitude.[71] Finitude is not only a determination of God's creation, but it has its ground and truth antecedently in God himself. "If we call God infinite, measureless, limitless, spaceless and timeless, this does not mean that we will try to exclude, deny or even question that He is the One who in His whole action posits beginning and end, measure and limit, space and time."[72]

God is not the infinite in the finite (as in Schleiermacher and Tillich), but God is the infinity that enters into fellowship with the finite. The finite can receive and bear the infinite because it springs from the infinite; it has its origin and basis in the infinite God.[73] The finite is not alien to God, for God can make himself finite (and he has done so in Jesus Christ). God can relate to finitude because God can and does experience finitude within himself.

Rational theism tends to make God detached and remote from the world of his creation. This is because it makes God suprapersonal—outside all time and space. Descartes understood God as "a substance which is infinite, independent, all-knowing, all-powerful and by which I myself and everything else, if anything else exists, have been created."[74] God is not a substance, however, but a living being who is at the same time being–itself. He is not a timeless infinity but an infinite person who seeks community with finite persons who reflect his image by virtue of their creation by his hand. He is not simply an all–powerful being or omnipotent force but the One who loves in freedom. It is noteworthy that Descartes had nothing to say of God as loving and forbearing. The God of the Bible is not infinite being but the almighty being who has infinite care for his people. He is not wholly independent of time and space, but he enters into time and space in order to have fellowship with his children. He is the infinite-personal God who does not simply create the world and then allow it to run by its own power but upholds and maintains the world by acting within it as well as upon it. In biblical supernaturalism being is not a substance but a "being–together," and God is not a pure essence but "a community of mutual otherness" (Jüngel).[75]

God's Almightiness in Question

One of the salient features of the contemporary theological panorama is the pronounced discomfort with the traditional notion of God's almightiness. A God who is all-powerful contradicts the democratic ethos in which decisions are arrived at by consensus rather than by arbitrary fiat. It also calls into question the individualism of Western culture, which prizes personal freedom over adhesion to community values and tradition.

The older liberal theology eagerly undertook to correct the traditional conception of God by emphasizing his love and empathy rather than his power and majesty. God is "the fellow sufferer who understands" (Whitehead) rather than the Lord and king of the universe. Walter Rauschenbusch sought a democratic God, one "with whom democratic and religious men could hold converse as their chief fellow worker."[76] For Edward Scribner Ames, God should embody the ideals of freedom and imaginative cooperation.[77]

Process theology has done much to bring God down to the human level. God is still supreme but not absolutely sovereign. For the fulfillment of his purposes he depends on human cooperation. We contribute to the enrichment of God just as he contributes to our growth and enrichment. We are not only enlisted by God in his service but also included in God as necessary ingredients of his creative advance. God works by rational persuasion, not by issuing edicts. For Schubert Ogden the model of God's relation to the world is that between the self and its body rather than between the self and another self.

The theology of hope associated with Jürgen Moltmann also signifies a decisive break with the God of power and glory, as envisioned in traditional Christian religion. Moltmann does not deny that God has power, but he reinterprets the nature of this power—as suffering love rather than irresistible causality. In his view a God who is only omnipotent could be respected but not loved. "Omnipotence can indeed be longed for and worshipped by helpless men, but omnipotence is never loved; it is only feared."[78] The God of biblical faith, in his view, is a God of hope, a God who invites us into a promising future, rather than a God who has foreordained the future even before the advent of humanity. Like the God of process theology, Moltmann's God is dependent on humanity for his own fulfillment. "Through his freedom he waits for man's love, for his compassion, for his own deliverance to his glory through man."[79]

In his theology of universal history Pannenberg also calls into question the claims of traditional or classical monotheism: "An almighty and omniscient being thought of as existing at the beginning of all temporal processes excludes freedom within the realm of his creation."[80] For Pannenberg God is "real" but not "an existent being," certainly not an absolute person, a self-contained being alongside others.[81] Nevertheless Pannenberg is unwilling to discard the idea of God's omnipotence; indeed, he sees it as indispensable for Christian faith. He frequently calls God "the all-determining Reality," though God's universal power does not abrogate human freedom. Instead, God realizes his goal by preparing a future that humans can enter and help to shape. God's power is not the power of irreversibility, of a predestinating decree before creation, but the building of a future that is congruent with human freedom and striving. This is why we can call God "the Power of the Future." The power of God over the world is the power of creative love that opens up new possibilities for those who respond to his offer of life and hope for fallen humanity.[82]

An even more daring attempt to reconceptualize God is evident in neo-mystical theology, represented by such luminaries as Nikos Kazantzakis, Miguel de Unamuno and Pierre Teilhard de Chardin. God is no longer the supreme being who brings the world into existence but a universal consciousness that seeks to realize itself through the creative striving of humanity. Kazantzakis declared: "Our God is not almighty, he is not all-holy, he is not certain that he will conquer, he is not certain that he will be conquered."[83] Indeed, "it is not God who will save us—it is we who will save God, by battling, by creating, and by transmuting matter into spirit."[84] Instead of a preordained future we face an open future that depends very much on human self-determination.

Feminist theology adds its voice to the many others that seek to redefine God in terms of the modern worldview. For feminist theology the principal adversaries are monarchism and patriarchalism. We need a conception of God that affirms the full equality of men and women and also the mutual dependence of divinity and humanity. According to Anna Case-Winters power should be reconceived as tender care and loving assistance rather than as domination and control.[85] God is not the majestic Lord of the universe but "the Roar of the Universe" or "the Lure of the Universe." God does not create by an act of his will but nurtures us and leads us much as a mother caring for her children. This God is not almighty Creator but the Womb of Being, the Primordial Matrix or the Immanent Mother.

For the most part Emil Brunner reaffirmed the traditional conception of God as majestic Lord and all-powerful Ruler; yet he insisted that these notions must be understood relationally rather than ontologically. "In Himself . . . God is not the Almighty, the Omniscient, the Righteous One; this is what He is in relation to the world which He has created."[86] "Revelation . . . teaches nothing about *omnipotentia*. The Biblical conception means God's power over the whole universe; but *omnipotentia* means the abstract idea that 'God can do everything.' "[87] Barth's position is different: God is Lord of the world because he is first of all Lord of himself. He exercises power not only toward the world but within himself as a trinitarian fellowship—the power of creative and holy love. Like Brunner, Barth saw the danger of conceiving of God as absolute power in the sense of unrestricted power. But we must still acknowledge the biblical truth that God has power and is power: "Absolutely everything depends on whether we know God as the One who is omnipotent in Himself."[88]

The affirmation of God as the "Father Almighty" has created difficulties for modern theology partly because of misinterpretations on the part of orthodoxy. Medieval scholastic theology relied too heavily on philosophical ideas in articulating a viable doctrine of God. God's power was conceived of in terms of his omnicausality rather than his sovereign freedom. The medieval scholastics viewed creaturely existence as "directly grounded in the eternity of God" rather than in his freedom and therefore could maintain only a blurred distinction between God and the world, one that threatened the biblical doctrine of creation.[89]

In Reformed orthodoxy God's predestinating decree came more and more to be interpreted in terms of causal determinism instead of the gracious initiative of a loving God. James Daane shares these pertinent observations:

> What the Reformers meant by the sovereignty of grace—that is, God's freedom to be gracious to whom he will—came increasingly, as it developed in Reformed thought, to mean merely that God is free from any concern about the plight of the world, free in the sense of being unmoved by any moment within history. More and more, God was seen as accounting for whatever comes to pass in history, but not free to respond in grace to what occurs in history.[90]

Daane rightly noted that if all things are ontologically necessary, if they flow necessarily from the essence of God, then God is fully responsible for sin and evil. The decretal theologians did not shrink from this conclusion.[91] For Herman Hoeksema God hates the reprobate and loves the elect. Yet because God is absolute and unconditioned he does not relate directly even to the elect. His love for them is really a love for the radiance of his own glory that is reflected in them. In decretal theology God is free to carry out his decree, but he is not free to alter his decree, since it proceeds from his very essence.

Daane boldly invites us to return to the more biblical outlook that God is free both to be himself and to go out of himself into history. "The peculiar character of the historical is that what happens might not have happened. The peculiar character of divine grace, similarly, lies in the fact that grace bestowed might not have been bestowed."[92] For Daane God's decree is "both eternal and event, and both as an eternal act of his freedom. As such, what God decreed is both absolute *and* historical, historical both as an event in God and as actualized in the world external to God."[93] The incarnation itself did not derive necessarily from the nature of God but was a free decision of God. God became historical without ceasing to be eternal; he became human without ceasing to be divine.

The gospel is not a proclamation that God necessarily wills both election and reprobation, and that all we can do is submit to our divinely appointed destiny. Rather it is an invitation to enter into the fellowship that God opens for all humanity. Grace sets us free to respond in decision and obedience to this offer of salvation. Grace is not the dawning of the realization that everything has been determined and that our task is simply to acknowledge this fact and to live accordingly. God may withhold grace from those who believe and give grace to those who do not believe or do not yet believe. The God of the Bible is not bound by the rigors of human logic. He relates freely and lovingly to his people and may even choose to alter his plans and purposes when he discerns either signs of true repentance or signs of obstinacy and folly. This is the kind of God to whom we can pray, in whom we can hope, whose promises we can trust.

With Barth and Brunner, Daane calls us to retrieve biblical insights long since buried in the often well-meaning attempt to make logical sense of the mystery of God's choosing to become historical in Jesus Christ. We should indeed strive for as much coherence as possible but at the same time recognize that no human mind can grasp the mystery of God's self-abasement in human history or fully understand or appreciate the immeasurable richness of his mercy as displayed in the agonizing suffering and death of our Lord Jesus Christ (cf. Rom 11:33).

·THREE·

THE
SELF-REVEALING
GₒD

You did not learn that from any human being;
it was revealed to you by my heavenly Father.

MATTHEW 16:17 REB

No one has ever seen God. It is God the only Son,
who is close to the Father's heart, who has made him known.

JOHN 1:18 NRSV

The God of the Bible . . . is not discovered.
He is not forced into the light, even of love,
by any power outside Himself, not even by our misery.

P. T. FORSYTH

The fact that God reveals Himself through His Word
presupposes that man is a being
who has been created for this kind of communication,
for communication through speech.

EMIL BRUNNER

Even the unbeliever encounters God, but he does not
penetrate through to the truth of God that is hidden from him.

KARL BARTH

God is the one who speaks *out of himself.*
To be addressed by God can therefore only and always be an *event.*

EBERHARD JÜNGEL

Theology has often drawn a distinction between the God who is hidden *(Deus absconditus)* and the God who is revealed *(Deus revelatus).*[1] This is to be understood not as a cleavage within God but as an acknowledgment of two different sides of God as he freely relates himself to us. This polarity is already found in Deuteronomy 29:29 (NEB): "There are things hidden, and they belong to the Lord our God, but what is revealed belongs to us and our children for ever; it is for us to observe all that is prescribed in this law."

The question that immediately arises is whether God is hidden because his essence is beyond human comprehension or whether God veils himself in order not to overwhelm us by the splendor of his majesty. Scripture makes clear that no one can see the face of God and live (Ex 33:20; Is 6:5); yet Moses was permitted to gain a glimpse of the "back" of God (Ex 33:23). He was also allowed to hear the voice of God address him personally and to formulate God's commands for the people in his charge.

The transcendence of God over human reason is also attested in the Bible, but God's will and purpose are hidden from mortals—not simply because of our finitude but primarily because of our sin. Our thoughts are not God's thoughts and our ways are not God's ways (Is 55:8-9), for our reasoning is corrupted by lustful ambition. We are separated from God, not only ontologically but also morally.

The mystical tradition of the church has so heightened the epistemological gulf between God and humanity that God becomes basically unknowable and incommunicable. In mysticism "the ultimately unspeakable God cannot be reached by way of language. The only sense which talk about him can have is to cause, with the help of language, something like a self-removal of the inauthenticity of human talk about God and thereby to reach God himself at least in silence."[2] Eberhard Jüngel reminds us that for Dionysius the Pseudo-Areopagite, one of the guiding lights of Christian mysticism, "it is not so much the affirming but rather the negating statements which are hermeneutically appropriate for expressing the divine, so that such talk does not completely miss God."[3]

In mysticism the principal way to God is the way of negation *(via negativa)* by which we fashion some kind of picture of God by emptying him of human attributes. The result is a hermeneutical skepticism that regards language as a barrier to knowledge of God rather than a conduit or channel. The mainstream of Christian mysticism also employed the way of affirmation *(via eminentiae)* in which we raise the attributes of things in the finite order to the infinite order. Thus we can speak of God analogically by seeing in God the perfection of qualities associated with creaturely being. Yet for both mystics and medieval scholastics the inner being of God infinitely transcends the probings of the human mind. We have at best a broken reflection or fleeting manifestation of the God who remains essentially unknowable and indescribable.

Against both mystical and scholastic theology I maintain that we cannot reach God by the way of virtue or of thought, but God can come to us and enable us to think what was previously unthinkable. Jüngel makes a telling point that in philosophy thought is prior to speech, but in biblical Christianity speech is prior to thought. We know as we are addressed.

> Since thought, in order to work through a concept of God, is dependent on God's *having* revealed himself, the word of God must *already have happened,* regardless of whether there might possibly be a further event of this word. The attempt to think God is meaningful only under the presupposition that God *has* spoken.[4]

We can know God because God truly reveals himself to us, though God does not communicate with us directly—face to face—but indirectly by means of his mighty deeds in biblical history culminating in Jesus Christ. Revelation, as Kierkegaard saw so clearly, is fundamentally indirect communication.[5] God may act directly on a person, but the understanding of this revealing action is mediated through historical testimony. Even hearing the voice of God in a dream (a common occurrence among the prophets) is still not seeing. God knows himself directly or immediately. While we may indeed hear the voice of God, this hearing does not lead to knowledge unless it is the inner hearing of faith. We know God indirectly through creaturely signs and works. We know God by faith, not by direct vision. Even in the act of revealing himself God veils himself so that we are not consumed by his splendor and can enter a relationship based on faith in which our pilgrimage has to depend on trust in his promises.

Mystery in the biblical vista is not a conundrum that baffles human reason and leaves us in a permanent state of bewilderment. Instead, mystery is the content of divine revelation—a word that can be grasped by faith but not mastered by human logic. A mystery as distinct from a riddle "cannot be resolved, uncovered, or exposed."[6] Yet it "permits itself to be grasped."[7] "A true mystery draws us to itself and into its confidence. It allows itself to be known in confidence *as* a mystery."[8] A mystery in the context of biblical faith enlightens even while it eludes comprehension.

Paul declares that the "mystery" of God's grace was made known to him by revelation (Eph 3:3; cf. Gal 1:12). In former generations this mystery was not known, but now with the coming of Christ we are allowed to see and to grasp the will and purpose of God for all humankind. It is incumbent on us to "make everyone see what is the plan of the mystery hidden for ages in God who created all things" (Eph 3:9 NRSV). We are to speak in such a manner that people of faith may be "encouraged and united in love, so that they may have all the riches of assured understanding and have the knowledge of God's mystery, that is, Christ himself" (Col 2:2 NRSV).

The mystery of God's self-manifestation in Jesus Christ is neither absurd nor opaque. Rather it is translucent to reality, since we see partly but not exhaustively. God's disclosure of his grace and mercy to us is intelligible but not finally comprehensible. Yet we should try to understand this mystery as much as possible (Rom 11:25), so that we can live in obedience to Christ's commands and finally arrive at our eternal home.

The mystery of faith is not the infinite abyss that transcends human reason but the wisdom of God becoming incarnate in human flesh. The Word of God is not a surd in human reason but the fount and ground of reason. God's Word is not a passing flash of light in the darkness but a definitive act of God in history, a happening that is "full of grace and truth" (Jn 1:14). The mystery of God's working is not an abysmal silence that defies intelligibility but a message that can be heard and communicated. We are called to be not simply pointers to this mystery but "stewards" of this mystery (1 Cor 4:1). Karl Barth referred to the mystery of God's saving work in Jesus Christ as an open mystery. It is incomprehensible and imperceptible with regard to its essence, but it is comprehensible and perceptible with regard to its work.[9]

The Protestant Reformers sometimes described the *Deus absconditus* as the unknown, inscrutable God behind his revelation in Jesus Christ. They associated his secret will with his wrathful judgment on sin and his revealed will with the love and mercy in Jesus Christ. They generally assumed that we are incapable of perceiving the very essence of God; we know only what he chooses to reveal to us in Christ. We know not God in himself but only his benefits toward us (Melanchthon). In Christ he is love, but outside Christ he is judgment and wrath.

Barth resolutely broke with this tradition by contending that we really know the hidden God in his self-revelation in Jesus Christ. What God is in himself is identical to what he is in his revelation in Christ. We know God to be love in his innermost nature, and this means that his wrath and judgment are not another side of God but actually expressions of his love. What God reveals is not something of himself but his very self, his own eternal being. Yet we know God's inner self not directly but indirectly—in the sign and work of his revealing acts in history. To know the *Deus revelatus* is to know the *Deus absconditus* and vice versa. God remains hidden even in his revelation, and he discloses himself precisely in the hiddenness of the mystery of Jesus Christ.[10]

Outside of Christ we still experience both the love and judgment of God, but we cannot begin to fathom these realities. Emil Brunner created a dichotomy between God in his work of love—known only to believers—and God in his work of wrath—known by human beings in their fallen condition.[11] I contend that even the wrath of God is fully disclosed only in Jesus Christ (Jn 12:31-32; Rom 1:16-18; 2:5, 16). Only in Christ can we discern the mystery that God's wrath is a form of God's love, that God's love is a consuming fire and not simply divine empathy with the human condition. We can speak of the secret will of God so long as it is always seen to be in the service of his revealed will, which is consistently kind and loving. The purposes of the hidden God *(Deus absconditus)* are at one with his will disclosed in Jesus Christ. God in his naked majesty *(Deus nudus)* is not to be separated from the God of revelation *(Deus revelatus)*.

The mystical tradition of the church considered it exemplary to get beyond the naive, anthropomorphic language about God in the Bible and embrace metaphors drawn from the world of philosophy that were supposedly more spiritual. Jüngel maintains on the contrary that the anthropomorphic speech about God that we encounter in biblical faith is singularly appropriate for theological discourse.[12] It reminds us that we are speaking of a personal God who confronts us in our sin and upholds us in our tribulation. An infinite God who can take the finite into himself, a divine God who can relate to us on the human level, is harder to understand than the pure being or transcendent good of mysticism and idealism. The God of the philosophers and mystics who in his aseity and impassibility remains untouched by human vulnerability and suffering is far easier for reason to grasp than the God who in his infinite power makes himself vulnerable to pain and crucifixion. The God who freely identifies with the human predicament is far more enveloped in mystery than the God who remains supremely detached from the world of temporality and materiality.

To really know the *Deus absconditus,* we must first know the *Deus revelatus,* the One who meets us in Jesus Christ. This meeting is more than an I-Thou relationship: it is being confronted by the very One who became incarnate in history at a particular time and place. God encounters us not only as being-as-subject but also as being-as-object—in the sacramental sign of the Jesus Christ of history (Jüngel).[13] The true God is not the God accessible to thought but the One who speaks, the One who acts, the One who redeems. God does not simply confound us as the Wholly Other, but he embraces us as the bridegroom embraces his bride (a truth readily acknowledged by many of the Christian mystics). An experience of the true God will indeed arouse awe and reverence in the human creature (Rudolf Otto).[14] But the evangelical experience in which we meet the living Christ convicts us of our sin and fills us with the joy and assurance of knowing that God is basically *for* us and has acted decisively and irrevocably on our behalf and on behalf of all humanity.

Natural Knowledge of God

Not all human beings believe in the gospel, but all are objects of God's care and protection. Reformed theology traditionally speaks of common grace in addition to saving grace, thereby attesting its belief that all people are inescapably related to the living God and all are therefore beneficiaries of his providential care. It follows that every person has some intimation of God's goodness as well as of his severity against sin and wrongdoing. This knowledge, however, is sufficient only to render us inexcusable because it is clouded by a sinful proclivity within the very heart of humanity (cf. Rom 1:20-21). It does not lead directly to God but only reinforces our prideful self-sufficiency and self-trust. The picture of God that it produces corresponds not to the true God but only to the vain imaginings of sinful humanity. The image we conjure up of God is what we would like God to be, not what God really is. Augustine perceived this when he confessed that the idea of God that informed his philosophical quest was not the God of Christian revelation.[15] There can be no bona fide natural theology because theology cannot rest on the universal human awareness of some higher power, an awareness that necessarily renders a distorted and idolatrous picture of God.

The mystics recognized that our intellectual effort could take us only to the boundary of reason: it could not procure positive knowledge of the true God. For Gregory of Nyssa the divine nature "transcends every act of comprehensive knowledge, and it cannot be approached or attained by our speculation."[16] There is no human "faculty to comprehend the incomprehensible; nor have we ever been able to devise an intellectual technique for grasping the inconceivable."[17] Yet though we cannot mount up to God by the ladder of speculation we can ascend to him by the ladder of love. Love alone can penetrate the veil that separates God and humanity. Reason can take us only part of the way, but love can pierce through the cloud of unknowing.[18]

Thomas Aquinas believed that we can demonstrate the existence of a higher power, but we cannot prove the God of biblical revelation. We can probe the mystery of the being of God, but we cannot penetrate this mystery. Human reason can describe God analogically, but it must finally bow before mystery in its attempt to define God. Jüngel raises the question whether scholastic theology "is not defining the concept of the mystery of God solely through the limits of human knowledge. But is God a mystery because we are not able to know him adequately? Or is he full of mystery in his being? Does not a mystery constitute itself only through itself?"[19]

The traditional proofs for the existence of God can be helpful in clarifying the relation of God and the world, but only faith can identify the God of rational demonstration with the God of divine revelation. Anselm proffered the so-called ontological proof for God in which we reason from our conception of a highest being to the reality of this being. Such a proof enables faith to understand itself, but it does not compel the person of unfaith to believe. Helmut Thielicke makes a telling point that Anselm's proof is simply a transposition of the certainty of faith into the certainty of thought. It is therefore not a proof in the strict sense.[20]

The cosmological proofs put forward by Thomas Aquinas throw light on the relation of God and the world, but they do not positively prove the existence of the God of the Bible. In these proofs we begin with the traces of God in nature and on this basis argue for the existence of a first cause or prime mover or designer. Victor Preller prefers to speak of Thomas's five arguments as "five ways" substantiating "the theological claim that the mind of man is ordered to an Unknown God," but they are not to be construed as proofs.[21] Preller argues that in Thomas's view "assent to the proofs in no way *contributes* to the reception of faith, and failure to follow and accept the proofs is not an impediment to election by God."[22] He reminds us that for Thomas the authority for theology rests primarily on the authority of Scripture and secondarily on the witness of the saints and the wisdom of the philosophers. "Only the first of these is both necessary and sufficient to establish the truth of any position taken in the *Summa Theologiae.*"[23]

Thomas Oden presents a welcome interpretation of the role of rational arguments for the existence of God, which he claims is rooted in the tradition of faith:

Classical Christian teaching has held that these rational arguments are confirmatory to faith. They corroborate what faith knows, rather than produce or establish faith. . . . They are not independent, airtight, unchallengeable "proofs"; but taken together, they tend to confirm and rationally to validate what faith already knows of God's existence and to corroborate faith's persistently intuited conviction that God exists.[24]

The mystical heritage of the church regarded inward purification as a necessary first step to knowledge of the true God. Before the grace of illumination must come the arduous work of purgation, though the more solidly Christian mystics contended that we cannot even begin to purify ourselves adequately without the assistance of prevenient grace. Nevertheless, the knowledge of God was often portrayed as beyond the ken of ordinary mortals and available only to those who make the difficult ascent from the earthly to the spiritual realm. In the words of Gregory of Nyssa, "The knowledge of God is a mountain steep indeed and difficult to climb—the majority of people scarcely reach its base."[25]

The priority of works of obedience over faith runs through the writings of the mystics, and it has some biblical basis. Our Lord declares, "Those who do what is true come to the light, so that it may be clearly seen that their deeds have been done in God" (Jn 3:21 NRSV; cf. Jn 8:31–32; Rom 6:4–14; 12:2; 1 Jn 4:7–8). Yet the context indicates that only those can do the truth who have been placed in the truth by God's undeserved grace. We cannot do the truth unless we are already in the truth (Jn 8:42-47; Rom 6:17-18). Once we are grasped by the Spirit of God and united with the Son of God, we can then make progress toward a fuller understanding of the mystery of redemption.

It is misleading to claim, as does the Catholic theologian Fernand Van Steenberghen, that "the knowledge of God . . . is always the fruit and the reward of good will. God shows himself only to those who seek him."[26] While God does hearken to those who seek him truly, Scripture is clear that unbelieving persons do not seek God but crave only their own security and well-being (Ps 14:1-3; Rom 3:9-18). In the biblical context knowledge of God is not the reward for good works, but good works spring inevitably out of faith in the redemptive work of God, and this knowledge given through faith is all the Christian needs to make the pilgrimage to the holy city, the new Jerusalem.

In the evangelical perspective, we cannot find God by ascending the ladder of love, the ladder of merit or the ladder of speculation. Instead, God must find us by descending to us on the ladder of grace (Luther).[27] The God of biblical revelation is not the object that is thought nor the act of thinking, the thinking subject, but the One who speaks and acts, the self-revealing and self-communicating Lord of all of creation (Brunner). God reveals himself through himself, by his Word and by his Spirit (Irenaeus).[28] As Torrance aptly puts it, "We can only know God in His self-objectification for us, not by seeking non-objective knowledge of Him."[29]

Evangelical Christians join with Christian mystics in acknowledging the infinite distance between God and humanity. It is God alone "who has immortality and dwells in unapproachable light, whom no one has ever seen or can see" (1 Tim 6:16 NRSV). For the biblical Christian there is no way from humanity to God, but God has opened a way by which he establishes communion with his creation—the way of the incarnation and the cross of Jesus Christ (cf. Jn 1:18). It is not any ladder of speculation or stairway of merit that brings us to God but the elevator of free grace; all we have to do is step into it by the simple act of faith.

The goal of our works is to show others the way by which God comes to us and raises us into his presence. They also demonstrate our praise and thankfulness for God's immeasurable act of mercy.

While real knowledge of God comes only through Jesus Christ, this does not mean that nature or history are bereft of the presence of God. I here agree with Moltmann: "Nature is not the revelation of God. Nor is it God's image. But it shows 'traces of God' everywhere, if we are able to perceive in it a mirror and reflection of God's beauty."[30] In the light of God's redeeming act in Jesus Christ, we are able to discern and to appreciate the many signs of God's work and mercy in nature and in cultures and religions outside the sphere of Christian faith. In his light we are enabled to see light (Ps 36:9), but these little lights do not generate light in and of themselves. They reflect the one great light—the Son of God—through whom the world was created and by whose work the world is redeemed. The role of the little lights is to direct us to the great light, and thus they may have a positive role in the plan of salvation.

God as Elector and Persuader

God reveals himself not only in history but also in the experience of believers. God not only gives grace but creates faith. God not only elects people to service in his kingdom but also persuades them to accept and believe his gracious offer of redemption. All the glory in the accomplishment of our salvation must therefore go to the living God *(soli Deo gloria)*.

God is the persuader as well as the elector, but this does not imply that we who believe must therefore sit back and do nothing. We need to present the gospel as clearly and forcefully as possible in the confident hope that God will act in and through us. Paul declares, "It pleased God through the folly of what we preach to save those who believe" (1 Cor 1:21). The world cannot receive the Spirit of truth (Jn 14:17), but the Spirit of God can reach out through human instrumentality and open people's inward eyes so that they can begin to understand, and empower their wills so that they can begin to believe.

As messengers and ambassadors of our Lord Jesus Christ we do not so much persuade people of the truth of the gospel as invite them to believe in the gospel. We should not expend our efforts on arguments in support of the faith (though these are not to be disregarded altogether) but proclaim a message that creates the possibility of faith. We can persuade insiders of the viability of our theological interpretations, but we cannot persuade outsiders of the credibility of the gospel. Our task is not to *argue* the case for the gospel, as though it needed our defense, but to *present* the gospel as the life–giving message that alone can redeem from sin and death.

We must be prepared to give answers to those who question the claims of faith (1 Pet 3:15-16), but we should bear in mind that no human explanation can move the hearts of hardened sinners, though indeed they may be prompted to inquire further and perhaps finally hear and grasp the mystery of God's unfathomable love as revealed in Jesus Christ. Yet this inward hearing and grasping are themselves gifts of the Holy Spirit, who works through the preached word of the cross (Rom 10:14-17). God gives not only faith but the very condition to receive it. No human faculty can of itself lay hold of the treasure of salvation, but this word from the beyond can enter into our faculties so that we can understand truly, though never fully or exhaustively. The apostle declares, "May he enlighten the eyes of your mind so that you can see what hope his call holds for you" (Eph 1:18 JB).

This is not to imply that the human subject is entirely passive when acted on by grace. Those enslaved by sin will first of all resist the incursion of divine grace into their inner being, but then they are finally overwhelmed by the grace that is always greater than human sin. Jeremiah puts this succinctly: "O Lord, you have enticed me, and I was enticed; you have overpowered me, and you have prevailed" (Jer 20:7 NRSV).

Grace does not leave us in a state of torpor, however, but so enlightens our understanding and activates our will that we are moved to commit our lives to Christ. The mystery of Christian salvation is that God does all—but in and through human effort. We must not conceive this in terms of synergism, in which salvation is worked partly by grace and partly by human free will. The paradox is that God does all and we do all, but our efforts are entirely dependent on God working in and through us (Phil 2:12, 13).

Yet the human mind is not content to bow before mystery. From the beginning of Christian history people have sought to resolve the paradox of salvation either in the direction of embracing divine determinism or in the direction of accentuating human responsibility and autonomy. These attempts to reduce mystery to logic have had a baleful effect on preaching. In hyper-Calvinistic pulpits the gospel is sometimes treated as a discourse on God's predestinating decrees; our task is simply to resign ourselves to his irreversible will and to give him glory.[31] In popular Arminian preaching God's electing grace is not included in the gospel but becomes an appendage to it. The high point of the gospel message is the call to decision, which rests primarily on human freedom. Grace is enabling but not transforming: it assists the human will but does not turn it around. The error in much Barthian preaching is simply to announce what God has already done for us and the whole world in Jesus Christ; our task is to respond in loving service to our neighbor. But the idea that God's grace is not completed until it finds its goal in a personal decision of faith, apart from which we remain lost in our sins, does not really figure in mainstream Barthianism (which is not always faithful to Barth's own perspective).[32] Much liberal preaching reduces the gospel to moral exhortation and celebrates Jesus primarily as our model for righteous living. Faith simply becomes a response to the divine call to service, a response that is rewarded by grace.

The way we understand the mystery of salvation is closely tied to the way we understand God himself. If we picture God as a remote, benevolent ruler who allows the world to run by its own laws, then our salvation depends on our ability to discover and to master these laws. If we view God as an impassible, self-sufficient Absolute who attracts our wonder by the beauty and grandeur that he possesses, then salvation is entirely a matter of self-purification and human striving, a product of eros rather than of agape. If we conceive of God as an absolute monarch with unlimited power who has predetermined whatever comes to pass, then salvation is a matter neither of grace nor of works but of abject resignation to fate.

The biblical view is not to be confounded with any of the above. The God of the Bible is not content to gaze on his own illimitable glory, but out of compassion he freely chooses to go out of himself to seek and to save his lost human creation. God's predestination is not an irreversible decree made and completed outside time but an electing grace that is realized in time. The electing God is a God who goes out of himself into history. The persuading God is a God who creates fellowship by the power of his vicarious, self-giving love.

Henry Ward Beecher, nineteenth-century Congregationalist pastor and theologian, graphically described the living God of biblical religion as "laborious and self-sacrificing, seeking the race, not because they are so good, but to make them good, stimulating them, inspiring them, and desiring above all things else that they shall be fashioned . . . toward his sonship."[33] He was insistent that "God is supreme and sovereign, not because he is perfect, and not because he is lifted above care and trouble, but because he has in him a heart and soul that feels for sin, for infirmities, for sorrows, for mistakes; for all that goes to wreck and ruin."[34] Beecher failed to do justice to the sovereignty of God's grace, however, when he warned, "God has already done his part in the work of your salvation. If you don't choose to do your part you will perish."[35] Such an approach overlooks that God is active not only in bringing salvation to the world but also in awakening people to the reality of this salvation, moving them to accept his grace through the power of grace. At times, Beecher grasped the paradox of salvation, recognizing that we could not attain our goal unless God were at work within us "to will and to do of his good pleasure."[36] Basically Beecher sounded a call to heroism with the aid of grace, holding that human destiny depends on "the upbuilding of character," which is "one of the most glorious ambitions" that we can essay.[37]

It is precisely because God's grace is sovereign that we are set free to believe and to obey. Our faith does not create salvation but receives it. Our obedience does not earn salvation but manifests and demonstrates it. God's grace does not pulverize us but liberates us for fellowship and service. Nor does grace simply enable us to believe and to overcome: it makes us want to believe and assures us that we will overcome. Grace is not a new possibility that we can dispose of but the actuality of the power of creative transformation at work in human life. God elects us before we believe, and God persuades us so that we are compelled to believe. His love constrains us (2 Cor 5:14) by dispelling all doubt and fear so that we can be bold not only in deciding for Christ but in professing Christ before others. Divine election means that we are saved by grace and also kept by grace.

But we must not take God's grace for granted. We must not presume on God's benevolence by acting and living as though Christ had not interceded on our behalf. The One who gives grace may withhold it. The One who reveals himself may hide himself (Is 45:15). The light of faith may be eclipsed by the darkness of unbelief that may again intrude into our lives as an impossible possibility. Yet even in the darkness and despair into which God may allow us to fall his yes is more powerful than our no, his faith in us is stronger than our lack of faith in him (Rom 3:4; 2 Tim 2:13). To affirm God as elector and persuader means to affirm a future of blessedness that can be denied and spurned but not overthrown. God's wisdom will triumph through our folly: even our self-damnation cannot permanently obstruct the realization of the divine plan of salvation. Even pertinacious human obduracy cannot finally thwart the efficacy of God's overflowing love, which reaches out to all creation, even to the depths of hell as well as to the heights of heaven.

The Authority of Holy Scripture
We do not really know God until he speaks and acts, and he has done

so decisively and definitively in the history mirrored in Holy Scripture, culminating in Jesus Christ—the center and goal of Scripture. God reveals himself through himself: through his Word, who became incarnate in human flesh, and through his Spirit. But at the same time he reveals himself through the historical witness to his incomparable act of incarnation and condescension. The Spirit confronts us in human words that bear the imprint of cultural and historical conditioning. Revelation is therefore a mediated immediacy. We hear and see but indirectly, through external means: the Scriptures and the church proclamation of the scriptural message.

The Scriptures are not the object of faith but the catalyst that the Spirit uses to create faith. It is not sufficient simply to possess the Scriptures as documents or even to investigate the Scriptures as literature and history. The Jews were entrusted with the Scriptures of God (Rom 3:2), but they failed to grasp the meaning of the promises of God because they were "under the power of sin" (Rom 3:9), and so they were no better than the Gentiles.

We must avoid both the objectifying of scriptural truth and its existentializing. Pannenberg represents the first aberration in his contention that the Spirit inheres in the scriptural word and is not added to it.[38] The words carry within them "the meaning that already belongs to the events to which they refer."[39] In seeming contradistinction to both Calvin and Luther, Pannenberg rejects the view that the meaning of the biblical words is unlocked by an inspired or authoritative interpretation.[40] Revelation constitutes not supernatural knowledge but historical knowledge that is "open to general reasonableness."[41]

One can also discern an objectifying of revelation in Daniel Fuller. In his view the inspired or intended meaning of the text can be unearthed simply by bringing the canons of biblical interpretation to bear upon the text in question. The Word of God is thus reduced to the historical-grammatical meaning of the text, a meaning that is accessible to any diligent observer. The role of the Holy Spirit is to empower the human will to assent to what the human intellect can know on its own. The idea that the Holy Spirit imparts the true understanding of the text is rejected by Fuller, whose position is representative of a significant strand of evangelical rationalism.[42]

The existentializing of biblical truth is exemplified by Theodore Jennings, who offers a reinterpretation of the Apostles' Creed divested of its "mythological" and supernatural elements. For Jennings faith is neither belief in God's existence nor assent to revealed propositions nor even the passion of inwardness but loyalty to "the way of God," which we see enacted in the ministry and mission of Jesus. The resurrection of Christ is not a "nature miracle" in which a person comes back bodily from the tomb but an unparalleled witness to the power of life-giving love that cannot be contained by death. The ascension of Christ is not a literal elevation into a heavenly realm but the power of his spirit in the proclamation and witness of his followers. Eternal life is not life with God in heaven but a life free from exploitation and deprivation. The general resurrection of the dead becomes the uprising of the crucified against their oppressors. One may well ask whether this is a revision rather than a reaffirmation of the faith once delivered to the saints.[43]

Against both rationalistic objectivism and existentialist subjectivism, I propose that we retrieve the dialectical approach of Irenaeus, Augustine and the Reformers, an approach reaffirmed by the theology of crisis in the twentieth century.[44] The Swiss Reformer Ulrich Zwingli may here be taken as representative of this third position, which holds together Word and Spirit in a dynamic and paradoxical unity. For Zwingli God's Word can be grasped not by human understanding alone but only by "the light and Spirit of God, illuminating and inspiring the words" so that "the divine content" is seen in its "own light."[45] The Word of God brings with it "its own clarity"; it acts upon the understanding in such a way that the recipient is enabled to ascertain what is seen and heard.[46] Geoffrey Bromiley wisely observes, "By refusing to make an exact equation of the Word and the Bible Zwingli holds fast to the truth that the Word in its full and true sense is living speech. The Word is mediated through written documents, but it has its character and effectiveness as

Word only in so far as it is directed and applied by the Holy Spirit."[47]

That Scripture bears the stamp of divine authority through the inspiring and revealing action of the Spirit is not really grasped in much current discussion. At the Presbyterian (PCUSA) General Assembly in Milwaukee in June 1992 the potentially explosive decision was made to substitute "unique and authoritative" for "ultimate, authoritative source" to describe biblical authority.[48] Elizabeth Achtemeier of Union Theological Seminary in Richmond, Virginia, gave this timely warning:

> There is a virus eating at the PCUSA, a deadly disease that is making us sick, gradually but surely destroying our life together. The disease is characterized by the attempt to turn the Scriptures into a relativistic document that takes two forms, and both of them are found in the majority report on abortion that was adopted by the General Assembly. . . . First, the Scriptures are viewed no longer as the ultimate authority for our faith and practice but only as a unique authority, one differing from other authorities yet not necessarily superior to them. Second, the Scriptures are said to have no objective meaning in themselves but rather contain only that message which the individual interpreter brings to them.[49]

From my perspective Holy Scripture is not simply a "unique" authority for faith among other supposed authorities but in its unity with the Spirit the ultimate authority, the infallible standard for faith and practice. Nor does it derive its meaning from the person who comes to it seeking after truth. It contains an objective meaning that the inquirer must bow before and accept by virtue of the Bible's past inspiration by the Spirit and its present illumination in which the Spirit confirms and clarifies what he already affirmed and revealed through the mouth of human authors.[50]

It is commonly said in contemporary academic circles that the Scriptures, reflecting another culture and period of history, need to be transposed into new language and symbolism so that they can continue to speak to people today. Scripture needs to be made relevant and credible to the democratic, pluralistic and egalitarian ethos that characterizes the progressive nations of the modern world. In face of this attempt to reinterpret and rephrase Scripture in the light of a current ideology or worldview, we should heed Thomas Torrance's trenchant admonition: "By their nature the Holy Scriptures, given by divine inspiration, cannot be revised, let alone rewritten. In them God has set his seal upon his self-naming as Father, Son, and Holy Spirit, and thereby set his seal upon the language we are bound to use in praying to him and speaking of him."[51] Torrance does not rule out the use of new concepts and metaphors drawn from contemporary thought and experience to clarify or to illuminate old meanings, but with Barth he is firmly convinced that we must finally return again and again to the language of Zion, in which the Bible was originally composed, and this is especially true in our times of worship.

Donald Mathers, former principal of Queens Theological College in Kingston, Ontario, has likened the Bible to a telescope through which we see the divine beauty and holiness mirrored in Christ. "It is for looking through, not looking at. It is not itself revealed, it is the witness to revelation."[52] This illustration has some merit, but it obscures the revelational fact that the truth of faith is received by hearing rather than by vision (Rom 10:14-17; Col 3:16; Gal 3:2, 5). The Bible does not simply point us to Christ, but is a testimony from Christ himself. It might be better likened to a letter that carries the seal of Christ. The letter comes alive as we read it in the power of the Spirit so that we hear the living voice of Christ in the very words of the letter.

We cannot come to God either by a dialectic of inwardness (as in Kierkegaard) or by arduous self-purification (as in the mystics), but God comes to us even while we are still in our sins. We cannot rise up to God either by a ladder of speculation or by a ladder of merit, but God comes down to us as rain pours forth from a cloud or lightning strikes out of darkness. The Bible is the record of this irrevocable divine incursion into human history, and it is also the mirror and echo of what transpired in the past. It is not God's direct voice, but it carries his voice by the power of the Spirit. It is not itself the light, but it reflects the light through the working of the Spirit.[53]

Revelation is more than an event in our inner history that brings "rationality and wholeness into the confused joys and sorrows of personal existence."[54] It is an event in which God personally confronts his people with a message that both enlightens and redeems.[55] God discloses not only himself but objective information concerning his plan for the world. Yet this information is not generally accessible to human reason; it must be given ever anew by the Spirit of God, who employs the biblical text not as a replica of divine revelation but as an instrument that brings us into contact with the revelation that remains hidden even in the act of divine unveiling.

What the Spirit brings through Scripture is not general knowledge of the cosmos but salvific knowledge—expressed by means of affirmations that entail existential involvement rather than propositions that articulate universal truth.[56] The divine content of Scripture is the mystery of God's self-revelation in Christ that saves from the terror of spiritual darkness rather than metaphysical truths that simply enlighten the mind. This mystery can be grasped neither by inductive reasoning (Warfield)[57] nor by deductive logic (Gordon Clark) but only by the eyes of faith—a gift of the Holy Spirit. Once meaning shines through the mystery of divine revelation, it then gives sense and purpose to the whole of human and cosmic existence.

·FOUR·

TRANSCENDENCE

& IMMANENCE

I live in the holy heights
but I am with the contrite and humble,
to revive the spirit of the humble,
to revive the heart of the contrite.
ISAIAH 57:15 NJB

There is . . . one God and Father of all,
who is above all and through all and in all.
EPHESIANS 4:6 NRSV

He alone possesses immortality, dwelling in unapproachable light;
him no one has ever seen or can ever see.
1 TIMOTHY 6:16 REB

The distance between the Divine being and all created being is infinite.
JOHN OF THE CROSS

God is only absolute Lord of the world if He is wholly
independent of it; thus if it is wholly a work of His freedom.
EMIL BRUNNER

God is before, above, and after all things.
KARL BARTH

Already within biblical history the debate over the transcendence and immanence of God had begun to occupy people of faith. The Hebrews vigorously defended the utter transcendence of God against the goddess spirituality of the Canaanites and other Near East Semitic peoples that blurred the lines between God and nature. The Hebrews insisted that the true God infinitely transcends sexuality, and therefore Yahweh has no consort (unlike the gods of the Canaanites).[1] God is not the superlative of human possibilities but challenges and baffles human ingenuity. As the mouthpiece of God, the prophet asks, "To whom will you compare me? Or who is my equal?" (Is 40:25 NIV). Yet this God is not remote and detached from his people, for though he lives in a high and holy place, he also makes his dwelling with the contrite and humble in spirit (Is 57:15). This is a God who sees the humiliation of his people and hears their cry for mercy (Ex 3:7).

The ethical monotheism that came to dominate Judaistic religion sharply opposed the naturistic pantheism of the animistic and polytheistic religions prevalent in the ancient world. Yet with the advent of Christianity ethical monotheism itself was challenged, for God was portrayed not only as the supreme being, ruler of the world, but also as the incarnate Savior who identifies himself with the travail of the world. This being is not simply a being beside others but one who includes the fullness of all being in himself. The stance of Christian faith is a trinitarian monotheism that transcends the polarity between the Sky Father and the Earth Mother. The God of the Bible understood in the light of the incarnation of Jesus Christ is not a monochrome God but a fellowship of persons existing in a dynamic unity. He radiates the splendor not of solitary majesty but of outgoing love.

In the early church an attempt was made to unite the biblical vision of God with the wisdom of Hellenistic and Roman philosophy. One of the heretical deviations that resulted from this apologetic strategy was subordinationism, which posited a God beyond the God who meets us in Jesus Christ. The Arians held that the true God is the unoriginated and that Christ is a being less than God, though higher than humanity. More orthodox subordinationists contended for the ontological superiority of the Father over the Son and the Spirit, referring to the Father as the source and ground of the Son and Spirit. Against these misunderstandings the church insisted on the absolute equality of the members of the Trinity, though assigning a priority in relationship to the Father. Against Arianism it also upheld the full deity of the Son of God. To contend that the Father alone is God is to make God totally transcendent. To affirm that the Christ and the Spirit who meet us in human experience are also fully divine is to acknowledge the radical immanence as well as the incomparable transcendence of deity.

Gnosticism posed another serious challenge to the faith of the church, for it virtually removed God from the world of temporality and materiality.[2] A syncretic movement that drew upon many sources, Gnosticism was world-negating though it also sought to be self-fulfilling. The goal in life was to break free from the bonds of the flesh and to ascend to the purely spiritual realm where we are reunited with divine being. Redemption is from an evil material environment rather than from the perversion of sin, which for orthodox Christians originates in the realm of spirit. Gnosticism posited two gods: the demiurge who created the world and the supreme and remote divine being who was described only as "abyss" and "silence." Contact with the God beyond creation is made by discovering the point of identity with this God within the soul. The knowledge that redeems is the knowledge of self-discovery—that the essence of the self is divine. The church fathers (especially Irenaeus and Tertullian) sought to combat Gnosticism on the grounds that it denied the unity of the God of the two Testaments and demeaned the goodness of the creation.

More subtle were the allurements of Platonism and Neoplatonism, which envisioned a God beyond the divine-human encounter, often called the One—impassible, undifferentiated and utterly tranquil. Christians seeking to accommodate to this perspective saw the Son and the Spirit as manifestations or emanations from the One, who alone is unconditionally supreme. Dionysius the Pseudo-Areopagite postulated a God beyond the trinitarian distinctions, calling God "the superessential darkness."[3]

In Neoplatonism Augustine found insights that helped to free him from Manichaeism (a form of Gnosticism). Unlike the Gnostics, he saw evil not as a natural principle opposed to the good but as the privation of the good. Against Neoplatonism he insisted that God created the world ex nihilo and incarnated himself in world history. The world is not an emanation from eternal being that simply reflects the splendor of eternity but the arena in which God confronts us and transforms us by his Spirit. Augustine tried to hold together the Hellenistic and biblical visions of God: "You love, but are not inflamed with passion; you are jealous, yet free from care; you repent, but do not sorrow; you grow angry, but remain tranquil."[4]

While trying to steer clear of the pantheistic implications in Neoplatonism, the church fathers also had to be alert to the heresies of patripassianism and theopaschitism, which located suffering in the Godhead.[5] Orthodoxy contended that God the Father cannot be acted upon, since he is pure actuality. To suffer is to be acted upon, but God can never be at the mercy of his creation. God did suffer in the human nature of Jesus Christ but not in his divine nature.

According to Thomas Aquinas the world was both created by God out of the boundlessness of his love and used by God to redeem a lost humanity. Nature prepares the way for grace, and grace leads us to glory. The natural is the groundwork for the supernatural. The signs of God's presence in the immanent order lead us to contemplate the glory of God transcendent.

With the dawning of the Renaissance the supernatural creationism of the church fathers and the doctors of the medieval church was challenged by a creeping pantheism. For Nicholas of Cusa God is both the center and circumference of the world; he is everywhere and nowhere.[6] God is not a supreme being outside the world but the infinite unity that holds the world together. For Giordano Bruno God is wholly in the world and "infinitely and totally in each of its parts."[7]

Renaissance themes reappeared in the Enlightenment of the eighteenth century and in the Romanticism of the nineteenth century. The emphasis in the newly arising modernity was on continuity rather than crisis. God was no longer an infinite being beyond the universe but the infinite in the finite, the soul and ground of the world. Spinoza referred to God as the indwelling cause of the world rather than the transcendent cause (as in Thomas). Schleiermacher wrote, "The usual conception of God as one single being outside of the world and behind the world . . . is only one manner of expressing God, seldom entirely pure and always inadequate."[8] According to Hegel, "The God outside of us who saves us by His grace, is a misleading pictorial expression for saving forces *intrinsic* to self-conscious Spirit, wherever this may be present."[9] In his philosophy the creation of the world is not a kind of emanation (from the perfect to the imperfect) but evolution (from the imperfect to the perfect). Hegel did not flatly identify the world with God but held to their inseparability: he perceived the world's progress as God in his development.

Even those who remained close to classical theism strove to overcome the gulf between God and humanity. God is to be found not simply in the history of the Bible but in nature, conscience and universal history. Henry Ward Beecher, whose theology constitutes an attenuated Calvinism, admonished: "Remember grace is only *nature blossomed out;* it is no new thing grafted in upon nature, but nature won and warmed into its *true* growth; that for which the God of nature made it."[10] His appeal was not to divine revelation alone but to natural sensibility as well: "Each one of our faculties, when well cultivated, becomes an interpreter of God, a window through which we can look out and see God."[11]

Although a mysticism of nature continued to make headway, especially with the rise of Romanticism, prophetic spirits in the church toiled unremittingly to combat the trend toward immanentism. In the nineteenth century Søren Kierkegaard was a particularly adamant foe of the religion of immanence. For him God was "the Absolutely Different" and "the Eternal," who towered above human nature and history even as he intervened decisively in it in the moment of the incarnation. "God and man are two qualities between which there is an infinite qualitative difference. Every doctrine which overlooks this difference is . . . blasphemy."[12] Against the Danish theologian Nikolai Grundtvig, who sought a synthesis of Christianity and Nordic mythology, Kierkegaard underscored the uniqueness and incomparability of the divine revelation in

Jesus Christ. Grundtvig held that both Odin and Christ could be deemed sons of God;[13] Kierkegaard stoutly maintained that Jesus Christ alone is the Son of the living God.[14]

In the twentieth century the theology of crisis, associated with Karl Barth and Emil Brunner among others, is to be seen as a herculean effort to stem the tide toward immanentism. In his groundbreaking *Epistle to the Romans* Barth described God as "the Wholly Other," who infinitely transcends the reach of human perception and conception.[15] For Barth "God stands at an infinite distance from everything else, not in the finite degree of difference with which created things stand towards each other."[16] Brunner insisted that "what the philosophers call 'revelation' is different from that which faith calls 'revelation.' The God who is discovered through thought is always different from the God who reveals Himself through revelation. The God who is 'proved,' just because He has been 'proved,' is not the God in whom man 'believes.' "[17] Indeed, "the God with whom we have to do in faith, is not a Being who has been discussed or 'conceived.' . . . He is not an object of thought—even though in a sublimated and abstract form—but the Subject who as 'I' addresses us as 'thou.' "[18] Brunner was willing to affirm a "transcendence of essence" in God in which God is "absolutely and irrevocably different from all other forms of being," but not a "transcendence of being," which in the absolute sense portrays God as not immanent in any sense at all but as radically separate from the world. The latter view ends in deism, which is as unacceptable to faith as pantheism and panentheism.[19]

Because the valid insights of crisis theology have been obscured by the new immanentalism associated with existentialist and process theologies, this book is an attempt to retrieve these insights in dialogue with the new theological movements described in a later section of this chapter. I am convinced that theology today sorely needs to recover a robust supernaturalism that avoids the overt dependence on Hellenistic philosophy as well as a naive biblicism that reduces God to "the Man Upstairs." The true God is neither the highest abstraction of human thought nor the superlative of human personhood but the One from the beyond who intervenes in human life and who turns around human thought so that we are given an entirely new horizon of meaning and an absolutely new motivation for living. Kierkegaard, Barth and Brunner have shown us the way, but we need to build on their contributions, for the church faces new challenges as it nears the end of the twentieth century. It must cope with new heterodoxies as it struggles to remain true to the faith once delivered to the saints. We do not need a neo-Barthianism, but we do need a refurbished evangelical Christianity that draws upon the heritage of the church catholic as well as upon the treasures within Holy Scripture as it seeks to articulate a doctrine of God that makes sense to thinking Christians, though it can never be palatable to the modern mind.

Infinity and Spirituality

The God of the Bible is infinite—free from all limitations. In philosophical tradition infinity carries the idea of being unlimited or immeasurable in extent of space and duration of time. Yet it must be emphasized that infinity in the theological sense connotes freedom from all *creaturely* limitations. It does not imply that God is formless or characterless. God is free to limit himself. He is also free to withhold himself from his creatures. He is free to create and free not to create.

The idea of "absolute infinity" is more philosophical than biblical.[20] Barth rightly reminds us that God is both infinite and finite: "God is certainly infinite, i.e., He has no basis which is not Himself, no goal which is not Himself and no standard or law which is not Himself. But He is also finite—without destroying, but in His infinity—in the fact that as love He is His own basis, goal, standard and law."[21] We may call God "infinite, measureless, limitless, spaceless and timeless," but "this does not mean that we will try to exclude, deny or even question that He is the One who in His whole action posits beginning and end, measure and limit, space and time."[22] God is infinite but he can enter into the finite, he can take the finite into himself. His being is infinite, but he can incarnate himself in the finite, he can realize his purposes in the arena of the finite. God can make himself finite without ceasing to be infinite and can unceasingly relate himself to the finite.

Eternity is closely associated with infinity; indeed, the two concepts are virtually interchangeable in some contexts. In philosophical tradition "eternal" indicates the absence of limits of time. It applies to what has no known beginning and presumably no end. In this sense it means everlasting. The classical notion of eternity (as in Boethius) is "a time-lessness where God experiences past, present and future simultaneous-ly."[23]

Barth made a valiant effort to bring the philosophical concept of eternity into the service of the biblical revelation.[24] As a result this concept was irremediably altered, for an absolute dichotomy between eternity and time is not found in the Bible. Protestant orthodoxy portrayed God as "action without movement," being "without time and beyond time."[25] According to Barth God's eternity is eminent temporality. God has his own time, "the absolutely real time."[26] God includes time within himself while still remaining eternal. God's eternity is not itself time, but it is the absolute basis for time and the absolute readiness for it. In Barth's view God is supratemporal rather than nontemporal. This idea corresponds to the biblical distinction between *chronos* and *kairos*. The first indicates what is fleeting or transitory. The second denotes the fulfillment of time in an enduring relationship with the eternal. Brunner phrases it well: "God's Being is not timeless; but it is full of time, fulfilling time; all that is temporal is present in Him in the same way."[27]

Otto Weber has also been helpful in articulating anew the paradoxical unity of time and eternity in God. Eternity is not timelessness but God's "absolute previousness in relation to all time."[28] "God's eternity accompanies time, carries it, and grants it to us." Eternity is the ground and goal of time. "Time is not advancing toward nothingness, but toward eternity. It does not peter out: it comes to its goal."[29] Eternity is not the antithesis of time but God's lordship over time. This "does not consist of his having once caused time to be, but of the fact that he always precedes our time. Thus his eternity is 'pretemporality.' "[30]

Another aspect of God's infinity is his immensity. According to the Reformed theologian Amandus Polanus, "God's *immensitas* is the essential attribute of God, through which the divine essence is signified as not being limited, circumscribed or bounded by any place, but as penetrating and filling places one and all everywhere and being present to all things."[31] The immensity of God means that God cannot be measured. His infinity means that the essence of God cannot be contained within any bounds. Scripture refers to the "immeasurable greatness" of the power of God "in us who believe, according to the working of his great might" (Eph 1:19). His power is "abundant" and "his understanding is beyond measure" (Ps 147:5).

Closely associated with God's immensity is his omnipresence or ubiquity. This does not mean that his being literally permeates all matter but that everything is included in his overall vision. Matter is a channel of his power but not a part of his nature. The Old Testament sage declares, "The eyes of the Lord are in every place, keeping watch on the evil and the good" (Prov 15:3). Omnipresence does not signify spacelessness but God's freedom to be in space. He is present to all his creatures, but there is no identity between God and the creature.

Theological speculation has often veered toward pantheism by incorporating the philosophical notion of omnipresence. In the biblical view omnipresence is not the inactive extension of divine being in the universe but "sovereign dominion over all space" (Küng).[32] Luther charged Zwingli with "imagining God as a vast, immense being that fills the world, pervades it and towers over it, just like a sack full of straw, bulging above and below."[33] But God "is no such extended, long, broad, thick, high, deep being. He is a supernatural, inscrutable being who exists at the same time in every little seed, whole and entire, and yet also in all and above all and outside all created things." Luther sought to safeguard the mystery that God infinitely transcends his creation and yet actively relates himself to every part of his creation. Pannenberg is helpful in his observation that while "God's eternity means that all things are always present *to him,* the stress in his omnipresence is that he is present *to all things at the place of their existence.*"[34] God's presence fills heaven and earth (Jer 23:24), but this is an act of his freedom, not a necessary implication of his essence.

God is supreme over all space and time, yet God has his own space and time. God's spatiality is identical with his being. There is a spatiality that belongs to him. Because God has time and space within himself, he does not contradict himself by creating historical time and creaturely space. Our time and space reflect the absolute time and space that constitute the very being of God and that alone are enduring. True eternity includes the potentiality of time and space. "True eternity has the power to take time [and space] to itself, this time, the time of the Word and Son of God."[35]

Another side of the infinity of God is his aseity—the quality of having life in and of oneself. Aseity means that God is radically independent of all creaturely power and being. God is self-sufficient, self-sustaining and self-existent. Yet here again philosophical meanings can undercut the biblical truth that this God who is sufficient unto himself and independent of everything outside himself nevertheless has the freedom to make himself dependent on those whom he has created. He exists by his own power, but he seeks to fulfill his plan and purpose in cooperation with his people whom he empowers by his Spirit.

Christian faith also insists upon the spirituality of God. In the words of John, "God is a Spirit: and they that worship him must worship him in spirit and in truth" (Jn 4:24 KJV).[36] The God of the Bible is not a material being, nor is he a composite being. He is invisible and spiritual, not visible and physical. But does this mean that he is unrelated to the material, that he exists in antithesis to the physical? The older theology portrayed God as absolute Form, but does he not also have a concrete nature—not a human nature to be sure but a divine nature? As already noted, Cochrane has observed that Scripture speaks not only of God as a Spirit but also of God's nature; God has wrath and mercy, even "face, arms, hands, and feet."[37] Much of this language must, of course, be taken symbolically, but it points to the truth that God exists in a unity of his spirit and nature. In idealistic philosophy the distinction between divine and human actuality is understood in terms of the polarity of spirit and nature, soul and body, internal and external, visible and invisible. Cochrane reminds us that the event of revelation "possesses natural, corporeal, and visible elements, as testified by the Creation (not only of heaven but of the earth), by the concrete existence of the people of Israel in Palestine, by the birth of Christ, his physical miracles, his suffering and dying under Pontius Pilate, and by his bodily resurrection."[38] To affirm God's spirituality does not mean the denigration of the visible and the material but its transfiguration in the light of God's glory. God is not a material being, but he can assume a material form, and he has done so in the incarnation of his Son, Jesus Christ. His Son was resurrected not as a pure spirit but in a bodily form that carried the earmarks of materiality. The resurrection means not liberation from the flesh but glorification of the flesh. Yet this glorification involves a transformation and elevation of flesh into a spiritualized form of existence.

In biblical parlance spirit is not opposed to body (as in the Hellenistic view). God has a spiritual body just as he has his own space and time. Nor is spirit opposed to nature. God assumed a human nature which he united with but never confounded with his divine nature. Spirituality in mystical tradition involves an attempt to disengage ourselves from the physical and rise to the realm of pure spirit. Spirituality in biblical perspective means the descent of the spiritual into the material. It involves meeting material and genuine human needs but with a spiritual purpose and goal. The spirituality of God is not to be confused with a spirit world beyond the material; instead it is to be seen as the light of the presence of God that breaks into the darkness of our world and sets us free to serve in the very midst of the degradation that surrounds us. God is a spirit, but he includes the phenomena of nature, humanity and history within his comprehensive vision. In contrast to an exaggerated Neoplatonism and Gnosticism, biblical faith asserts that God's spirituality "is not exclusive opposition to matter which is regarded as evil, but power infinitely superior to all created things."[39] To say that God is invisible and spiritual does not suggest that he is limited to the invisible and spiritual, excluded from the visible, material and physical.

To affirm God's spirituality is also to affirm his simplicity. Christian faith is adamant that God is one and indivisible, that he does not encompass within himself disparate parts or quantities.[40] Nor is his relation to the world to be understood as an amalgamation or combination with the world process. This does not imply that God is monochrome or solitary. He exists as a triune fellowship within himself and relates himself to the world in a multitude of ways. He is not simply personal but interpersonal. He has many faces and countless modes of action. But within and behind this irrefragable diversity is an underlying unity—in being and in purpose. In Barth's words:

> Being simple in the sense described, God is incomparably free, sovereign and majestic. In this quality of simplicity are rooted, fixed and included all the other attributes of His majesty: His constancy and eternity, His omnipresence, omnipotence and glory. Nothing can affect Him, or be far from Him, or contradict or withstand Him, because in Himself there is no separation, distance, contradiction or opposition.[41]

Barth nevertheless reminds us that although God is simple, the simple is not God. The human mind has little difficulty in conceiving of a whole that is indivisible or an indivisible that is a whole.[42] But when we try to "think out the idea of the simple to its conclusion," the simple becomes "an utterly unmoved being, remote from this world altogether, incapable of sound or action, influence on or relation to anything else."[43]

Both the spirituality and simplicity of God sharply distinguish him from the world that he has created, from the humanity that he sustains and nurtures, from the history that he directs and judges. Yet we must not mistake God's spirituality for a reality that can never be joined to the material nor God's simplicity for a conceptual abstraction that isolates him from the real world in which we live. The paradox that biblical faith celebrates is that the spiritual has entered into the material in order to redeem and transform it. The simple has entered into the world of complexity and confusion in order to give it purpose and direction. God is Spirit, but Spirit is not discovered in the depths of human selfhood but is unveiled in the dramas of human history, most of all in the life, death and resurrection of Jesus Christ, who brings us the promise of a new earth as well as a new heaven.

Immutability and Impassibility

Classical theism, which sought to employ philosophical concepts in elucidating the biblical vision of God, presented a picture of God that often stood at variance with the biblical witness. God's perfection was envisaged in terms of his total unchangeability *(immutabilitas)*, his invulnerability to suffering *(impassibilitas)*, his completeness *(actus purus)*, and his possession of all possible values *(ens realissimum)*. This depiction of God was commonplace among the church fathers and the doctors of the medieval church, including Augustine, Anselm and Thomas Aquinas.[44] It was also reflected in Reformation and post–Reformation orthodoxy[45] as well as in the idealistic philosophy of Descartes and Leibniz (seventeenth and eighteenth centuries). More recently the doctrine of God's immutability and impassibility has been reaffirmed by Baron von Hügel, who maintained that God in himself is "pure joy, an ocean of it" with "not one drop of sin or suffering or of the possibility of either."[46] Although he acknowledged that this pure joy includes compassion and sympathy, he was adamant that "religion itself requires the transcendence of God in a form and a degree which exclude suffering in him."[47] H. P. Owen, who defends traditional theism in his *Concepts of Deity*, recognizes that suffering may be included in God's love for his creation but insists that such suffering is "immediately transfigured by the joy that is necessarily his within his uncreated Godhead."[48] Similarly E. L. Mascall acknowledged that God "sympathizes with our sorrows" but "even this is infinitely surpassed by the beatitude which God enjoys in the interior fulness of his own divine life."[49] Paul Fiddes questions whether this can be deemed real suffering.[50]

Scripture itself is very firm on the abiding reality and utter transcendence of the living God, but whether this kind of vision can be reconciled with the Greek view of immutability and impassibility is another matter. "The grass withers, the flower fades," says Isaiah, "but the word of our God will stand for ever" (40:8). The psalmist contends that the heavens and earth "will pass away, but you remain. . . . You are the same and your years will have no end" (Ps 102:26-27 REB). This theme is reiterated in Hebrews: The earth and heavens "shall perish, while you endure. . . . They shall undergo change. . . . But you remain ever the same" (1:11-12 GNC). In Malachi we read, "I the Lord do not change; therefore you, O sons of Jacob, are not consumed" (3:6). The Epistle of James strikes a similar note: "Every good endowment and every perfect gift is from above, coming down from the Father of lights with whom there is no variation or shadow due to change" (1:17). Adrio König maintains convincingly that the passages in Psalm 102 and Hebrews 1 are concerned with the eternity and incorruptibility of God and cannot be used to endorse the Greek idea of God's total unchangeability.[51] The Malachi text is indeed speaking of God's unchangeability, but the meaning is that God "reacts in accordance with what he has promised; that is, he is faithful. This does not imply remoteness or detachment, but rather the most radical involvement in history."[52] Similarly the citation from James does not support the Greek conception of a God "who cannot react, is not involved with his creation, knows no repentance and cannot change his intentions."[53] The biblical view is that God is true to himself and unchangeably faithful to his people, not that he is incapable of being affected by the sufferings of his people.

Martin Luther posed a significant challenge to the biblical-classical synthesis on the grounds that God himself shared in the humiliation and passion of Jesus. "If I believe that the human nature alone suffered for me, then is Christ worse than no Saviour to me."[54] This is not patripassianism but deipassianism.[55] God the Father did not suffer and die on the cross, but he suffered in Christ. Luther sometimes distinguished between the nature of God as he relates to the world and the person of the Son of God as he relates to the Trinity. For Luther, suffering in this context pertains only to the first, though he did not hold fast to this distinction.[56]

Barth affirmed the notions of immutability and impassibility as applied to God, but radically reinterpreted them. Immutability describes "the living God in His freedom and love, God Himself. He is what He is in eternal actuality. He never is it only potentially (not even in part). He never is it at any point intermittently. But always at every place He is what He is continually and self-consistently."[57] Barth preferred the term "constancy" to "immutability," since it retains the idea of God's fidelity to himself and to his people. Constancy means that there "neither is nor can be, nor is to be expected or even thought possible in Him, the One and omnipresent being, any deviation, diminution or addition, nor any degeneration or rejuvenation, any alteration or non-identity or discontinuity. The one, omnipresent God remains the One He is."[58]

While Barth was critical of the traditional notion of impassibility, which portrays God as unfeeling and supremely detached, he recognized the truth that God cannot be moved by anything outside himself except by his own volition. God possesses in himself a perfect beatitude that cannot be shaken, even by the pleadings of his people, but he wills to suspend this beatitude and hearken to their cries. "He could have remained satisfied with Himself and with the impassible glory and blessedness of His own inner life. But He did not so do."[59] The God who is impassible in himself can be passible in the world. Barth was not willing to speak of a cleft in the inner being of God, but he did acknowledge that God freely chose to enter into a history of contradiction. In a direct challenge to classical theism Barth contended for a "holy mutability" in God: "He is above all ages. But above them as their Lord . . . and therefore as the One who—as Master and in His own way—partakes in their alteration, so that there is something corresponding to that alteration in His own essence."[60]

Jürgen Moltmann goes further than Barth in maintaining that the travail of the world is necessarily included in God himself. Yet he tries to stay clear of patripassianism by contending that only the Son undergoes the experience of dying; the Father suffers the grief of the Son. In a strikingly un–Barthian stance Moltmann maintains that not only do we need God's compassion but also God needs ours for his perfection to be complete.

Tillich, too, recoiled from patripassianism with its implication that God's purposes can be thwarted or defeated. Tillich acknowledged non-being within God himself, but this negative element is constantly being overcome and superseded. The truth in the traditional notion of God's impassibility is that there is an eternal conquest of the negative in God.[61]

I believe that we must continue to affirm the immutability of God not in the sense that God is static and unbending but in the sense that God remains true to himself and to his purposes. It might be better to speak with Barth of God's constancy or with Thomas Oden of God's reliability.[62] As Barth phrases it, "God is certainly the immutable, but as the immutable He is the living God and He possesses a mobility and elasticity which is no less divine than His perseverance."[63] Or in the words of Hans Küng: God's immutability "must be understood as essential fidelity to himself in all his active vitality."[64] God's being is indestructible, his plan and purpose are unalterable. His love is unfailing and inexorable. His grace is irreversible and persevering. This is the biblical picture of God's unchangeableness.

The notion of impassibility can be retained so long as it does not mean that God is impassive and unfeeling. According to James Packer the biblical meaning of impassibility is that "no created beings can inflict pain, suffering and distress on him at their own will. . . . The Christian mainstream has construed impassibility as meaning not that God is a stranger to joy and delight, but rather that his joy is permanent, clouded by no involuntary pain."[65]

The impassibility of God must not be confused with imperturbability (ataraxia) or apathy (apatheia). God freely involves himself in the travail of his creation, yet he does not cease to be joyous as he looks forward to the overcoming of this travail. God remains above pain and suffering even while descending into the world of confusion and misery. He is not invulnerable to pain and suffering, but he rises above them. He transforms our pain into his joy. He does not simply empathize with our pain but he enters into it, he experiences it. Against Moltmann I contend that a theology of the cross must be completed in a theology of glory. The cross is not the last word, for Jesus Christ rose from the dead and ascended into heaven. God in Christ drinks from the bitter cup of suffering, but this suffering is transfigured by the joy of his resurrection triumph.[66]

Suffering is not inherent in God, but God freely wills to enter into our suffering so that it can be overcome. God cannot be changed by either heavenly or earthly powers, but God can change himself. He remains unchanging in his will for the world, but he alters his ways with his people in conjunction with their response to his gracious initiative. God enters into a reciprocal relationship with his people so that we can have a role in the realization of his plan and purpose. He makes us covenant partners with him in the drama of redemption, but our role is to receive and celebrate, to witness and proclaim. He alone is the efficient cause that moves the world. We are, at the most, instrumental causes that he uses to accomplish his purposes.

To view God's immutability as "devoid of all succession, change or variation" as in the older orthodoxy is to render God powerless.[67] God has the freedom to alter the course of events in order to realize his overall purposes more effectively. In so doing he remains true to his nature, faithful to his plan, constant in his love and devotion. God allows himself to be affected by the prayers of his children, he allows himself to be hurt by the hardness of their hearts. The risen Christ made clear that he was sorely afflicted by the persecution of Saul (Acts 9:4-5; 22:6-8). And the apostle urges the Ephesians, "Do not give pain to God's Holy Spirit, whose seal you have had set upon you, so as to mark you out for the Day of Redemption" (4:30 GNC).

The biblical idea of God's freedom has been subverted not only by mainstream Christian orthodoxy but also by the idealistic-mystical tradition that has infiltrated both church and culture. The Renaissance philosopher Nicholas of Cusa envisioned divine perfection as "the infinite actualization of all that is simply and absolutely possible."[68] This is a reaffirmation of the Neoplatonic principle of plenitude in which divine perfection invariably entails the fullness of being.[69] Such a position makes the world a necessary implication of God's essence. It does not consider that God in his freedom has passed over some possibilities. God is neither completed actuality nor infinite potentiality but a dynamic actuality that is constantly coming to himself, reclaiming and experiencing anew what he already is.

Reinterpretations of Transcendence

Theological movements receive their distinctiveness from the manner in which they conceive of God. The major movements in theology today signify sophisticated attempts to redefine transcendence. Existentialism finds transcendence at the outer limits of reason. God exceeds the bounds of human apprehension, but this does not imply that God is ontologically prior to the world. In a theologian like Tillich we meet God in the depths of human existence rather than in the heavenly heights. God becomes the infinite ground and depth of all being. Here we see a synthesis between existentialism and the new mysticism of the earth. Similarly J. A. T. Robinson contended that God is to be found not "out there" or "up there" but "in here," in the center of the soul.[70] Drawing upon the panentheism of Hegel, Hans Küng concludes that God "is not separate from the world and man; he is not outside all that is; inherent in the world and man, he determines their being from within."[71]

No theological movement has focused more attention on the doctrine of God than has process theology. The process God is not a God who acts in history but a superconsciousness that resides in the processes of nature. He is not "a rigid ground of being" but "the lure of becoming."[72] For Whitehead and Hartshorne God is not infinite but finite, though irreversibly moving toward an infinity yet to be realized. God's transcendence is conceived of in terms of self-surpassing excellence rather than radical independence from the world of creation. Whitehead envisaged a world of eternal objects, corresponding to Plato's eternal ideas, that guided the actual entities of the world in their quest for fulfillment. Transcendence is here found in abiding ideals that lure nature onward toward new spiritual heights. Hartshorne distinguished between the "perfection" of God and his "completion."[73] God is perfect in that he is whole and inclusive, but he has not realized all his potentialities. David Pailin sees transcendence in the unrealized open future that is being realized as God and the world move toward an ever higher perfection.[74]

In the theology of hope associated with Moltmann and the early Pannenberg, transcendence is the power of the future—the eschatological consummation of all things that is anticipated now as we move toward a higher degree of justice.[75] Moltmann prefers to think of God as the "God before us" as opposed to the "God above us" and the "God within us."[76] In his view God is not a sovereign being transcendent over the world but "the event of self-liberating love." God is "transcendent as Father, immanent as Son and opens up the future of history as the Spirit."[77]

Detecting in Marxism a continuity with the prophetic tradition of the Bible, liberation theology locates transcendence in the new world of hope and promise that is realized in the ongoing struggle against oppression and injustice. Transcendence is not in a God over history, but it is the dynamic of history itself that brings us a new horizon of meaning. According to Ronaldo Muñoz: "The Bible . . . reflects the primitive beliefs of a people on their journey, whose faith had to be continuously purified by the blows of history . . . and finally, radicalized by the witness of Jesus Christ."[78]

In narrative theology transcendence is being caught up by the creative power that directs and shapes world history as we identify with the trials and hopes of the heroes of biblical faith, as we relive the stories of men and women of God.[79] Metaphysical explanations of transcendence are for the most part eschewed in favor of making experiential contact with the Spiritual Presence that molds and guides people of faith. Christianity is seen as an invitation to pilgrimage rather than a summation of propositional truths that give correct information on the nature, will and purpose of God.[80]

Cultic aberrations that come out of Christian faith often drastically alter the understanding of transcendence. In Mormonism transcendence consists in other worlds within the vast cosmos of the universe, for the most part hidden from human perception.[81] In Spiritualism transcendence lies in spirit worlds beyond the earthly mode of existence but still part of the evolutionary world process. The hope is to make contact with these higher planes of existence through shamans or mediums.[82] A similar idea is expressed in the New Age movement, which views some persons endowed with unusual psychic gifts as channels through which ascended masters communicate with ordinary mortals.[83]

New forms of biblical or evangelical theology stand forthrightly for a supernatural creationism that conceives of God as a supreme being who by a free act of decision brings the worlds into being. Barth basically saw transcendence as the presence of God, a presence involving both spatiality and temporality but always sharply distinct from the historical world of space and time.[84] Karl Heim conceived of transcendence as another space-time dimension that lies beyond the polarities of human experience.[85] This "suprapolar space" is not to be confused with the eternal reality of God himself, however. It is the medium through which God makes contact with us, but it does not exhaust the mystery of the inner life of God. God is still the *Deus absconditus* even as he reveals himself to us in the witness of Holy Scripture.[86] But we know enough about God to mount an effective apologetic for the claims of Christian supernaturalism against the naturalism and relativism that dominate the centers of university life. Heim freely drew upon the new breakthroughs in the natural sciences as he tried to bring words like "supramundane," "super-historical" and "supernatural" back into Christian discourse.[87] Among scholars in more recent times who argue for the credibility of supernaturalism (in the sense I have defined it) and who are thoroughly conversant with modern science are T. F. Torrance,[88] John Polkinghorne[89] and Phillip E. Johnson. Johnson shows with considerable acumen that the theory of evolution lacks scientific basis and that Christian supernaturalism can make a persuasive case in the intellectual arena.[90]

Dynamic Transcendence

We must avoid the Charybdis of deism and the Scylla of pantheism and panentheism by affirming a dynamic biblical theism that does justice to both God's otherness and his personalness. God is present to us but not inherent in us. He upholds us but is not identical with us. God is both the Wholly Other and the Infinitely Near. He is both God transcendent and God *with* us and *for* us. Richard Keyes here reflects my own sentiments:

> God is immanent, close to us, available to us. But that does not make Him a tame God, controllable, at our disposal. . . . God is also transcendent. He is great beyond greatness. He is the Alpha and the Omega, the beginning and the end. But that does not make Him distant, impersonal, impotent, arbitrary, or beyond moral categories.[91]

If we conceive of God as infinitely other, we must at the same time envisage him as infinitely close. If we picture him as wholly transcendent, we must at the same time allow for the truth that he is radically immanent in the sense of being present with us and for us. But he is never immanent without being essentially transcendent, just as he does not remain transcendent without making himself for our sakes immanent. God's immanence is an act of his freedom, not a quality of his being. Just as he freely relates to his creation, so he is also free to withdraw from his creation.

God is both "beneath" and "above," but he is the latter before he is the former. He is the living Creator, not simply the *source* of all things. In the Hellenistic conception God *cannot* change, for his nature is unalterable and incorrigible. In Christian doctrine God *does not* change, for he wills to remain true to his nature. The God of mysticism is "the God always at rest" *(Deus semper quietus)*. The God of prophetic religion is the ever active God *(Deus semper agens)*. God is best described not as the Absolutely Other (as in mysticism and existentialism) nor as the Creative Energy or Vital Force (as in process thought and New Age religion) but as the majestic Lord and loving Savior (as in biblical religion).

God has new experiences, but they do not so much enrich his being or add to his perfection as bring out the perfection that he already possesses.[92] God's anger does not subtract from his goodness, nor does his forbearance add to his goodness. He already has the fullness of perfection and glory in himself, but he radiates this glory in different ways, as he freely interacts with his people and with all humankind. In the words of Adrio König, "To suggest that God could not will any *new* things would be to make of him a thing, a ground of being, instead of the living God of Israel. *New* things (creation, incarnation) do not *change* his will, but are acts of his will that give form to his being in new situations."[93]

God enters the realm of contingency, though he does not himself become contingent but remains the Eternal. As Barth phrases it so well, "God gives Himself, but He does not give Himself away. He does not give up being God in becoming a creature, in becoming man. He does not cease to be God. He does not come into conflict with Himself."[94] God identifies with the pain and misery caused by our sin, but he does not succumb to this malady: he overcomes it not simply through an act of creative imagination but through the cross and resurrection of his Son, Jesus Christ. As the victim hanging on the cross he was already the victor over the powers of sin, death and the devil.

God wills his own being, and his being is fully consonant with his will. His will expresses his being, and his being is manifested through his will. "God is His own will," said Barth, "and He wills His own being. Thus will and being are equally real in God, but they are not opposed to one another in the sense that the will can or must precede or follow

TRANSCENDENCE & IMMANENCE

the being or the being the will."[95]

Much of what I contend for is in accord with classical theism. The differences lie in my envisaging God as a person who freely interacts with his creation rather than a first cause or principle of being. H. P. Owen, who presents a contemporary case for classical theism, sees the basic attributes of God as his "unity, personality, transcendence, creativity and moral holiness."[96] This comes close to the biblical theism that I uphold, but surprisingly he leaves out love, and it is love that constitutes the biblical understanding of God as dynamic transcendence.[97] It is love that gives meaning to the interaction of God with the world of his creatures.

God's transcendence is nowhere more graphically expressed than in his free decision to make his second dwelling place with the contrite and humble in spirit (Is 57:15). This decision is nowhere more powerfully revealed than in the incarnation of Jesus Christ, in which God makes himself weak and vulnerable for the sake of his people. In countering the Hellenistic conception of a remote, monarchial deity, Gregory of Nyssa insightfully declared, "God's transcendent power is not so much displayed in the vastness of the heavens, or the luster of the stars, or the orderly arrangement of the universe or his perpetual oversight of it, as in his condescension to our weak nature."[98]

According to the renowned scholar of Judaism George Foot Moore, the Old Testament viewed God as imminent-eminent.[99] The Hebrews affirmed the imminence of God, meaning that God is very close to humanity. But they gave equal emphasis to his eminence—God is much more lofty than humanity, though this in no way limits his contact with humanity. He is "supramundane but not extramundane" in the sense of not having contact with the world. He is "exalted but not remote."[100] This notion of imminence-eminence contrasts with that of the Jews of Alexandria, who upheld extreme transcendence.

The God of the Bible is supernatural not in the sense of being the essence of the natural but in the sense of being the creator of the natural. Creation originates not in the eternally creative divine life (as with Tillich) but in God's creative decree. The supernatural is not the upper story of a two-story house (as in a not truly adequate understanding of Thomism), nor is it the basement of the house, the lower depths (as in a mysticism of the earth). Instead, the supernatural is the enduring reality outside and beyond the house altogether. The house could not exist apart from this otherness that encompasses it and upholds it. The house is transitory whereas the reality of this otherness is abiding.

The living God alone is immortal and his home is in "inaccessible light" that no human being has ever seen or can see (1 Tim 6:13-16 JB). We cannot see him, but he can and does see us. We can experience his loving care and redeeming power, but we cannot penetrate the veil that separates God from a fallen and finite humanity. We can gain a glimpse of the light that shines in the darkness, though this glimpse is not the vision of sight but the inner seeing of faith, which alone is sufficient to guide us to our eternal destiny. We seek him, but only because he first seeks us and has indeed found us. Our goal is not to be lost in God but to be found in Christ (James Denney). It is in Christ that we come to know God as dynamic transcendence, as the unbounded love that reaches out to us even in our sin and depravity in order to draw us toward himself so that we might share the glory of his eternity.

· F I V E ·

P O W E R
& W I S D O M

The Lord by wisdom founded the earth;
by understanding he established the heavens.
P R O V E R B S   3 : 1 9   N R S V

I create both light and darkness;
I bring both blessing and disaster.
I S A I A H   4 5 : 7   G N B

God made the earth by his power,
fixed the world in place by his wisdom,
unfurled the skies by his understanding.
J E R E M I A H   1 0 : 1 2   N E B

He is the radiance of God's glory, the stamp of God's very being,
and he sustains the universe by his word of power.
H E B R E W S   1 : 3   R E B

God can do all that He wills,
even though He does not will all things that He can do—
for He can destroy creation, but He does not will to do so.
J O H N   O F   D A M A S C U S

God's power is greater than His work, in which
He permits other things outside Himself also to have power.
K A R L   B A R T H

I n the classical tradition with its focus on the great chain of being,
the essence of God is power—productive, creative or generative
power.[1] Love is the overflowing power of God. Plato, it seems, had
two gods: the Idea of the Good and Creative Goodness or Infinite Fecundity.[2] In this perspective goodness lies in abundance. A good god will

be generous and will by necessity share his goodness. He will diffuse his goodness throughout creation. Creation itself is the product of his streaming forth out of himself. As this tradition developed it was held that a creative, generous God will fulfill every conceivable possibility, and this is why goodness results in plenitude—a full world with a hierarchy of gradation. That which is closer to being–itself is at the same time closer to the good, and that which has less being is on a lower rung of the ladder of being.

Church theology was unduly influenced by this philosophical legacy that depicted God as overflowing or absolute power *(potestas absoluta)*. Omnipotence came to be conceived in terms of self–expansion, not self–emptying or self–limitation. God was defined in terms of his power to create or produce. His love was subordinated to or made an aspect of his power. Duns Scotus and the nominalists who succeeded him envisaged God as absolute will, a will that is universally creative.[3]

Some statements of John Calvin might suggest a God of unrestricted power, though Calvin himself sought to counter this idea by relating God's power directly to his love and mercy. He warned against the "fiction" of a God of "absolute might,"[4] a god who is "a law unto himself." The God of the Bible is not lawless but embodies "the law of all laws."[5]

Nevertheless, in Reformed theology the idea of a God of unrestrained power persisted, though various theologians tried to modify this notion. A distinction was frequently drawn between "God's absolute power," by which he is "capable of everything that can throw light on His glory," and "God's ordered or actual power," by which "He has willed what He decreed to do from eternity."[6] For the older Reformed theologians, "Omnipotence is the omnipotent nature of God Himself and is therefore eternal, bound to no means and infinite, since it is never exhausted in what it produces."[7] Here the Neoplatonic conception of power as productive or creative is very much in evidence.

Whereas Calvin endeavored to hold to the view that God's decrees spring out of his sovereign freedom, many orthodox theologians emphasized that the decrees are an eternal aspect of his nature. Divine sovereignty came to be confused with omnipotent causality. Reformed de-cretal theologians envisaged "an all-comprehensive divine decree that 'accounts for all that happens in the world.' "[8] This means that God necessarily wills whatever comes to pass. If all things are ontologically necessary, if they flow necessarily from the essence of God, then God is fully responsible for sin and evil. Thus Gordon Clark can make the palpably heterodox statement that Scripture "explicitly teaches that God creates sin."[9]

Karl Barth sought to correct classical and Reformed tradition by view-ing God's power in the service of his love. The Bible, he said, "is not interested in God's power over everything, the power that creates, up-holds and moves the world,"[10] but its focus is on God's infinite readiness to redeem and heal. His power is not unrestrained but has "a definite direction and content. It is both His power to will and His power not to will."[11] God's power must never be reduced to omnicausality because this would make God necessarily bound to a reality distinct from him-self. It "belongs to God's will not to will many things."[12]

Otto Weber also rebelled against the notion of absolute power asso-ciated with classical theism:

If God's omnipotence is nothing other than the all-conditioning "power," "will," and "knowledge" of God, then it is not an attribute of God in his freedom, but is rather the forcing of God into the system of necessary laws as we see or presume them to be. And they are then nothing other than the expression of what God "wills"—better, what he basically "must" will or have wanted to will.[13]

In his *Letters and Papers from Prison* Dietrich Bonhoeffer spoke of the need to conceive of God in terms of his powerlessness rather than al-mightiness. God has power, but this is paradoxically the power of the powerlessness of his love. "God allows himself to be edged out of the world and on to the cross. God is weak and powerless in the world, and that is exactly the way, the only way, in which he can be with us and help us."[14] God conquers power and space in the world precisely by his weakness.

Jürgen Moltmann too has sought to reconceive divine omnipotence. Instead of speaking of a God without limits he prefers to speak of a God in whom there are no limits to his vulnerability. A God who is only omnipotent could not be loved, only feared. A God who is exclusively omnipotence is an incomplete being, "for he cannot experience helplessness and powerlessness."[15]

One should keep in mind that Scripture itself can describe God as having unbounded power. The psalmist rejoices, "Great is our Lord, and mighty in power; His understanding is infinite" (147:5 NKJ). And again: "Ours is the God whose will is sovereign in the heavens and on earth" (Ps 115:3 JB). Job confesses, "I know that thou canst do all things, and that no purpose of thine can be thwarted" (42:2). Yet in the fuller biblical perspective God's unbounded power can be shown to be none other than the boundlessness of his love. God is not power in and of itself but the One who exercises his power to liberate and redeem a lost human race. God's power is not unrestricted or arbitrary but is the power of his suffering love. He loves us with an everlasting love (Jer 31:3) and therefore acts to save us (cf. Ps 136; Jon 4:2). His anger is provisional, but his love is eternal (Is 54:7-8).[16]

In the biblical view God's power is manifested not in arbitrary decrees but in sacrificial, other-serving love. God is a destroyer as well as a redeemer, but he destroys in order to redeem, he judges in order to set free those who are bound. His power is to be understood not in terms of omnipotent causality but in terms of invincible, personal freedom. His omnipotence is the sovereign freedom of a God who is both holy and merciful and who acts to vindicate his righteousness as well as to console and to deliver. He does not cause evil, but he acts in the midst of evil in order to bring good out of evil. He is not the direct cause of all things but is sovereign over all causes and realities. God is not the sole actor, but all events are under his control.

Biblical Christians do not affirm the God of absolute power, the one who can do anything. God's power does not violate his love. He is the God who can do everything to express and fulfill his love. His power is his conquering love. His almightiness is his persevering and indefatigable will—to love, heal and restore.

The Messiah of God, too, is characterized by the enduring power that springs out of an unquenchable love. The Old Testament links the Messiah to the strength of God as well as to his caring concern (cf. Is 9:5; 11:2; Ps 110:2; Mic 5:4). The Messiah's power is both prophetic and kingly. This prophetic aspect acquires special prominence in the New Testament (Mt 21:10-11; Lk 7:16; 13:33; 24:19; Acts 3:22-23). Jesus is more than a prophet endowed with power: his whole being "is peculiarly determined by the power of God."[17] Jesus Christ does not so much personify power in itself as reveal "the power of God" that "works victoriously in history and brings it to its goal."[18] God anointed Jesus with the Holy Ghost and with power (Acts 10:38), thus enabling him to liberate the captives and to restore sight to the blind (Lk 4:18-19).

As an all-powerful being, God is not consigned to be separated from his creation. He has the power to relate himself actively to his creation and to share in its trials and sufferings. In and of himself he has no need or deficiency, but he has chosen to create within himself a need for the creature so that he can relate to the creature in dialogical fellowship as well as in self-giving love. God creates a need within himself for the creature, but because he foreknows that this need will be fully met in Jesus Christ, his need is not devoid of joy. His need is one that is already satisfied and will be satisfied when all things are brought into subjection to Jesus Christ in the consummation of world history.

In contrast to the detached, remote being of Hellenistic philosophy, the God of biblical faith is a caring, active being—constantly in relationship to his people. His unchangeableness is his perpetual concern to help and deliver. He creates us and redeems us apart from our assistance, but he enlists us in the service of his kingdom as his heralds and ambassadors. He does not need our love, but he loves us. He does not need our help but he lets us help (Mary Shideler)[19]—not as co-creators or co-redeemers but as witnesses and proclaimers of a redemption already accomplished on our behalf and on behalf of the whole world. The power to create and redeem belongs to God alone, but this power can be reflected and radiated in the words and lives of people dedicated to the service of his glory.

Creator and Redeemer

Biblical faith affirms God as the creator of all that exists. The doctrine of *creatio ex nihilo* ("creation out of nothing") is firmly rooted in biblical and apostolic tradition, though this idea dawned only gradually upon the biblical prophets. Genesis 1 portrays God as Lord over both light and darkness; the implication is that God is the creator of darkness as well as light, though this is not explicitly stated.[20] The priestly writer is undoubtedly working with mythological materials that depicted the world as founded upon a watery abyss—the deep or the *tehom*.[21] The author finds the ultimate source of the universe not in a primeval, uncreated darkness but in the creative speech of God whereby he calls the worlds into being.[22] The recognition that God created both light and darkness is more overt in Second Isaiah (Is 45:7). He did not create the world to be a chaos but formed it to be inhabited (45:18). The darkness that belongs to the shadow side of the creation is the outcome of the creative action of God, but the demonic darkness, which indicates a reversion to disorder and formlessness, contradicts God's creative purposes, though it is allowed by God for the purpose of magnifying the light that overcomes the darkness.[23]

The doctrine of *creatio ex nihilo*, which is definitely implied in Proverbs 8:22-24, is forcefully stated in the apocryphal book of 2 Maccabees 7:28: "I beg you, my child, to look at the heaven and the earth and see everything that is in them, and recognize that God did not make them out of things that existed. And in the same way the human race came into being" (NRSV). By the time of the New Testament this view had become deeply ingrained in the Judaic consciousness as well as in the emergent apostolic faith. Paul affirmed that God "calls into existence the things that do not exist" (Rom 4:17; cf. Heb 11:3). "It is he who is the creator of heaven, of the earth, of the sea, and of all the creatures in them" (Acts 14:15 GNC; cf. Acts 4:24). *Creatio ex nihilo* implies creation by divine fiat: "Worthy art Thou, our Lord and our God, to receive glory and honor and power; for Thou didst create all things, and because of Thy will they existed, and were created" (Rev 4:11 NASB).

Creatio ex nihilo does not necessarily imply, however, that everything was created by God at the same time or even in a brief period. God not only created in the past, but he continues to create. New forms of existence come into being and old forms are renewed by the Spirit of God. The psalmist exclaims, "When you send your Spirit, they are created, and you renew the face of the earth" (Ps 104:30 NIV). Those who hold to progressive creation can allow for evolution within a species, but they insist that every single species has its origin in the direct creative action of God.[24] The six-day schema of creation in Genesis 1 would seem to indicate some form of progressive creation.

With considerable acumen Ted Peters draws upon the latest insights in physics to support a refurbished biblical theism: "What is at stake for the theist is to understand God as a contemporary factor—not merely a past factor—in world events. This means that God's creative work is not limited to a one-time event in the ancient past, but it continues now, and we can expect more things yet in the future. Today's research in physics challenges us to think through what this means." In the light of the new scientific worldview Peters contends that there could be "a possible eternal reality" beyond time.[25]

The biblical view of creation stands in marked contrast to the ancient view prevalent in the Middle East and in Platonism that God formed the world out of a preexistent chaos or matter. God in this sense is a demiurge who fashions the world out of existing materials rather than the One who calls the world into being by his creative word. This position was revived by Teilhard de Chardin, who claimed that at the beginning there were two poles of existence—God and pure multiplicity. "To create is to condense, concentrate, organize—to unify."[26] Likewise Mormon theology sees God not so much as creator as organizer. According to Bruce McConkie, "To *create* is to *organize*. It is an utterly false and uninspired notion to believe that the world or any other thing was created out of nothing."[27] In the words of John Widtsoe: "God, the supreme Power, cannot conceivably originate matter; he can only organize matter. Neither can he destroy matter; he can only disorganize it."[28]

In process theology, which includes Teilhard, Whitehead, Hartshorne and many other eminent thinkers, creation is interpreted as an ongoing process in which new worlds come into being through cosmic evolution. God is the director of the evolutionary process, and some of these thinkers would view themselves as proponents of theistic evolution.[29] For Hartshorne God is the cosmic memory that takes all things of value into itself. For Wieman God is the power of creative transformation that draws the world toward higher possibilities.[30]

Classical mysticism, which has its basis in Platonism and Neoplatonism, sees the world as the product of divine emanation rather than creation. For Plotinus the physical universe is the outpouring and extension of divinity rather than a special creation of God. God goes out of himself by the necessary overflowing of his being, but he then returns to himself as light flooding back to its source. John Scotus Erigena (c. 810-877) viewed the creation of the world as "a creation by God of everything out of *himself*."[31] The implication is pantheism, since there is then a direct continuity between uncreated being and the world of appearances in which this being is manifested.

In Gnosticism, which could be deemed an exaggerated form of Platonism,[32] creation was viewed as a cosmic catastrophe, literally a fall of divinity into multiplicity and temporality. The world is not a product of a beneficent Creator but a prison house that constitutes an obstruction to the upward ascent of the individual soul. Our goal is to reunite with the infinite abyss of silence beyond materiality and temporality, and this can be realized by discovering the divine spark within the human ego, which links us to the higher reality. Some forms of early Gnosticism regarded the creator god as an agent of evil, since creation is the cause of our entanglement in the flesh that prevents spirit from returning to its source.[33]

Paul Tillich, who leaned heavily on Hegel and the Platonist tradition, concluded that creation has its origin not in a divine decree but in the eternally creative divine life. God does not create at a certain point in time but is continuously creating, for in this way he actualizes himself. Creation is his destiny rather than an act of sovereign freedom.[34]

A more agnostic position is represented by Rudolf Bultmann, who held that God's creative action can be understood only existentially, not theoretically. To affirm God as Creator can only mean a personal confession of the believer who understands the human self to be a finite creature owing its existence to God. Creation is the experience of being upheld and sustained by the unconditioned.

The Neoplatonic view explains the world in terms of a necessary derivation of essences. In the biblical view creation is a free act of a sovereign God who would still be God even if he had not created. Charles Williams expressed it well: "The web of created glory, exterior to Himself, is unnecessary to Himself. So the Divine Word need not have had a Mother, but exquisitely decreed that He would."[35]

Biblical religion regards God not only as Creator but also as Redeemer and Lord. He creates in order to redeem, for he foresees the fall of humanity in time and acts to heal the breach between himself and the crown of his creation—the human species. In Neoplatonism sin means separation from the ground of our being, and salvation is achieved through a reunion with this infinite ground. In biblical Christianity sin consists in transgression of the law of God, and salvation in reconciliation and forgiveness by a compassionate heavenly Father. The pilgrimage of faith lies not in the return of the soul to its uncreated source but in the deliverance of the soul from the web of unfreedom into which it has fallen. We are created for the glory of God, and we are redeemed to celebrate this glory in the arena of world history.

The God of classical mysticism, being fully self-sufficient and the absolute maximum of all perfection, remains unaffected by the world, even though he is the ultimate cause of all worldly existence. Meister Eckhart confessed that "God has been immovably disinterested from the beginning and still is and that his creation of the heavens and the earth affected him as little as if he had not made a single creature. . . . All the prayers a man may offer and the good works he may do will affect the disinterested God as little as if there were neither prayers nor works, nor will God be any more compassionate or stoop down to man any more because of his prayers and works than if they were omitted."[36] In the biblical view God identifies himself with the trials and sufferings of his people to the extent of incarnating himself in human flesh and experiencing the pain of death on a cross so that fallen humanity might have a new and glorious future. God has perfect fellowship within himself, but he wills also to have fellowship with his human creation, and the key to such fellowship lies in the initiative of free grace.

Theologians and philosophers have debated through the ages whether this world is the best possible one, since it was created by a God who is at the same time perfectly good and all-powerful. Leibniz drew such a conclusion, but he recoiled from intimating that this is the *only* possible world for fear of making the world a metaphysical necessity rather than an act of divine freedom.[37] While acknowledging this world as created by God, Simone Weil saw it not as the best possible but as containing the whole range of good and evil and now having reached the point "where it is as bad as possible."[38] In my view this world is neither the best nor the worst possible, but it is the best way to the best possible world—the eschatological kingdom of glory that will usher in a transfigured heaven and earth. The vision of the best possible world already resides within God, and this vision is being realized as the kingdom of God advances in a world marred by evil and discord. This is neither an exorcised nor a demonized world but a world that is being exorcised by the Spirit of God working through the evangelical proclamation of the church, itself a creation of the word of God.

Lord and Ruler

God is not only the creator and redeemer of the world but also its lord and master. He not only calls the worlds into being but directs the course of world history. The God of the Bible is neither the soul of the world (as in Platonism) nor the order of nature (as in Stoicism) but the governor and ruler of the world. His relationship to the world is to be understood not in the sense of a vague omnipresence that penetrates all things (the Stoic view) but as a compelling presence that engages all things.

Theology refers to God's foreseeing and fore-ordering of world history as his providence. God not only sets the world in motion but preserves it from chaos and destruction. Providence also involves his cooperation with his created entities in shaping a durable and viable future. God is not remote and detached from his creation (as in deism), but he actively guides all things toward their ultimate purpose. Providence refers to the mysterious interplay of divine action and human reaction that brings the divine plan to fruition. Providence is the predetermination of God in that he sets the stage and then follows through with his willing and not-so-willing subjects.

God's providential rule is to be seen in close relationship to Jesus Christ. All things are created for the sake of Christ, and all things are directed toward their goal in Christ. Christ is the "appointed heir of all things" through whom he "created the worlds" (Heb 1:2 NRSV; cf. Eph 1:10). General providence, whereby God upholds and sustains all things, is in the service of special providence in which God manifests his will through prophetic figures in the history of the people of God, especially in Jesus Christ. His common grace is for the sake of his special grace by which he crowns and glorifies his creation.

Providence in the Christian sense must be sharply distinguished from the classical notion of fate, which abrogates rather than restores human freedom.[39] In the ancient world fate was portrayed as a dark, sinister power that casts a shadow over all human endeavors. Fate is the transcendent necessity that shapes and conditions human life. Freedom, though not denied, was seen as entangled in fate and therefore limited and finally self-defeating. We have the freedom to rebel against our fate, but we cannot escape the doom that the gods have decreed for us—

suffering and death. Fate in the Hellenistic ethos therefore has a tragic dimension. It is the tragic flaw that arouses pity for the heroes, who courageously strive to transcend their limitations. Fate implies an inevitable and usually adverse outcome. Consequently the dominant anxiety in the ancient world was the anxiety of fate or death.

Providence challenges the rule of fate by allowing for divine intervention in history that creates a new future for humankind. Whereas fate thwarts and overrules human freedom, providence liberates human beings to fulfill the destiny for which they were created. Fate entails the abrogation of human freedom; providence assures the realization of authentic freedom through submission to divine guidance. Providence is the direction and support of a loving God, which makes life ultimately bearable; fate is the working out of an iron necessity that casts a pall over all human endeavors. Whereas fate makes the future precarious and uncertain, providence fills the future with hope. Fate is impersonal and irrational; providence is supremely personal and suprarational.[40]

One must also differentiate providence from chance, called by the ancients *Tychē* (Greek) or *Fortuna* (Latin). While the Stoics were inclined to fall into a fatalistic determinism to which we must resolutely resign ourselves, the Epicureans upheld radical contingency and a future that is totally open. They denied the intervention of the gods in history on the grounds that the divine is immutable, whereas the Stoics emphasized the providential ordering of the world in all details on the basis of God's omnipresence.[41] Chance implies that events are unexpected, random and unforeseeable. It suggests the total absence of design or predictability.[42]

In the biblical view God is not infinitely removed from his creation but actively engaged in shaping the destiny of his people. The world is not out of his control but wholly within his purview and guidance. Even the casting of lots is governed by the free decision of God (Prov 16:33). Moreover, God does not act arbitrarily or irrationally but always in accord with his innermost purposes—steadfast love and righteousness. God's power is not capricious, "for it expresses his will and is thus determined by his righteousness"[43] (cf. Is 5:16). Barth keenly observed that "the sovereignty of God bears no relation whatever to the sovereignty of whim or chance or caprice. On the contrary, we learn from the revelation of this sovereignty that the power of whim and chance and caprice is not a sovereign power."[44]

God is in ultimate control of nature and history, but this is not to be interpreted deterministically. All things are within his vision, and all things are ordained to give him glory. His foreknowledge means his foreordination, for what he foresees he brings about. Christianity is neither determinism nor indeterminism but a divine foreordination that respects rather than annuls human freedom. God realizes his purposes in covenant partnership with his people. He draws out possibilities within them for the creation of a promising future for the whole of humankind. He leads them toward a new order of existence rather than imposing on them an order alien to their being. His omnipotence in no way threatens or destroys the independence of his creatures. On the contrary, his omnipotence is poignantly displayed in the freedom of his creatures.[45]

God's providence is his mysterious care for his creation as he works out his purposes in and through and sometimes over and against his human subjects. God is not the sole actor in the drama of history, for he allows his people a certain autonomy. God is the ultimate cause of world order and redemption, but he works through human instrumentality. We may even speak of secondary causes—not alongside God but in and under him.

He does not directly cause all things, but all things are under his beneficent oversight and power. Even those things that are done against his will are not done without his will (Augustine).[46] God controls all events, though he is not the exclusive actor in all events. His hand is in all events—always working to bring good out of evil. The mystery of God's providential care and oversight is illustrated in the Exodus account of the hardening of Pharaoh's heart. This hardening is described at one place as self-imposed (Ex 9:34) and at another as the work of

God (4:21). Still another text indicates that Pharaoh's heart "just gets hard—unaccountably but unmistakably" (7:13).[47] How God accomplishes his purposes in conjunction with human effort and striving is a mystery that lies beyond human comprehension. Like creation and redemption, providence is a mystery open only to faith. When we try to make it too amenable to the demands of logic we invariably fall into some heresy—in this case either determinism or indeterminism.

God's omnipotence includes his omniscience, by which he knows all things—even before they happen. Theologians as well as philosophers have had difficulty in reconciling God's foreknowledge and foreordination with the incontestable fact that history includes the emergence of genuinely new things—new experiences and new outcomes. Thomas Aquinas held that God knows the world not as a succession of events but as a single, timeless present. But the question then arises whether God really knows the world as actual.[48] For the Protestant orthodox thinker J. H. Heidegger "actual future events" or any phenomena in the world "cannot be the object of God's knowledge," because "in our mode of understanding the object moves the faculty and is in a sense the cause of the act arising from it."[49] Cocceius declared, "If we admit something new in God, He cannot be eternal. Therefore neither can a new object come to God's knowledge; for new knowledge would exist in God."[50] This seems to limit God's capacity to know as well as call into question the reality of time and history. Is history only a picture in the mind of God, or does God really involve himself in human history? Is God only an eternal present, or does God genuinely experience futurity?

It is important to emphasize (as did Calvin in his time and Barth in more recent times) that human freedom and divine providence are by no means mutually exclusive. Our freedom comes from God, and it is realized as God works with us and in us. God's sovereignty liberates the human creature for responsible obedience. The paradox is that the more the human will submits to God the more free it becomes. Human freedom is upheld and fulfilled by divine providence, not annulled.

Barth challenged the synthesis with Greek philosophical thought by affirming a God who dynamically intersects with time and even includes time within himself. Yet in his effort to uphold divine omniscience he sometimes lapsed into the position that he was trying to overcome. "God's knowledge," he said, "does not consist only in His knowing all things before they are and have been," but in "His actually knowing them when they are still future."[51] Barth held that God knows all things—past, present and future—and that He knows them equally well at all times. My question is: But does he know them in the same way? Can God know the future before it happens? God certainly has conceptual knowledge of the future, but can God experience the future before it happens? At times Barth viewed God as eminent temporality, at others as a timeless eternal now.[52] Colin Gunton observes that on occasion Barth

> appears to hold that the eschatological future is future only in being so for "our experience and thought," that it is a matter of ignorance rather than time. The corollary would be that *objectively*, so far as God is concerned, there is no divine futurity, and all has been already decided in a timeless past.[53]

William Hill, who stands in the tradition of Thomism, is willing to allow that God is affected by changes in the human situation:

> When finite entities change, God knows and loves them in their changed situation, thus it has to be granted that the divine knowing and loving change at least on the part of their terminative objects. God then knows and loves something new *in the world* and though he gathers this novelty into himself, this need not mean any increment to his own plenitude of being which already pre-contains everything that is or possibly could be.[54]

Process theology has tried to resolve the dilemma by positing a God who really does experience temporality, but it has done so at the price of letting go of the biblical truth that God is in full control of history. While recognizing God's continuing presence in the world, John Cobb contends that "God does not know what the result will be."[55] Daniel Day Williams held that God's knowledge "does not encompass all the specific aspects of future free decisions," but "God's being includes his knowledge of all possible outcomes."[56] Hartshorne maintained that God "flexibly controls" the world process, but he "does not and cannot completely determine all things."[57] Both Hartshorne and Charles Peirce were convinced of the reality of chance in all human decision and therefore saw the future as filled with both risk and uncertainty. Process theologians usually claim that God moves the world by persuasion rather than by coercive power,[58] but if his persuasion is not invincible or sufficient to assure the desired result, then it is not God but chance that is sovereign in the universe.

Tillich tried to reconcile destiny and freedom by affirming their coalescence in human planning and decision. "Destiny is not a strange power which determines what shall happen to me. It is myself as given, formed by nature, history, and myself. My destiny is the basis of my freedom; my freedom participates in shaping my destiny."[59] The source of the ontological anxiety that plagues the human race is that we are "threatened with the loss of freedom" by the "necessities" implied in our destiny, and we are equally threatened with the loss of our destiny by the "contingencies" implied in our freedom.[60] Tillich's solution is anthropocentric rather than theocentric, since it regards human striving as the key to the realization of human destiny. Providence is not the active working of God in human life and affairs but the human person working out his or her own destiny with courage in the face of adversity. "The man who believes in providence does not believe that a special divine activity will alter the conditions of finitude and estrangement. He believes, and asserts with the courage of faith, that no situation whatsoever can frustrate the fulfillment of his ultimate destiny."[61]

The theological task is to affirm both the inscrutable reality of divine providence whereby God unfailingly guides the world to its true destination and the ineradicable reality of human freedom by which we cooperate with God in fulfilling the divine purposes. The mystery is that our cooperation is possible only on the basis of divine superintendence and empowering (cf. 1 Cor 15:10; Phil 2:12-13; Col 1:29). It also includes the fact that God's purposes are realized even in our contumacy and rebellion. Heinz Cassirer brings out this point in his translation of Jude 4: "Certain fellows have wormed their way into our company, indeed, the very people whom scripture marked out long ages ago for the doom which they have in fact brought upon themselves" (GNC). God's will will be done but not without human effort—even when this effort is consciously motivated to obstruct the divine purposes.

God's providence is not a law of iron necessity, for this would be a reversion to fatalism. Neither is it a sometimes ill-fated attempt to bring order into a world that is unpredictable and chaotic. Providence is the mysterious, hidden hand of God at work in all phenomena of nature and events in history, bringing into temporal reality what has already been envisaged and ordained by God from all eternity—but in cooperation with, not in negation of, creaturely freedom. To affirm the providential rule and supervision of God over the whole of creaturely existence is to affirm nature as the theater of God's grace and history as the arena of God's glory. Nature is not the body of God (as the Stoics maintained) but the handiwork of God that witnesses to the marvel of his creation as well as the glory of his redemption. History is not the random interplay of forces beyond any human or divine control but the field in which the drama of redemption is played out amid conflict between the forces of righteousness and of iniquity. The outcome of this struggle is already assured, but the way in which we arrive at this outcome is partly dependent on how God chooses to interact with and respond to human initiatives. We are not masters of our fates and captains of our souls (as the Enlightenment envisioned), but we are nevertheless by the grace of God covenant partners with him in building a future that fulfills the hopes and dreams of a lost and fallen humanity through the ages.

Wisdom

The God of the Bible has not only indomitable power but also indelible wisdom by which he exercises his power. Wisdom and power are closely related throughout Scripture. It was by wisdom (Hebrew *hokmah*, Greek *sophia*) that the Lord "founded the earth" and by understanding that he "established the heavens" (Prov 3:19 NRSV; cf. Jer 10:12). The psalmist rejoices, "Our Lord is great, all-powerful, his wisdom beyond all telling" (Ps 147:5 NJB). By his power God "stilled the sea," and by his understanding "he smote Rahab" (Job 26:12). Power, glory and wisdom are ascribed to the Son of God, who was slain in sacrifice (Rev 5:12).

The Wisdom literature of the Old Testament and Apocrypha personified wisdom as a mediator of salvation and a teacher (Prov 8:1–21). She streamed forth from God prior to all his works of creation, disclosing to humanity the original order inherent in creation.[62] She was not only present at creation but is herself the "mother" of all things, and in her hands are innumerable riches (Wisdom of Solomon 7:11, 12).

Proverbs 8 has been a matter of theological debate through the ages. Is wisdom "created" by God or "possessed" by God?[63] In the apocryphal Wisdom of Solomon she is described as the "breath of the power of God, and a pure emanation of the glory of the Almighty" (7:25 NRSV). According to Ecclesiasticus 1:4, "Wisdom was created before all other things, and prudent understanding from eternity" (NRSV; cf. 24:8-9). She has come into being prior to all created things and is a fellow worker with God in the creation of the universe.

R. B. Y. Scott makes a fairly convincing case that the poem in Proverbs 8 was produced after the "monolatry of early Israel had become an unequivocal monotheism."[64] What we probably have in Proverbs 8 is not a hypostasis of Yahweh endowed with a personal identity but "an unusually striking example of personification for poetic effect."[65] This personification of wisdom must be understood as referring not to an ontological divide within the Godhead but simply to the sagacity by which God brought the worlds into being.[66] Wisdom is not a separate being carrying out the commands of God but God himself in action imprinting his plan upon the whole of creation. Another Old Testament scholar, C. H. Toy, saw in this poem a valiant attempt to affirm that wisdom was manifest in the creation of the world, an attempt that approaches the concept of hypostasis but is "not more than an approach."[67]

It is well to note that both the orthodox and the heretical parties within the church appealed to Proverbs 8. Does it suggest the eternal generation of the Son by the Father (the orthodox position) or an intermediate being less than God but higher than humanity who assisted in the creation of the world (as Arius maintained)? Still another possibility is that the creation of wisdom might refer to the eternal decision of God to unite himself with the humanity of Jesus, for Jesus Christ is explicitly identified with wisdom in the New Testament. That wisdom is sometimes portrayed as the breath of God (cf. Wisdom of Solomon 7:25; Ecclus 24:3) suggests an affinity with the Holy Spirit, but none of these texts can be used to prove that the Holy Spirit is the third person of the Trinity.[68] It is probably most in keeping with the wider tradition of the church to see the wisdom of Proverbs 8 as a foreshadowing of the preexistent Logos in John's Gospel, but for John the Logos or Word was consubstantial with the Father, whereas this idea is definitely not found in Proverbs.

The Old Testament ascribes wisdom not only to God but also to the messianic king. The prophet Isaiah declares that "the Spirit of the Lord shall rest upon him, the spirit of wisdom and understanding, the spirit of counsel and might, the spirit of knowledge and the fear of the Lord" (Is 11:2; cf. Mt 3:16; Lk 2:40, 52; Jn 1:32).

The New Testament applies wisdom—not surprisingly—to the person of Christ. Jesus is referred to as wisdom itself, the wisdom of God (Mt 11:19; Lk 11:49). In 1 Corinthians 1:24 Christ is called "the power of God and the wisdom of God." In verse 30 Paul declares that God made Christ "our wisdom, our righteousness and sanctification and redemption" (cf. Col 2:3). Like the wisdom of Proverbs, Christ has a role in the creation and preservation of the world (Col 1:16-17). The prologue of John attributes the characteristics of creative wisdom to the preexistent Word that became incarnate in Christ (Jn 1:1-5; cf. Jn 6:33-35). Luke 11:49 equates the wisdom of God with the Word of God (cf. 7:35). The book of Revelation depicts wisdom as an attribute of God (7:12) and also of the exalted Christ (5:12). Moreover, there is striking parallelism between

Wisdom of Solomon 7:25, which describes wisdom as "a clear effluence from the glory of the Almighty" (REB), and Hebrews 1:3, which depicts Christ as "the radiance of God's glory, the stamp of God's very being" (REB).

Wisdom is not only an attribute of God but also a gift from God (cf. Prov 2:6). God gives wisdom to his sons: Solomon (1 Kings 4:29-34), Daniel (Dan 5:14) and Ezra (Ezra 7:25). He also imparts this gift to holy souls who become his friends (Wisdom of Solomon 7:25-28). This gift is preeminently seen in exemplars of piety, but it is also available for all God's elect. Since we as Christians have the Holy Spirit dwelling within us, we are now in actual contact with the wisdom of God, but we need to draw upon this wisdom if it is to become manifest in our lives. We need constantly to seek wisdom if we are to have truth in our innermost being (Ps 51:6). In 1 Corinthians 12:8 Paul describes wisdom as a charism of the Spirit, but the highest gift is love, apart from which even knowledge of the mysteries of faith has no redeeming efficacy (1 Cor 13:1-3, 13).

Isaac Watts makes a telling point when he declares that "the glorious names of wisdom, love and power" are "all too poor to speak His worth," too poor to set forth the glory of the Savior.[69] This may be why wisdom was personified in the Wisdom literature. Finally wisdom became identified with the Word of God incarnate in human flesh. Wisdom is an attribute of God, to be sure, but it is more than an attribute in the wider biblical witness: it is God himself in the person of Jesus Christ. It is the Spirit of God empowering Christians from within to believe, to rejoice, to bear public witness to the faith once delivered to the saints. This wisdom makes those who believe invulnerable to the darts of the devil, unconquerable in their battle against the powers of darkness. We read that the revilers of Christ "could not withstand the wisdom and the Spirit" with which Stephen made his witness that finally brought him martyrdom (Acts 6:10).

Wisdom came to be identified with the Torah by Ecclesiasticus, but the New Testament perceives wisdom as deeper and higher than law:

it is the living Christ who fulfills the law. This living Christ is the image of God, the radiance of the glory of God, the spirit that proceeds from the mouth of God. We can participate in this wisdom through the outpouring of the Holy Spirit, and we can give evidence of our commitment to the wisdom of God by exercising self-control, by practicing gentleness and loving-kindness, by speaking words that convict and empower. These words challenge the wisdom of the wise of this world (Is 29:14; 1 Cor 1:19), for they point to the incapacity of natural reason to fathom the mysteries of faith. They call for the exercise of humility that alone renders the human person teachable by the Spirit of God. Worldly astuteness can be made to serve the spiritual discernment that comes from above, but standing by itself it can only make one proud and thereby vulnerable to the nemesis that invariably follows hubris.

Our wisdom, like our righteousness, lies outside ourselves in the living God incarnate in Christ, but we can reflect this transcendent wisdom through lives of fidelity, vigilance and diligence. Through our broken and fallible witness others may come to know the wisdom that resides within God himself, the wisdom that became incarnate in human flesh, the wisdom that is associated with the gift of the Holy Spirit to the community of faith.

The Wisdom literature indicates that in wisdom we see the maternal face of God. Wisdom is our mother who nurtures and sustains us;[70] Wisdom is our sister who accompanies us on our spiritual journey;[71] Wisdom is our providential provider who cares for us and assists us.[72] Wisdom, however, is not the name by which we ordinarily address God, for the God of biblical faith is not a dyad—partly male and partly female—but a Trinity—Father, Son and Holy Spirit.[73] Yet this triune deity has a motherly as well as fatherly dimension, and the depiction of God as wisdom reminds us of this fact.

Glory

Glory in the Bible indicates the ineffable majesty and shining splendor of God. The key words are *kabod* (Heb), which also carries the nuances of weightiness and importance, and *doxa* (Gk), indicating honor and awesomeness when applied to God. *Shekinah,* used in postbiblical Judaism, refers to the radiant presence of God that dwelt with the people of faith. It was thought of as a cloud that rested above the tabernacle by day and the fire that supplanted that cloud by night. Shekinah was not a being or reality separate from God but for the most part a title or designation of God in post-Old Testament writings (despite Philo's speculations). In the priestly writings the glory of God appears as a fiery presence associated with Mount Sinai.

The glory of God is the transcendent beauty of God manifest in his mighty works in sacred history. Occasionally "glory" and "God" become synonymous in Old Testament writing (cf. Ex 33:22; Lev 9:6, 23; Ps 113:4; Zech 2:5). Ezekiel 1 has a vision of the divine glory descending from heaven in a chariot drawn by four chimeric creatures. The glory of God is his glowing light and immensity, which can be overwhelming and awe-inspiring for the person of faith.

God's glory is closely associated with both his power and his wisdom. His power serves to manifest and magnify his glory (Ps 24:8). The author of Hebrews declares that it is the Son "who radiates forth God's glory . . . who sustains all things by his mighty word of command" (Heb 1:3 GNC). In the book of Revelation the divine power is virtually identical with the divine glory (Rev 1:16; 19:1). Power, glory and wisdom are ascribed to the Lamb who was slain in sacrifice (Rev 5:12). The apocryphal Wisdom of Solomon pictures wisdom as proceeding from the throne of glory (9:10; cf. 7:25).

Just as God's glory was manifest in Israel in the tabernacling Presence (Heb 9:2), so it is now manifest in Christ (2 Cor 4:6; Heb 9:11-14). As the source and wellspring of glory, the mighty God gives his glory to the transfigured Jesus (Jn 1:14; 2 Pet 1:17) and to the resurrected Christ (1 Pet 1:21; 1 Cor 2:8; Heb 2:7, 9; Rev 5:12-13). Christ is also glorified in his suffering and death (Jn 12:23), being exalted in his humiliation (Phil 2:8-9). In addition, glory is a hallmark of Christ's second coming as the Son of Man (Mt 24:30; Mark 8:38; Tit 2:13). God is the Father of glory

(Eph 1:17) and Jesus Christ the Lord of glory (1 Cor 2:8; 2 Cor 4:4; Jas 2:1).

God's glory is also associated with the Holy Spirit. 1 Peter gives these words of comfort: "You have resting upon you all that pertains to glory, in fact, the very Spirit of God" (4:14 GNC). Paul assures his hearers that "out of the treasures of his glory" God will grant them "inward strength and power through his Spirit" (Eph 3:16 REB). The Spirit is the pledge of the new reality that brings glory to the world.

The divine glory also has an unmistakably eschatological thrust throughout Scripture. It will make the deserts bloom (Is 35:2) and the temple the recipient of the riches and glory of the nations (Is 60:13; 66:12). The new Jerusalem will exude an abundant glory (Is 66:11; Zech 12:7) that will be seen and celebrated among the peoples of the world (Is 66:18-19). This glory will be universally known (Hab 2:14; Lk 3:6) and feared (Is 59:19). The hope of the redeemed in Christ is the appearing of the glory of Jesus Christ (Tit 2:13).

In the Old Testament the cloud that accompanied Israel on its journey simultaneously veiled the glory of God and revealed it (Ex 16:10; 33:9, 20; cf. Lk 9:31-32, 34-35; 2 Pet 1:17). God's glory is not seen directly, but its effects are experienced. Moses asked the Lord to show him his glory, but he was told that no human being can see the face of God and live (Ex 33:18-20). He was allowed to see the "back" of God—the traces of God's glory in physical phenomena—but not the very face of God. We can have an intimation or foretaste of the glory of God through dreams, visions and ecstatic experiences, but we cannot penetrate the inner being of God, for we would then be overwhelmed by the majesty of his countenance and reduced to nothingness.

This note reappears in the New Testament: "No one has ever seen God. It is God the only Son, who is close to the Father's heart, who has made him known" (Jn 1:18 NRSV). God alone "has immortality and dwells in unapproachable light, whom no one has ever seen or can see" (I Tim 6:16 NRSV). The disciples of Christ had beheld God's glory in the earthly Jesus (Jn 1:14); yet this was not a direct seeing, for his glory was concealed in his human garb (cf. Mt 16:17). Paul wrote that the "hope of glory" lies in the indwelling Christ (Col 1:27), but this inner presence of Christ is "hidden from sight" or general human perception (Col 2:3 GNC). God reveals the glory of his name in the cross of Christ (Jn 12:28; 17:5), but only those who had been chosen to be his witnesses could apprehend this glory, not directly—by sight—but by the perception of faith.[74] We shall see him as he is, when he comes again in power and glory to set up the kingdom that shall have no end, but now we walk by faith, not sight (cf. 1 Cor 13:12-13; 2 Cor 5:7).

The mandate of the church is to give glory to God and to him alone *(soli Deo gloria)*. This was a salient emphasis of the Protestant Reformation.[75] Glory cannot be ascribed to the church, to the sacramental bread and wine, to the saints, to their relics, to the pope, but only to God. He alone is the object worthy of our devotion and reverence, for he alone is the source and ground of our being and the hope of our salvation. Holy souls can become transparent to the glory of God, but they cannot claim our unconditional allegiance. Nature can be the theater of the glory of God, but it is not the source of this glory. It is not the locus of the sacred but more appropriately a sign and witness to the sacred. Similarly the church can reflect the glory of God but cannot claim to be the object of glorification, for this would be rank idolatry. The role of the saints and of the church is to direct us to the glory of God by introducing us to Jesus Christ, in whom God's glory has been revealed decisively and definitively for all humankind.

God glorifies himself by revealing and communicating his power and mercy. Barth put it well: "God stands in need of nothing else. He has full satisfaction in Himself. Nothing else can even remotely satisfy Him. Yet He satisfies Himself by showing and manifesting and communicating Himself as the One who He is."[76]

God loves us not in order to give himself greater glory, but he glorifies himself in the act of self-giving love. In loving us "God wills His own glory and our salvation. But He does not love us because He wills this. He wills it for the sake of His love."[77] Through his love he communicates his glory, but he does not seek to gain glory by loving, for glory already belongs to him.

As mortals we cannot add to the glory of God because God is not deficient in any perfection. We cannot contribute to God's enrichment, but the fullness of his glory and perfection can be reflected in our lives— in our words and acts. We can radiate the glory of God by being salt and light to the world (Mt 5:13-16). We can witness to this glory by upholding Jesus Christ before others; in this way we carry forward his glory in the world. We can heighten the esteem and respect that mortals give to God, but we cannot increase the inherent excellence of God.[78]

It is helpful in this connection to distinguish between the intrinsic and extrinsic glory of God, as does the Eastern Orthodox theologian Petro Bilaniuk:

> The intrinsic glory of God is His holiness, goodness, beauty and all the other attributes. The extrinsic glory of God is the true goal of creation, for it is a reflection and manifestation, through creatures, of the intrinsic and substantial glory that is God Himself. Therefore God necessarily ordered all things to His extrinsic glory. Consequently the intrinsic perfection of any creature is in reality the extrinsic glory of God.[79]

The divine purpose in creation and redemption is not to procure glory for either the Father or the Son but to communicate and manifest the eternal glory to the whole of creation. The goal is the transfiguration of the cosmos; the motivation is self-giving love that proceeds out of a heart of boundless compassion. God's loving acts redound to his glory, but they proceed out of his own free decision to share the goodness of his being. He has no need to go out of himself to create and redeem, for he already possesses creative love within himself. He already shares his bountiful capacity to love within the fellowship of the persons of the Trinity. He is not metaphysically bound to go out of himself to the creation, but he wills to do so out of inexplicable love that gives him glory but does not make him more worthy to receive glory.

The Problem of Evil

In the history of philosophy the problem of evil has proved to be the most difficult to resolve. No solution advanced by the greatest minds in the world has gone unchallenged. Theodicy, the valiant attempt to justify the ways of God before humanity, is the most ambitious of all human intellectual enterprises and the one that seems most destined to failure.

A purview of the philosophical answers reveals the diversity in the way great minds have grappled with this issue. Heraclitus traced the source of evil to the strife and discord in the universe, but he saw order and disorder, justice and strife, reconciled in a universal cosmic force. Aristotle identified evil with strife but took care not to locate this in God himself. In Platonism evil is associated with the privation of being and the resistance of matter to form and structure. The cosmic, nonmoral evil of the deficiency in being inherent in matter becomes the source of moral evil in the human soul. Among the gnostics evil is located in the cosmic fall of spirit into materiality and temporality. Hans Jonas observed, "The sublime unity of cosmos and God is broken up, the two are torn apart, and a gulf never completely to be closed again is opened: God and world, God and nature, spirit and nature, become divorced, alien to each other, even contraries."[80] Also verging toward a cosmic dualism is Zoroastrianism, which posits two spiritual powers arrayed against one another through all the ages, though the future belongs to the power of good. In Buddhism the fulcrum of evil is unrequited desire, and the solution to evil is the extinction of desire.[81] In modern humanism, drawing upon Platonism, Stoicism and Aristotelianism, evil is reduced to ignorance, and the antidote to evil is self-understanding. In fatalism, widespread in the ancient world and continuing today, the human creature is at the mercy of sinister powers beyond human and divine control that irrevocably fashion human destiny.[82]

The Bible does not offer a theodicy, nor does it present an explanation for evil that is readily credible, but it does throw considerable light upon the human condition. First of all it does not deny the harsh reality of evil. Evil is not an appearance of good or a necessary steppingstone to the good (as in John Hick).[83] Nor is it ignorance that needs only to be remedied by education. Plato was convinced that once people have knowledge of the real situation they will invariably do the good. Paul the apostle was more realistic. He saw that the good we desire to do we inexplicably fail to do because of an evil proclivity within us (Rom 7:15-20). Reinhold Niebuhr was probably right when he contended that original sin is the only Christian doctrine that has solid empirical verification. The origin of evil lies in the perversion of the will evident among both angels and mortals. Such malformation is to be attributed not to the gift of freedom but to the willful abuse of our freedom, an abuse that is not comprehensible to human reason. This is why Scripture can speak of "the mystery of iniquity" (2 Thess 2:7 KJV). Some light is shed on the human fall into sin by the recognition of a demonic fall prior to human sin, which sets the stage for both moral and physical evil in the world. The devil does not cause humans to sin but tempts them to sin, and once they yield to temptation they fall precipitously into spiritual bondage.

The Bible posits a moral but not a metaphysical dualism, for biblical faith is adamant that the devil and his hosts are both restrained and used by the living God, to whom alone belongs ultimate power.[84] God allows evil to happen for purposes that elude human comprehension, but he does not create moral evil. The King James rendition of Isaiah 45:7, "I make peace, and create evil," has led to the erroneous impression that God is the author of sin. The RSV translation, "I make weal and create woe," is more accurate, since the Hebrew word for "evil" *(ra)* probably refers here to physical calamity rather than moral evil.[85] In the Bible the onus for moral evil lies on the human creature, not on the Creator. Ezekiel answers those who claim that "the way of the Lord is not just": "Hear, O house of Israel: Is my way unjust? Is it not your ways that are unjust?" (18:25 NIV).

Yet biblical religion is unequivocal that although evil is not directly willed by God it is under his controlling power. Behind the afflictions and sufferings of the human race lies the malevolent work of Satan, and behind this abysmal power lies the inscrutable hand of the living God. In Job 2:10 we read: "If we take happiness from God's hand, must we not take sorrow too?" (NJB). And in Lamentations: "Do not both bad and good proceed from the mouth of the Most High?" (3:38 REB). Yet it is also expressly stated that God himself does not lead his human creation into evil nor can he be tempted by evil (Jas 1:13).

On the basis of Isaiah 28:21-22 theologians in the tradition of the Reformation have spoken of the proper work of God and of his strange or alien work. To kill and destroy is the alien work of God; to love and forgive is his proper work. God puts down an arrogant and rebellious humanity with his left hand and raises up a repentant and chastened humanity with his right. He uses coercive power to keep evil in check, but he uses redemptive power—the power of suffering love—to replace evil by good. This is not a bifurcation in the being of God, for his coercion is for the purpose of his redemption, his alien work is in the service of his proper work. He governs humanity both through the devil and cruel tyrants on the one hand and through just rulers on the other. He redeems humanity through the power of the cross and the evangelical proclamation.

Some theologians have located evil or nonbeing in the very heart of God. Drawing upon Schelling and Jacob Boehme, Tillich saw a dynamic movement in God by which being continually overcomes nonbeing.[86] Grace Jantzen sees evil in God but not God as evil.[87] God is not evil because God does not have an evil will. But he contains within himself all things, all contradictories, light and darkness. Bernard Loomer saw in God both "an expansive urge toward greater good" and "a passion for greater evil."[88] The New Age philosopher Joseph Campbell regarded evil as the shadow side of the good and the devil as a god who has not yet been recognized.[89] These views patently contradict the biblical confession that "God is light and in him is no darkness at all" (1 Jn 1:5; cf. Ps 92:15).

Barth seized upon the existentialist concept of the Nothingness to expound a somewhat novel approach to evil that is consistent, he maintained, with the biblical claims.[90] Evil is the darkness that is passed over at the creation (Gen 1:1-5) but allowed a certain provisional existence in order to prepare the way for a world transfigured by the light and truth of Jesus Christ. Evil is not created by God but negated and thereby takes on a semblance of reality and power. Yet already at the creation evil was vanquished, for the light of God's truth encompassed the whole of the creation. The conquest of evil was confirmed at the cross and resurrection of Christ, which exposed the power of evil as having its basis in a lie. In this schema the demons are not fallen angels but agents of disorder that have their seat in the chaos or nothingness that is excluded rather than included in the good creation of God. The demons wear masks that fill the world with dread, but in and of themselves they have no viable ontological power. Evil is what God does not will rather than what he expressly sanctions. Evil is the antithesis to good rather than a steppingstone to the good (as in Schleiermacher, John Hick and the New Age). But evil has no future, it does not pose a real danger, since God has already demonstrated his absolute sovereignty over the darkness.

One should note that Barth did not offer a theodicy but an insightful recognition that evil escapes the bounds of rationality. The Nothingness is really a metaphor in his theology for the persistent threat to the creation of falling into formlessness and disorder. Barth seemed to envisage the darkness in Genesis 1 as both an uncreated surd that intrudes into creation and a necessary element in the unfolding of creation itself. He would have nothing to do with the view that the chaos furnishes the material by which God molds the created order, for this would be to lapse into a cosmic dualism. The chaos arises not out of God's positive but out of his negative willing.

While recognizing with Barth that Genesis 1 speaks of spiritual as well as physical darkness, I wish to bring this perception into a vital relationship with a later tradition that becomes dominant in the New Testament—the emergence of Satan as the leader of an angelic conspiracy against God.[91] One may guardedly speak of the demonic darkness as the chaos in its destructive proclivity, but the reference is not to an uncreated chaotic matter but to an angelic rebellion that plunges the good created world into chaos. This kind of happening that circumvents human experience can be described adequately only in poetic language. The devil is not a shadow figure that lacks substantial reality but a divine anti-divine being who foments rebellion and discord in God's good world. While Barth conceded that a few biblical texts speak of fallen angels, he dismissed them as belonging to the periphery of the biblical witness. Yet many texts are relevant to this theme (Gen 6:1-4; Job 4:18; 15:15; Ps 82:6-7; Is 14:12; Lk 10:18; Jn 12:31; Eph 6:11-12; 2 Pet 2:4; Jude 6; Rev 9:1; 12:7-17; 20:1-3).[92] In the position I am advancing, moral evil is prior to physical evil. The source of evil is not a remnant of primeval darkness but the will of a malevolent being who reflects the light of creation, and this accounts for the disturbing reality of his power, though to be sure it is drastically curtailed by the providential will of God.

Evil in the biblical perspective is not a netherworld of darkness outside of creation that intrudes into the order of created being (as in Barth). Nor is it the resistance of chaotic matter to form and structure (as in Platonism). Instead, it is the misdirection and perversion of spirit. Evil has a spiritual origin—in the will of the creature rather than in either created being or the privation of being. Evil is not primarily a disorder that needs to be brought under rational control but a malevolent controller who needs to be overthrown.

Whereas Barth tied evil to the negation of God, Calvin saw evil as included in the express will of God but serving the wider purposes of God—the triumph of his kingdom. Calvin refused to take refuge in the divine permission, since this implies two contrary wills in God. God is ultimately responsible for evil but is absolved from guilt, since he always uses evil for a good purpose. The will of God is the underlying cause of all things that happen in the world, yet "God is not the author of evil."[93] Calvin recognized that evil is often opaque, that there is no silver lining visible even to the discerning eye. Evil is real, yet fundamentally incomprehensible. We need to go forward in the confidence that God is in control of our destiny and that his purposes will be realized—in our lives and in the world.[94] The unity of the divine will is to be found in the divine glory, which is served equally in election and reprobation.

Drawing on both Barth and Calvin, Ronald Goetz regards evil as initiated by God for the purpose of preparing for a greater good.[95] It proceeds from his sovereign will rather than being something merely allowed by God. God becomes the ultimate source of evil rather than its antithesis. For Goetz this is an imperfect world on the way to being perfected. There was no fall from a historical paradise: there has always been strife and discord in world history. God makes us mutual partners in shaping a livable world, a task that involves an ongoing struggle to transmute evil into good. For Goetz God is primarily responsible for sin, but he allows us to have a share in its defeat and mastery. The atonement of Christ is not only God's atoning sacrifice for the sins of humanity but also his "own atonement for being the ultimate agent of evil as well as good."[96] Goetz also posits a tension or division within the Godhead "over the ruthlessness of the divine means—inevitable violence, sin, suffering and death—and the love, self-sacrifice and mercy of God's redemptive ends."[97] "Must not Christ cry out to the Father at all times as every pestilence and famine, every war and act of genocide, every personal betrayal and every star-crossed life is added to the Father's burden?"[98] Goetz sees the world in an evolutionary uprise sparked by violence and tragedy but made tolerable by the love of a suffering God who identifies with us and upholds us in the midst of severe agony and affliction. To affirm the culpability of God in human tragedy and evil signifies a marked divergence from classical tradition as well as from Barth.[99]

Another contemporary effort, also daringly innovative, to come to grips with the enormity and banality of evil is that of Wendy Farley, whose mentors include Boehme, Tillich and Rosemary Radford Ruether.[100] Evil represents a rupture in creation caused by a tragic conflict in values and the restlessness of desire. Yet this rupture is the price that God must pay for creating a world where discord and strife are inevitable.[101] "The tragic structure of finitude and the human capacity for deception and cruelty together account for the possibility and actuality of suffering and evil."[102] Creation is fragile and God's power is not absolute, and this combination culminates in "the tragedy and rupture of history."[103] Evil must be defied and resisted in the knowledge that the vision of the good can be kept alive in succeeding generations. Farley speaks of a "tragic love" that battles against evil and that more often than not ends in death and radical suffering. Yet "even in defeat, a vision of justice remains to vindicate the tragic hero. The defiance of the hero enacts and recovers human dignity even in the teeth of destruction."[104] The cross symbolizes the struggle of God to preserve and redeem the world in cooperation with his creatures. The life and death of Jesus opens up the vision of a transcendent moral order that should inspire heroic perseverance in every age. Divine love contains the risk of bringing about a world "in which real and terrible resistance to God is possible."[105] Because God continues to incarnate himself in history all possibilities are imbued with "redemptive power." "Care for nature, the desire for justice, the struggle for peace, affection for one another are all sacraments of God's living presence in the world."[106] Farley presents a picture of God and the world where God is not fully in control, nor does he possess the plenitude of perfected love within himself. God needs the world in order to realize his desire for fulfillment in relationship to that which is outside himself. She also makes God responsible for evil by envisaging God as going out of himself in reckless love. "Tragedy is the price paid for existence," but the diversity and fecundity of nature suggest that "the price is not too high."[107]

In expounding my own position I find myself in many respects closer to Luther than to most other theologians who have addressed this issue.[108] For Luther the source of evil lies in the prideful rebellion of the angel of light against his appointed place in the hierarchy of being and in the spell that he is able to cast upon the whole of the created order. Evil is not basically a deprivation of being or a sliding away from being (as in Platonism), nor is it a natural principle coeternal with God (as in gnosticism). Nor is it rooted in a tragic conflict of values that creation makes inevitable (as in Wendy Farley). Rather evil lies in the strategy of demonic powers—greater than humans but less than God—to corrupt and enslave the human race. The devil is not omnipresent (as Luther sometimes described him), but the reach of his power is omnipresent, for he has working for him a host of fallen angelic beings—the demons of Christian mythology. While the language describing the demonic powers is indeed figurative, we cannot afford to demythologize these powers (as Barth advocates), for this would reduce them to an impersonal or subpersonal chaos. We should acknowledge, however, our inability to comprehend what took place before the creation of humankind in the transcendent heavens of biblical imagination. The devil must be seen as a superhuman intelligence with a strategy and agenda all his own, not as the chaos in its dynamic manifestation (as in Barth). Luther astutely recognized that the devil is able to make real gains in the world, though he is unwittingly carrying out the alien work of God—to destroy that which is evil through coercive power.[109]

The devil is always God's devil in Luther's theology while at the same time being God's foremost adversary. He has not been divested of his power (as we often find in Barth), but his power has been severely curtailed. He is still able to wreak havoc on the basis of the lies that he spreads, but he cannot reverse the impending triumph of the kingdom of God. He is like a monster that has been mortally wounded and thereby becomes all the more dangerous. The devil is in his death throes but still has the power to attack and bring down those mortals who have not remained vigilant and watchful (Eph 6:10-17; 1 Pet 5:8-9).

We need, of course, to include the human fall into sin as an integral part of the drama of the demonic conquest of the world of creation. While the story of the Fall is assuredly clothed in mythopoetic language, it conveys the truth that the human race as a species has been poisoned and corrupted from its beginning by the misuse of divinely given freedom. Sin is not simply ignorance (as in Platonism), nor is it unrequited desire (as in Buddhism). It is the prideful attempt of finite mortals to be as God. We are not unwilling victims of fate but willing accomplices in the ongoing spiritual rebellion against the authority of God.

Evil is not the lack of harmony in the cosmic process of evolution (as in process theology), nor is it the shadow side of creation (as in New Age theology). It is not the inertia of nature (Whitehead) or the resistance of matter (Plato) but the degeneration of spirit, which corrupts wholesome natural desire and makes it the servant of the lust for power. Against process theology I maintain that evil is not simply or fundamentally obstructive but is at its very core ruthlessly and often mindlessly destructive.[110] It is not a minus point but a virus of unholy contagion that can be counteracted only by the medicine of the blood of Christ applied through the word and the sacraments of the church.

Theology cannot offer a fully satisfying explanation for evil, but it does point to a spiritual solution—the incarnation and atoning sacrifice of our Lord Jesus Christ. Something has gone radically wrong with creation, but God has acted to bring good out of evil. He has acted to reverse the work of the powers of darkness and disorder by himself becoming human flesh and dying on a cross, taking upon himself the retribution that we deserve because of sin. That he rose again on the third day shows that the powers of sin, death and the devil could not defeat him. The cross proved to be the key to their undoing, for he rose from the dead and triumphed over them.

The conflict between good and evil continues, but the future belongs irreversibly to Jesus Christ, for his victory over the powers of evil has already been secured. What lies ahead is the all-encompassing glory of God—a transfigured heaven and earth—but the way to this glory lies in taking up the cross and joining the divine battle against the forces of unrighteousness that still cling to their diminished and fast-eroding power. The dawning of the millennium will be accompanied by a final stand of the devil against the holy catholic church—now on the offensive and looking forward to the coming age of glory.

· S I X ·

HOLINESS
& LOVE

Holy, holy, holy is the Lord of hosts;
the whole earth is full of his glory.

ISAIAH 6:3 NRSV

In overflowing wrath for a moment I hid my face from you,
but with everlasting love I will have compassion on you.

ISAIAH 54:8

The wrath of God is the highest strained energy
of the holy will of God, the zeal of His wounded love.

GUSTAV FRIEDRICH OEHLER

God is a God of holy love whose love
we do not only enjoy but worship.

P. T. FORSYTH

His love is not the passion to possess
but the loving-kindness that bestows.

DONALD M. MATHERS

Holiness in the Bible (Hebrew *qadosh;* Greek *hagios*) has both cultic and ethical meanings. Its basic connotation is separateness from all that is unclean, transcendence over all that belongs to this passing world. When applied to God, holiness signifies his majesty and inviolability. An encounter with the Holy is always accompanied by awe and dread (cf. Gen 28:10-22; Job 4:12-17; Is 6:1-5).

In his classic *Idea of the Holy* Rudolf Otto makes a telling point that holiness includes the ethical but goes beyond it.[1] The numinous represents the nonmoral, irrational side of the Holy that both attracts and repels. Holiness is not simply the good but the dynamic energy of God that consumes and overwhelms the one who experiences it. "Holiness" is a transmoral term that does not annul the ethical but opens up a new dimension of reality for the seeker after truth.

In Israel's history holiness could be applied to nonpersonal things, places and even pagan gods (cf. Dan 4:8, 9; 5:11). The ground around the burning bush is holy (Ex 3:5) as are the temple (Is 64:11; Jon 2:4; Hab 2:20), days (Ex 20:8; Deut 5:12; Is 58:13), utensils (1 Chron 9:29), garments (Ex 29:21; Lev 16:4), food (1 Sam 21:4; Neh 7:65), oil (Ex 30:25, 31; Num 35:25; Ps 89:20) and offerings (2 Chron 35:13; Ezek 42:13). The mountain on which God will manifest himself is called holy (Ps 87:1; Is 11:9; 56:7; Ezek 20:40).

At the same time, holiness came ever more to be associated in the consciousness of Israel with righteousness and moral purity. The prophets were constantly protesting against reducing holiness to rites and ceremonies (1 Sam 15:22; Ps 40:6-8; Prov 21:3; Hos 6:6). It is the Lord whom we must revere (Is 1:4; 8:13; 31:1; 55:5; 60:9; Hos 11:9). To be sanctified means to observe all the commandments (Deut 26:16). Isaiah confesses, "The LORD of hosts is exalted by justice, and the Holy God shows himself holy by righteousness" (Is 5:16 NRSV; cf. Ps 99:4-5). God's eyes are too pure to sanction evil (Hab 1:13). The holy God of Israel is described as a "mighty king" who loves justice and establishes equity (Ps 99:4). More and more it came to be recognized that cultic purity entails personal purity. The living God of biblical religion demands not simply surrender and submission but obedience and love. The holiness of God stands arrayed against both idolatry and injustice. The so-called code of holiness in Leviticus 17-26 contains both cultic and moral requirements.

In biblical faith God alone is the fount and source of holiness, though the awesome presence of God can leave its imprint on places and things as well as be reflected in the lives of people. God is referred to as "the Holy One" (Prov 9:10; Is 40:25; Hos 11:9; 1 Jn 2:20) and "the Holy One of Israel" (Is 1:4; 5:19, 24; 41:14; 43:14) and is acclaimed as "majestic in holiness" (Ex 15:11; cf. Is 45:15). Holiness is God's innermost nature, embracing power, eternity and glory (Rev 4:8). The angels sing "Holy, holy, holy" to the God of transcendent majesty (Is 6:3; cf. Rev 4:8). Jesus calls God "Holy Father" (Jn 17:11), and God's name is to be "hallowed" (Mt 6:9; cf. Ex 20:7; Ps 97:12; 103:1; Ezek 36:22; 43:7). In Rev 6:10 God is invoked as "Sovereign Lord, holy and true" (NIV; cf. 16:5–7).

The New Testament also ascribes holiness to Jesus, the Messiah of Israel and Savior of the world. He is "full of the Holy Spirit" (Lk 4:1) and is acclaimed as "the Holy One of God" (Mk 1:24; Lk 4:34; Jn 6:69; Acts 3:14). Even more striking is the common association of the Spirit of God with holiness, thus laying the foundations for the church's confession of the Holy Spirit as the third person of the Trinity.

Thomas Oden sees a "profound ethical and political import" in the biblical affirmation of God's holiness. "God is free from every moral evil; therefore those who are called to holiness of heart and life . . . are thereby called to consecrate themselves to a life of radical responsiveness to God's love and accountability to God's own justice."[2] Just as God is holy, so the people of God must be holy—in their words and in their conduct (1 Pet 1:15–16). We are to walk in his ways and thereby give him glory and honor.

Holiness together with love is the quintessential attribute of God. It includes his majesty, glory and power. James Leo Garrett expresses this well: "Eternity is the duration of God's holiness. Changelessness is the continuing stability or constancy of God's holiness. Wisdom is the truth of God's holiness. Power is the strength of God's holiness. . . . Glory is the recognized manifestation of God's holiness as majesty."[3] Righteousness, one might add, connotes the moral purity of God's holiness. It reminds us that obedience to the holy God involves moral excellence as well as separateness and apartness.

Two Sides of God

Biblical faith portrays God as having two sides: holiness and love. These are the perfections that shape the interaction of God with his people.

They are integrally related, and yet they coexist in a certain tension, one that highlights their paradoxical unity rather than dissolves it. God's holiness is his majestic purity that cannot tolerate moral evil. God's love is his outgoing, tenderhearted embrace of the sinner. God's holiness is his separateness from what is unclean and profane. God's love is his willingness to identify with those who are unclean in order to help them. God's holiness transcends the passing world of decay and death. God's love incarnates itself in this world corrupted by sin.

It has been fashionable in some theologies to subordinate God's holiness to his love and to identify the latter with the essence of God. Henry Ward Beecher regarded "power, wisdom and justice" as "God's lesser ways" which reflect "that side of His Being where there would be restriction if anywhere; while love and mercy are God's peculiar glory." In these are found "the most glorious liberty of the Divine Nature."[4] In the earlier, liberal phase of his theology, Reinhold Niebuhr could declare, "There is only one standard that has any business being read into the heart of God and that is this ultimate standard of love."[5] Other theologians who practically equate God and love include Nels Ferré, Anders Nygren and Eberhard Jüngel.

Another strand of theology in Christian faith gives preeminence to God's holiness. In Calvin the theme of God's love is not nearly as prominent as that of God's sovereignty and majesty.[6] According to W. G. T. Shedd holiness belongs to the essence of God's nature, whereas mercy is involved in God's disposition.[7] A. H. Strong held that justice is "a principle of God's nature, not only independent of love, but superior to love."[8] P. T. Forsyth reacted sharply against the deemphasis of God's holiness in liberal theology: "The love of God has ousted the glory of God, and the grace has been declared at the cost of the holiness."[9] He was adamant that the "prime thing in God is His holiness. From His holiness flows His love."[10] Forsyth aimed for a blending of divine holiness and love, though he gave a slight priority to the first. Similarly David Wells says that what defines God essentially is holiness, of which love is an inescapable manifestation.[11]

While Karl Barth included holiness under the rubric of divine loving, he nevertheless sought to hold the two together in a paradoxical relationship. "The holiness of God consists in the unity of His judgment with His grace. God is holy because His grace judges and His judgment is gracious."[12] For Barth God's holiness is ultimately in the service of his love, which emanates from the depth of God's being. Barth associated the Father with holiness, the Son with mercy and the Spirit with love.

Even more than Barth, Emil Brunner stoutly affirmed the mutual interpenetration of divine holiness and love. He discerned in the holiness of God "a twofold movement of the Divine Will—at first sight a contradictory movement, namely, a movement of withdrawal and exclusion, and a movement of expansion and inclusion."[13] God's holiness cannot be reduced to his love, but it is informed by his love: "The Holiness of God is fulfilled . . . in His merciful love, but it is not absorbed into that Love of God; it still remains distinct, and must be recognized by us as part of the Nature of God."[14] Brunner was sharply critical of the agape reductionism that he discerned in much modern theology.

From my perspective God's love and holiness constitute the inner nature of the living God. These two perfections coalesce in such a way that we may speak of the holy love of God (as did Forsyth) and of his merciful holiness. In the depth of God's love is revealed the beauty of his holiness. In the glory of his holiness is revealed the breadth of his love. The apex of God's holiness is the holiness of his love. The apex of God's love is the beauty of his holiness. God's love transcends his holiness even while it infuses and upholds it. His holiness is adorned and crowned by the magnitude of his love.

The Bible also speaks of God's anger and jealousy. It is customary in the mystical-idealistic tradition of the church to regard these as figurative expressions reflecting the projection of human feelings upon God. Angelus Silesius declared, "God stands far above the anger, rage and indignation ascribed to Him by primitive imagination."[15] In the controversial affirmation, "Jacob I loved, but Esau I hated" (Rom 9:13), liberal theologians discern in Paul a throwback to the Old Testament concept of a God of wrath, which is superseded by the New Testament depiction of God as inexhaustible love. Conservatives err by using this verse as a basis for double predestination, whereas it actually indicates God's by-passing of Esau and his election of Jacob for a special role in salvation history.[16]

In the Hellenistic conception of God, which entered into the speculation of both Catholic and Protestant theologians, God does not punish anyone. He allows us to be punished by our own sins. This approach is reflected in C. H. Dodd's contention that Paul "retains the concept of 'the Wrath of God' . . . not to describe the attitude of God to man, but to describe an inevitable process of cause and effect in a moral universe."[17] Ernst Käsemann takes issue with Dodd for explaining the wrath of God as an impersonal process, an immanent causality. On the contrary, God himself is secretly at work to exact retribution.[18]

We must recognize that God's wrath is a real, objective power, but it is qualitatively different from human anger. As Adrio König observes, "The prophets never speak of his wrath as an uncontrolled explosion, unpredictable and irrational. Indeed, his wrath is never spontaneous but is always a reaction, caused or provoked by the behaviour of people."[19] According to Wolfhart Pannenberg, wrath is not an attribute of God but "the annihilating outworking of his holiness when it comes into contact with what is unclean."[20] Paul Jewett's position is similar: "Wrath describes not God as he is in himself, but rather as he is related to the sinner who spurns his love and dishonors his name."[21]

Holiness and love are alone the true nature of God. Wrath is the reaction of God, the necessary reaction of God's holiness against sin. But wrath is an objective reality. For Luther wrath is the strange work of God, and love in Christ is his real work. Wrath is an objective reality emanating from the nature of God himself. But it is not identical with his true nature, which is revealed in Christ. At the same time, the wrath of God cannot be reduced to a subjective experience.

The wrath of God may be seen as the strange work of his love that destroys that which is against love (Tillich).[22] Gustav Friedrich Oehler gave a poignant articulation of this mystery: "The wrath of God is the highest strained energy of the holy will of God, the zeal of His wounded love."[23] Wrath is not what God is in himself but how God relates to sinners who stubbornly refuse his grace and mercy. Just as a caring mother disciplines her child who refuses to heed her warnings against playing on a busy street, so God reproves and chastises his children who wander into sin against his express will.

The older theology frequently drew a bifurcation between God's justice and his mercy, his holiness and his love. It was said that from all eternity God hated those on his left hand and loved those on his right hand.[24] On the contemporary scene Larry Dixon argues that God not only hates the sin but also hates the sinner with a hatred devoid of love.[25] Hell is a creation of his wrath and judgment, and this wrath must therefore be eternal. Despite an earnest appeal to Scripture for support, these theologians fail to take into consideration the wider biblical witness that God's wrath is provisional whereas his love is eternal (cf. Is 54:8; Rom 11:32). Apart from God's self-revelation in Jesus Christ, where God reveals himself as holy love, we would be compelled to see God as divided and consequently as the author of a double predestination where the elect people of God are foreordained to heaven and the reprobate to an eternal hell. I do not deny the dreaded reality of hell, but we need to envision hell as a creation of his love as well as of his justice. It is also incumbent on us to see the grace of God reaching into hell as well as reigning in heaven, for otherwise we are forced to posit a co-eternal evil that would take away from the glory and beatitude of heaven.[26]

I find some measure of agreement with the biblical scholar Gustav Stählin: "God's wrath is undoubtedly lasting as his holy resistance to everything unholy (Rev. 20:10, 14; 21:8). Eternity of wrath, however, is definitely not meant in 1 Th. 2:16 (cf. Rom. 9-11), where the *eis télos* might mean 'forever' in the sense of 'eternally' but has here a weaker rhetorical sense, and may even mean up to the dawn of the last time."[27] Stählin rightly recognizes that the New Testament does not stand opposed to the Old Testament "in an antithesis of love and wrath. Love and wrath are present in both. If, however, human arrogance is the occasion of divine wrath (cf. Rom. 2:4ff.), it does not cause eternal hostility between God and humanity, for God's love stands alongside and above his wrath."[28]

God's grace is greater than his judgment (Rom 3:3-4; Jas 2:13), his love is deeper than his wrath (Is 54:8; Hos 14:4). His holiness cannot be violated without just retribution, but the good news is that God in his infinite love has taken the retribution that we deserve upon himself in the life and death of his Son, Jesus Christ. He turns his wrath upon himself in order to save a lost and fallen human race. The cross of Christ signifies the vindication of his holiness as well as the incommensurability of his love. God still becomes angry when we continue to sin, but his anger is always in the service of his love, which is unquenchable and inexorable.[29] Hell is a reality because some mortals in their contumacy and folly refuse to acknowledge God's grace and choose to live apart from his love. But hell is not the final word on human destiny because God's grace pursues the sinner into hell (cf. Ps 139:7-12). I am here suggesting not a translation from hell into heaven but the penetration of hell by divine grace, which means that hell itself is made to serve the eschatological glory of God. The transcendent beauty of God is enhanced rather than diminished by the continuing polarity of grace and judgment, love and holiness.

Process theology depicts God as unbounded love (Ogden) or the power of creativity (Wieman, Cobb) rather than the unity of majestic holiness and self-sacrificing love. God moves us to higher levels of human striving by the magnetism of his beauty and the lure of his suffering love. In biblical perspective God is a God whose holiness repels and overwhelms rather than a God who simply lures or invites. Process theologians regard the anger and jealousy of God as metaphors reflecting human experience. But God's anger is "the other side of his love, of his holy will, the expression—that is—of his aversion from all that is evil and of his displeasure in the sinner."[30] His jealousy does not stem from envy or fear but is "the expression of his uniqueness which permits no other gods beside himself, the consequence of the will of him who insists absolutely on his directives for man's good."³¹ God is jealous for the sake of our preservation and salvation. He is wrathful for the sake of our redemption from the powers of sin, death and hell. Apart from his wrath we cannot understand God's love as holy love nor his grace as judging grace. Love is then reduced to sentimentality whereas God's love is a conquering power that does not simply urge us to pursue the ideal of the good but rescues us from dreaded evil. The psalmist rejoices, "The God who loves me is coming, God will show me my enemies defeated" (Ps 59:10 JB). God's love is inseparable from God's power as well as from God's holiness. His holiness is infused by his incomparable love and is therefore a source of comfort as well as fear, of confidence as well as dread. God's loving holiness uplifts us in the midst of divine affliction; it consoles us in the depths of gnawing despair. But all of these things remain incomprehensible apart from God's self-revelation in Jesus Christ, for only there do we come to understand the unity of his mercy and holiness, the inseparability of his love and wrath.

Divine and Human Love

No less integral to the divine being than his holiness is his immeasurable and incomparable love. In the New Testament this is described as agape—an outgoing and other-regarding concern for a lost and distraught humanity. God loves not in order to enhance or adorn himself but simply because he wills to give of himself unreservedly to those who are inferior to himself. Agape is not the urge to possess and to enjoy but the readiness to serve without condition. Agape love, says Anders Nygren, is unmotivated in the sense that it is not contingent on any value or worth in the object of love.³² It is spontaneous and heedless, for it does not determine beforehand whether love will be effective or appropriate in any particular case. It is a lost love (*verlorene Liebe*—Luther), a love that "squanders itself."³³ It "wants to radiate out into the realm of lovelessness" (Jüngel).³⁴ Agape goes out to good and evil alike (Mt

5:45), though it always seeks to turn evil toward the good. Agape is not indifferent to the moral state of the one loved, but it goes out to all persons irrespective of their moral preparedness or holiness.

Agape is often contrasted with eros, which is not found in the New Testament though it is prominent in Greek philosophy. Eros can refer to a vulgar, carnal love, but in the context of Hellenic thought it takes the form of a spiritual love that aspires to procure the highest good. Eros is the desire to possess and to enjoy; agape is the willingness to serve without reservations. Eros is an ascending love that proceeds from the earthly to the heavenly. Agape is a descending love that proceeds from the heavenly to the sinful. Eros is attracted to that which has greatest value; agape goes out to the least worthy. Eros discovers value whereas agape creates value. Agape is a gift love whereas eros is a need love. Eros springs from a deficiency that must be satisfied. Agape is the overflowing abundance of divine grace. For Plato eros is not found in God, for God is devoid of passion. Plotinus, on the other hand, made a place for eros in God, but this was simply God reflecting upon his own goodness.

In Christian perspective divine love is agape, not eros. But can agape also take the form of human love directed to God? Agape is not rooted in human nature as are eros and *philia* ("friendship"), but once agape streams into a person's life that person is enabled to participate in this creative energy that transforms and heals. We can love with agape through the power of God's grace; once our love is separated from this grace, however, it immediately becomes mutual love rather than pure sacrificial love (Reinhold Niebuhr). Our love for God and neighbor can correspond to God's love for us, but it cannot duplicate this love so long as it remains an entirely human act.

The supreme revelation of agape is God's self-condescension in Jesus Christ, for there he willingly took upon himself the pain and guilt of the human race for the sake of their salvation. This act of unmerited grace was at the same time the overflowing of his illimitable love, which humans cannot achieve or create but through grace can receive and celebrate. Agape as practiced by Spirit-filled Christians goes out to the neighbor without desire for merit or personal fulfillment. Reinhold Niebuhr put it succinctly: "The service of God is to be performed not only without hope of any concrete or obvious reward, but at the price of sacrifice, abnegation and loss."[35] Agape when directed to God by his sons and daughters is simply the upwelling of joy for a salvation already realized, a communion already attained. Agape directed toward God is still a thanking, serving love. It is not motivated to win special favor in the sight of God or to become as God. When eros is directed toward the neighbor, it is never the neighbor as a person but the divine core within that person that commands our devotion. Neighbor love is a ladder that leads us toward the higher love—the love of perfect being (John of the Cross).

Helmut Thielicke helps to clarify the qualitative difference between agape and eros:

> Eros as the human form of love needs the other to inflame and provoke it. It needs the other for its own completion. God's *agape*, however, is fundamentally different. It needs neither provocation nor completion. Hence it does not have to depend upon the partnership of the man who is able to respond in love. It does not come to itself only by means of this partnership.[36]

Eros is not the only form of natural love. Natural love may also appear as friendship *(philia)*, involving a mutual bond of affection between persons who share a common interest. Friendship is basically egocentric (as is eros), but it contains an altruistic element, since we seek the welfare of our friend though always at least partly to realize an inner need. Natural love may also take the form of familial affection *(storgē)*. Like friendship this is a preferential love, but it is necessary for the preservation of the family and for human happiness. Still another form of love is *epithymia,* the natural drive for life in everything that is.[37] In one sense *epithymia* can be considered a variation of eros. It is not the spiritual eros, however—the love of transcendent ideals—but the desire for life in all its immeasurable richness. *Epithymia* is the heroic will to power that expands and revitalizes the self, whereas eros in classical mysticism fosters the denial of the self for the sake of the ultimate perfection of the self.

Nygren rightly pointed to the cleavage between agape in the New Testament and the legalistic understanding of love in Rabbinic Judaism.[38] In the latter the command of love reduces love to law *(nomos)*, whereas agape reminds us that love is both gift and command: it is a gift that fulfills and transcends law. When love is seen primarily in terms of *nomos,* it becomes an external standard rather than a creative power within us. It is related more to merit than to grace. It is calculating rather than heedless, conditional rather than unconditional. It proceeds from a sense of obligation rather than from an overflowing heart. Love becomes obedience to law rather than a spontaneous display of mercy. In evangelical religion love is neither unrequited longing (eros) nor submission to a moral code *(nomos)* but unmerited grace (agape). It is not the passion to possess (eros) nor the duty to attend *(nomos)* but the loving-kindness that bestows (agape).

Divine love does not indicate the power of love as such but the living God who loves. In the mystical-idealistic tradition God is portrayed as beyond any kind of emotion or passion—including that of love. Meister Eckhart could say that God "is nonloving, being above love and affection."[39] For Charles Fillmore, cofounder of the Unity School of Christianity, which is deeply embedded in American transcendentalism, "God is not loving, God does not love anybody. . . . God is the love in everybody and everything."[40] In biblical religion God not only loves but demonstrates his love by incarnating himself in human flesh and going to the cross.

In some forms of liberationist and feminist theologies love is redefined as compassion—a caring concern that takes the form of justice and courage.[41] According to Wendy Farley, "Compassion labors to penetrate the darkness of pain and mediate to the sufferer the taste of love and the power of courage. . . . The power of compassion is incarnational, interactive. It is present to sufferers as the power to resist their suffering in whatever ways are possible."[42] Compassion in this sense can serve the cause of the kingdom, but it must never be confounded with agape. Whereas compassion teaches the right use of power, agape willingly gives up power and triumphs through powerlessness. Whereas compassion focuses on satisfying human need, agape is inexplicable grace. Compassion enables oppressed persons to resist their suffering; agape willingly takes suffering upon itself. Compassion is motivated to redress human wrongs; agape is unmotivated. Compassion instills resistance to entrenched evil; agape is nonresistance to evil (Mt 5:39-42; Lk 6:27-29). Compassion is a triumphal love that spearheads the struggle for righteousness. Agape is the love of the cross that willingly endures unrighteousness. Compassion conquers by enabling the oppressed to liberate and advance themselves. Agape conquers by shaming the oppressor into repentance (cf. Rom 12:20-21).

While natural love is not the same as divine love, it can be used and thereby transformed by divine love. The struggle for justice can be transfigured by the humility that discerns that even the just fall short of the radical love that Christ demands. Under the impact of agape, friendship *(philia)* can be transformed into fellowship (koinonia), where preferential treatment is subordinated to caring concern for the wider family of faith. The self-regarding love of eros can be converted into a regard for the integrity and personhood of others. Married love can be salvaged by subordinating the desire for sexual gratification to a genuine concern for the needs of one's partner. The drive for heroism can be transposed into an aspiration for holiness.

A modicum of self-love will always remain in the Christian life not only because of our sin but also because of our created nature as finite mortals. Agape does not annul the needs of the self, but it subordinates concern for the self to the service of God and neighbor. Agape does not extinguish hope for a better life or for eternal salvation, but it rises above hope for oneself in a service to others that is oblivious to one's own advancement or safety. In our love we do not expect anything in return, but we hope that through our efforts the kingdom of God will be served in some small way.

I agree with Reinhold Niebuhr that "self-love is never justified, but self-realization is allowed as the unintended but inevitable consequence of unselfish action."[43] We should not seek the security and happiness of the self above all else, but we can hope that God will bless us as we seek his kingdom first of all and most of all. Our natural needs are not repugnant to our Creator God, and he sanctions these things because he knows that they enable us to survive in the kind of world in which we live. But God calls us to give up our *craving* for the goods of this world in order to serve the crying needs of our neighbor. When we lose ourselves for God's sake and for the sake of neighbor, we shall then find ourselves in the end (Mt 6:33).

Reinhold Niebuhr again reminds us that the highest kind of love is neither humanitarian assistance nor self-sacrifice: it is forgiveness.[44] Behind the self-sacrifice of the Son of God on the cross lies God's unmerited forgiveness of a fallen humanity, which from the human perspective is totally inexplicable. When forgiving love is practiced by mortals, it is wholly contingent on their repentance and faith. As Niebuhr aptly phrased it, "Forgiving love is a possibility only for those who know that they are not good, who feel themselves in need of divine mercy, who live in a dimension deeper and higher than that of moral idealism."[45]

Niebuhr allowed that the paradoxical love of the cross could be experienced in human history, but it could never really take permanent lodging in history because of the continuing sinfulness of humanity. I believe that Niebuhr underestimated the reality and power of the Holy Spirit, who enables us to do what cannot be done through our own resources. We cannot love just as God loves, but we can love like God loves. The kingdom of God is not simply beyond history (as Niebuhr sometimes alleged), but it takes root in history. Our hope is not simply sporadic foretastes of the coming glory of God but the creation of a fellowship of love that mediates this glory to the world.

I also have difficulty with Niebuhr, especially in his earlier theology, as well as with Nygren, for tending to view God as exclusively love and thereby underplaying his holiness and majesty. They both rightly contend that God is not eros, but does not God contain law or torah within himself? I concur with Brunner that "the modern, unilateral, monistic Idea of God," who is bare agape, contradicts the biblical picture of God who is both agape and *nomos,* "both love and holiness, both hidden and revealed," who combines mercy with an anger that is real and objective and in the face of which and outside Christ humanity is in deadly peril.[46] God does not have unrequited longing for ever-greater perfection, but he surely has reverence for the holy law that he reveals, for this law mirrors his very nature—that of holy love. Unless we see God as lawgiver and moral ruler as well as redeemer, we render his redemption superfluous and his forgiveness meaningless. The love of God is not only something to be enjoyed but also something to be worshiped (Forsyth). But God cannot elicit our worship unless he is a consuming fire—a love that uproots sin as well as consoles in times of despair. Agape transcends *nomos,* but it does not cancel *nomos.* The gospel fulfills the law; it does not annul the law (Mt 5:17). We are made free for obedience to the law but in a spirit of love. Agape is the law of freedom that does not render external law superfluous but realizes its innermost intent and purpose.

It is fashionable in modern theology to regard God's love as eros rather than agape. According to Sallie McFague God has a passionate desire to be united with the world, which implies that the world is intrinsically valuable to God.[47] For Moltmann, "The creative Spirit of God is himself Eros, for out of his creations and in his creations his beauty shines forth and again awakens eros in its turn."[48] If God is inherently deficient and in need of the world for self-fulfillment and greater perfection, then he is no longer the almighty God of biblical faith.

In agape God loves us despite what we are and have become. God's very act of loving us makes us valuable—to God and to ourselves. We must not say that God loves us because of who we are, that he sees something in us that is fantastic and admirable. Luther brings out the qualitative difference between agape and eros: "Sinners are loved not because they are beautiful; they are beautiful because they are loved."[49]

In imitation of Christ we are called to love others as God loved us (Jn 15:9-10; Eph 5:1-2). We love others not because they are equally divine (as in Stoicism) but because God loves them equally.[50] By loving and serving others we show our love and gratitude to God for what he has done for us and for the whole world in Jesus Christ. Augustine betrayed a Platonic mindset when he said, "The more we love God the more we love ourselves."[51] The more biblical way of expressing it is: the more we love God the more we forget ourselves in service to our neighbor. I take issue with Moltmann's contention that "self-love is the strength to love our neighbor."[52] On the contrary, self-love is superseded when we love our neighbor. The selfless love of neighbor paradoxically brings us a sense of our dignity and respect as children of God, but this is because we now live outside ourselves in the service of the kingdom of God, and in this service we derive meaning and purpose in life. Love is not "the urge for the reunion of the separated"[53] but bringing light to those who now dwell in darkness. We do not seek the unity of God and the self but the liberation of the self for service to God in ministry to the lost and despairing of the world. General William Booth, founder of the Salvation Army, gave pithy expression to the Christian mandate: "Go for souls and go for the worst." Agape love is a love that descends into the affliction and misery of a sinful world, but paradoxically in this very descent we are elevated into the presence of the living God whose light is hidden in the darkness of the squalor and poverty of sinful humankind.

Holiness and Justice

Just as divine love is not the same as human love, so divine righteousness is not the same as human righteousness. But just as human love can correspond to divine love, so human righteousness can anticipate and foreshadow divine righteousness.

God's righteousness is the ethical dimension of his holiness. Holiness and righteousness are joined together in the messianic expectation in

Luke 1:75. Righteousness connotes moral purity, but it has its basis in God's illimitable mercy. Righteousness is the grace that equips us to live a moral life. It not only sets a standard but grants the freedom to live up to this standard.

Human righteousness is conformity to the universal dictates of conscience. It means giving each person his or her due or deepening respect for human dignity and freedom.[54] Divine righteousness is bringing people into a right relationship with one another and with God. Social justice is guaranteeing that the rights and just claims of people are duly satisfied. Divine righteousness is making people willing to forego their rights and claims for the sake of another. Social justice is preventing the wounds that estrange people from each other from festering by the resort to law and force.[55] Divine righteousness brings healing to these wounds.

The infinite qualitative difference between God and humanity is reflected in the polarity between divine holiness and human decency, love and law, divine righteousness and social justice, the kingdom of God and a righteous nation. Human justice is a worthy goal, for it means a society in which the rights of the marginalized are respected and the weak are protected from the strong. Yet social justice as a viable possibility in a fallen world is not to be confounded with divine holiness—the impossible possibility realized only through grace. In the former the claims of wronged individuals are rightly adjudicated; in the latter persons are accepted and loved as brothers and sisters. A just society by human standards falls drastically short of the ideal of love exemplified in the life and death of Jesus Christ.

This tension between the two moralities is illumined by comparing humanitarian love with agape, the paradoxical love of the cross.[56] Humanitarianism, which has its roots in the Hellenistic ethos, indicates an impersonal love for humanity that transcends all parochialism and insularism. Agape, by contrast, focuses on love for the individual person—even while it is universal in its outreach. Humanitarianism contains an element of paternalism: it seeks to raise the unfortunate to a higher level in society where their dignity can be recognized and appreciated. Agape descends into the depths of human misery and affliction and ministers to people on their level. Humanitarianism lends a helping hand to the deprived and forsaken; agape vicariously identifies with the castaways of society. Humanitarianism holds up before the disinherited the ideal of a better world. Agape creates a new world for the despised and helpless in the form of an ongoing fellowship of love. Humanitarianism necessarily makes a place for self-love, since in promoting humanity we also promote ourselves. Agape leads us to deny ourselves for the sake of our neighbor in need. Humanitarian love is altruistic without negating the self's quest for well-being and security. Agape love is transmoral—calling people to a higher ideal than self-interest—the service of the glory of God.

Humanitarianism was given a new lease on life by the Enlightenment. The humanitarian ideal has been salutary in the struggle for human freedom and justice, but it also contains the seeds of self-deception and self-righteousness. According to Reinhold Niebuhr, "Philanthropy always compounds the display of power with the expression of pity. Sometimes it is even used as a conscious effort to evade the requirements of justice."[57] Dietrich Bonhoeffer detected the driving force of ambition in much of what goes under the name of humanitarianism: "Self-love plays itself up as altruism and charity . . . as socially concerned love, as love of humanity, and does not want to be identified."[58]

Niebuhr has been helpful in trying to link up the striving for a just social order with the transcendent ideal of agape. Our exposure to this ideal will quicken us in our efforts to bring about a more humane world. The person who has experienced the love of Christ and the holiness of God will become more sensitive to social wrongs and be motivated to redress these wrongs. The danger arises when we are willing to settle for the rule of law in society and do not look further to the coming of a new social order—the kingdom of God that alone can satisfy the longings of the human heart for community and holiness. Social justice always employs coercion; kingdom righteousness imbues people with such a burning love for God and neighbor that external restraints are rendered superfluous. In a sinful world coercion will always be necessary, and to assume that a brotherhood of mutual love can supplant the need for force in resolving social conflict is to allow society to fall into chaos. Human beings have the capacity to humanize society, but they cannot of and by themselves Christianize society. Niebuhr astutely perceived that there will never be a "Christian civilization"—a society "with which a sensitive soul ought not feel itself in conflict."[59]

Civil law by itself cannot change the human condition, but it can better the human lot. Niebuhr saw this clearly: "The whip of the law cannot change the heart. But . . . it can restrain the heartless until they change their mind and heart."[60] In his view, "All political justice is achieved by coercing the anarchy of collective self-interest into some kind of decent order by the most attainable balance of power."[61] At the same time, the striving for justice must be seen in the light of the transcendent standards of the kingdom of God, which is not of this world but whose light illuminates our worldly tasks and saves us from despair. The law of love is not only a source for the norms of justice but also an ultimate criterion by which we measure our gains toward justice.

Brunner made a helpful distinction between "critical cooperation," in which Christians work with others toward a higher degree of justice in society, and "apostolic action," in which we try to change the value system and worldview of our fellow citizens.[62] Only an inner change can facilitate the vision of a new social order that reflects the values of the kingdom of God. But this does not mean that we should therefore abandon the social task of preserving order and of trying to make the world a better place in which to live.

Jacques Ellul, the French professor of law and sociology who passionately resisted Nazism and was himself active in politics after the war, shared this realistic discernment of the continuing imperfection in the structures of social existence.[63] We must be politically involved but without confusing our efforts to improve society with the coming of the kingdom of God. We should engage ourselves in social and political life not in the hope of making the world into a paradise but simply to make it tolerable, not to bring in the kingdom of God but to ensure that people are free to proclaim the gospel.[64]

Barth gave more meaning to social engagement when he asserted that Christians can set up signs and parables of the coming kingdom that quicken the hope for God's final intervention in world history.[65] We cannot duplicate the righteousness and holiness of God, but by his grace we can attain an approximation of this higher righteousness. Our ultimate purpose in political involvement is to give glory to God and to motivate people to prepare themselves for the inbreaking of God's kingdom in history.

The polarity between divine holiness and social justice has its basis in the biblical polarity between the law and the gospel.[66] The law does not redeem, but it can keep intact the fabric that holds society together. The law points to the gospel, but it cannot induce faith in the gospel. The gospel releases us from the burden of the law, but it does not cancel the need for law. On the contrary, it sends us back to the law, motivating us to apply its demands to the social arena—but in the spirit of love. We are saved for obedience to the gospel-law, the law illumined by the gospel and the gospel fulfilling the demands of the law. The divine command prepares us to hear the divine promise; the divine promise equips us to obey the divine command. Energized by the grace of the living God, we can strive for personal and social holiness and thereby help mold a society that reflects this holiness even while it is still subject to the corrosive power of sin and death. The continuing irruption of sin can unravel any society unless it is filled with people who fear God and earnestly strive to honor him in the public as well as in the private sphere of life.

In place of a natural law ethic (classical Catholicism) and a justice-peace ethic (liberation-feminist theology),[67] I propose an ethic of the divine command, which brings together the commandments and principles in Holy Scripture with the gospel of redeeming grace that created

Scripture and forms its inner content.[68] In this view the hope for a more just social order lies in an encounter with the God of holy love who alone gives meaning to life and direction in works of social amelioration. Our ultimate norm for personal and social conduct is the divine command in its paradoxical unity with the divine promise, and this command is mediated to people of faith through Holy Scripture and the sacred tradition that builds upon Scripture. In the light of divine holiness and love as we see this revealed in Jesus Christ, we can pour content and meaning into the immediate tasks of redressing social wrongs and humanizing social structures. The realization that we are sinners saved only by grace should prevent us from taking pride in our social achievements and ingloriously damning our opponents. The awareness that we are upheld in our feeble efforts to build a better world by the Spirit of the living God who transcends this world should make our political involvement worthwhile. Niebuhr put it well: "The hope of Christian faith that the divine power which bears history can complete what even the highest human striving must leave incomplete, and can purify the corruptions which appear in even the purest human aspirations, is an indispensable prerequisite for diligent fulfillment of our historic tasks."[69]

Niebuhr himself was attracted to a modified form of the natural law ethic, often appealing to universal principles such as equality, freedom and humaneness. Yet his primary commitment was to the law of love that incorporated these norms but also transcended them. Niebuhr believed mutual love to be the highest possibility within history and therefore failed to do justice to the abiding reality of the Holy Spirit in the fellowship of the saints.[70] It is the Spirit who makes it possible for human beings to love others more than themselves. Niebuhr can nonetheless be appreciated for his persistent awareness that the kingdom of God contradicts the social achievements of even an enlightened humanity and that this kingdom will always be an undeserved gift from a gracious God. For Niebuhr the kingdom is a gift that can be experienced in history but can never be an all-pervasive force that shapes history.[71]

Bonhoeffer saw the realization of the kingdom of God in the practice of costly discipleship where we actually endeavor to follow Christ in the midst of the world's afflictions.[72] More than Niebuhr, Bonhoeffer was convinced that Christians can be light and salt in an unfriendly and even loveless world and can thereby effect real changes. Yet he too perceived that justice as the world understands it is qualitatively different from the love that characterizes the kingdom of God: "Where justice seems to command us to keep a record of rights and wrongs, love is blind, knowingly blind. It sees the wrong, but does not keep a record of it."[73] Love is the spontaneous outburst of a converted heart; justice is the conscious deliberation of righting human wrongs. Bonhoeffer recognized that often we must first address penultimate concerns—such as land, peace and bread—before we can bring people to a realization of the ultimate—the last things and salvation.[74] By giving ourselves to the cause of justice and service of the needy, we can set the stage for introducing people to the claims of Jesus Christ and his gospel. Whereas Niebuhr was inclined to see works of justice as the fruit and evidence of a living faith rather than as a preparation for faith, both men rightly perceived the inseparability of faith in the gospel and engagement in political affairs. Both refused to identify God's unique work in bringing in the kingdom of transcendent righteousness and holiness with the social achievements of men and women whose consciences have been sensitized to the evils of oppression and exploitation. Perhaps Niebuhr thought more dialectically than Bonhoeffer, but both keenly realized that Christian service can be sustained only by the hope in God's promises to create a new heaven and a new earth.[75]

The Call to Holiness

As majestic holiness and unquenchable love, God wills that his nature be reflected in his people. Being a holy God he is satisfied with nothing less than holiness in all manner of conduct (cf. Lev 11:44; 19:2; Is 52:11). Being a loving God he strives to instill this love in the people he has created and called to service in his kingdom.

All people have a vocation to holiness. We are all created for the glory of God. All are called to fear God and to keep his commandments (Eccles 12:13). Our Lord declared, "Come to me, *all* who labor and are heavy laden, and I will give you rest. Take my yoke upon you, and learn from me" (Mt 11:28-29, italics mine; cf. Is 45:22).

People of faith, however, are especially singled out for a vocation to holiness. "Aim at peace with everyone and a holy life, for without that no one will see the Lord" (Heb 12:14 REB); "As obedient children, be yourselves holy in all your activity, after the model of the Holy One who calls us" (1 Pet 1:14-15 NJB); "He saved us and called us to a consecrated life, not for anything we had done, but of his own accord and out of the mercy which he bestowed upon us ages ago through Christ Jesus" (2 Tim 1:9 AAT).

Not only individuals but whole peoples can be set apart for the service of God's glory in the world. The children of Israel were told: "You are a people holy to the Lord your God, and he has chosen you out of all peoples on earth to be his special possession" (Deut 7:6 REB; cf. 1 Pet 2:9).

Holiness is not wholeness as the world understands it but faithfulness, perseverance in obedience. It means wholehearted dedication to the living God through service in his name. To aspire to holiness is to aspire to something other than a virtuous life or even a fulfilled life. What makes the holy person distinctive is not so much adherence to conventional moral standards as consecration to the Wholly Other, who stands in judgment over all human values and aspirations. Holiness excludes not only immorality but also mediocrity. It involves not only obedience to the law but also zeal for the faith.

The Christian life is characterized by passive sanctity and active holiness. The Holy Spirit secretly works sanctity within us (Calvin); our task is to manifest this work of the Spirit in our everyday activities. We do not procure sanctity or holiness, but we can do works that reveal the holiness of Christ. We do not earn holiness, but we can demonstrate, celebrate and proclaim his holiness. Christ has broken down the wall of hostility that divides peoples (Eph 2:13-16), but we can give concrete witness to this fact by being peacemakers and catalysts of social change.

Faith entails both passive surrender and active obedience. We are justified by faith alone; yet faith does not remain alone but issues forth in faith working through love (Gal 5:6). In the act of faith we become dead to the world so that we may live in Christ. In the life of faith we die with Christ so that the world may live.

In Matthew 5:13-16 we are summoned to live out our vocation as salt and light. The metaphor of light in the New Testament can refer to Jesus Christ, to the message of his saving work and even to the disciples. Basically the significance of our vocation lies not in what we are but in what we bring. We are commissioned to carry the salt of the gospel to the world, to radiate the light that is in Christ.

Just as Jesus is the light (Mt 4:16; Jn 8:12), so must his disciples be as well. Yet our light is reflective. It is his light that must shine through us. Our task is to make visible not ourselves but the living God in Christ. We are not to advance ourselves but to lose ourselves in service to God. Our Lord enjoins us: "Let your light shine before others, so that they may see your good works and give glory to your Father in heaven" (Mt 5:16 NRSV).

We are also sent out into the world as "sheep among wolves" (Mt 10:16 REB). Sheep are helpless, unable to defend themselves, but when they follow their shepherd they have nothing to fear. It is not the strong and mighty who will conquer the world but the meek who rely not on themselves but on their God and Savior (Mt 5:5). The Christian overcomes by the powerlessness of love, by which the holy will of God is implemented in the world.

We are commanded to let our light shine, to be rich in good works (1 Tim 6:18). Our righteousness does not lie in our works: our works proceed from our righteousness—hidden with Christ in God (Col 3:3). This righteousness, which has its basis in Christ and is received by faith (Rom 3:21-31; 9:30-32), will produce works that redound to the glory of God.

Among the duties that constitute the Christian life are deeds of piety. Calvin defined piety as the fear of God and zeal for the honor of God.[76] Piety concerns obligations that we owe to God alone, and one of these is believing in the gospel. "This is the work that God requires," said our Lord, "to believe in the one whom he has sent" (Jn 6:29 REB). To believe in Jesus Christ and to uphold him as Lord and Savior of the world is the one crowning work of the Christian. Luther put it succinctly: "In this work all good works exist, and from faith these works receive a borrowed goodness."[77]

Other works of piety are persevering prayer and worship that is done in spirit and in truth. Christians should not only pray but be warriors of prayer, praying both in the Spirit and with the understanding (1 Cor 14:15). If we do not pray, we will lose our saltiness and our light will grow dim.

Works of piety also include exhorting and reproving our fellow believers in a spirit of love—and being willing to receive such reproof from others. We are to be gatekeepers as well as servants (Ezek 3:17). We do our brothers and sisters no favor if we stand by passively while they openly flout God's holy law and careen down the slippery slope toward perdition.

Works of evangelism, too, will have a prominent role in our holy vocation. Worshiping God is integral to the Christian life, but so is bearing witness to what God has done for us in Christ. We have been chosen by God to "declare the wonderful deeds of him" who called us "out of darkness into his marvelous light" (1 Pet 2:9).

It is the responsibility of *all* Christians to tell the story of salvation. Fanny Crosby underlined this imperative in her much-loved hymn "Tell Me the Story of Jesus."[78] This prolific hymn writer was herself a model of holiness. Although blind and in need of the comforts of life, she blithely gave away all the royalties on her hymns to missions and charities.

Evangelism also consists in sharing our experience of Jesus Christ. The essential content of our proclamation is the gospel itself, but we need not keep secret the way the gospel comes alive for us personally. Paul spoke boldly of his Damascus Road experience, although his aim was to elevate not himself but Jesus Christ alone (cf. 2 Cor 4:5).

Part of the ministry of evangelism is interceding for the world, praying for the conversion of the lost. Unless our spoken witness is grounded in prayer, it will not avail for the salvation of others. Conversely, unless our prayer is accompanied by an earnest effort to bring the knowledge of Christ's atoning work to others, its value will certainly be diminished.

Works of mercy are still another way in which Christians manifest the righteousness and love of a holy God. As Brunner said, "When a man turns to Him, desiring to serve Him, God directs his attention to the world and its need. It is His will that our service of Him should be expressed as our service to the world—through Him, and for His sake."[79]

Being salt and light for the world certainly involves helping the poor and needy—providing hospitality, visiting the sick and people in prison, caring for the lonely and the abandoned, serving in the myriad of ways presented by the challenges of daily living. By ministering to others in the name of Christ, we give tangible reality to the royal priesthood of all believers. Works of mercy serve the Christian mission of bringing people into a right relationship with Christ. Through our Good Samaritan service we make it possible for those in need to sense the presence of Christ in our silent witness. Our hope is that they will thereby become open to our spoken witness when it is given. William Booth of the Salvation Army had as his motto "soup, soap, and salvation," wisely discerning that sometimes physical needs have to be met before there will be a positive response to our message. Our motivation is love, but our goal is evangelism: to confront people with the message of the gospel that alone can redeem and sanctify the human heart.

Finally, Christians should be involved in works of justice—correcting abuses in the social order. These too can be holy works—works that serve the glory of God. We are to "let justice roll down like waters, and righteousness like an ever-flowing stream" (Amos 5:24). For the Old Testament prophets justice entails redressing social wrongs and bringing about an equitable distribution of the goods of society.

Salt when applied to an open wound will sting; light when it breaks into darkness will expose the darkness. This is why salt and light will always be resisted. Speaking out in defense of the poor and disinherited will engender hostility from those who have vested interests in maintaining the status quo. But we must speak out in the name of Christ and for the sake of the gospel, not out of a desire to build an earthly utopia. Any justice that is not informed by piety—the fear of the living God— is bound to lead to greater injustice in the long run.

The church should preach against social sin and point the way to a practical solution. Its mission is to change the attitudes of people and thus provide an impetus to social reform. The church must seldom if ever be a political lobby, but the people of God are called to be agents in bringing about social holiness. Works of justice are not simply exercises in politics but parabolic acts that point beyond themselves to God's redeeming work in Christ. Our works are to be seen as a witness to the light of Christ, as signs and parables of the coming kingdom of God. Human justice must never be confounded with divine justice. It may, however, correspond to divine justice. When we defend the rights of the poor, the helpless and the oppressed, we are calling attention to the spiritual liberation that Christ brings through the outpouring of his Holy Spirit.

Works that are pleasing to God spring from faith in his mercy and power as revealed in Jesus Christ. Christians are not only to speak of light and salt but to *be* light and salt. Good fruit can only come from a good tree (Mt 7:17). Being is prior to action. "Faith in the heart leads to righteousness, and confession on the lips leads to salvation" (Rom 10:10 REB). The hope for a new social order rests on a new kind of person. Yet regeneration by the Spirit is only the beginning. We must be trained in righteousness so that we can apply the spiritual vision given us to the concrete needs and problems of society.

Being in Christ will invariably give rise to acting in the name of Christ. The one who "confesses and believes," says Barth, "shall live by righteousness."[80] If we truly accept Christ as Savior, we will be motivated to follow him as Lord wherever he takes us. Just as faith produces obedience, so obedience gives rise to understanding. According to 1 John 2:3 (REB), "It is by keeping God's commands that we can be sure we know him." Faith brings assurance as it works through love.

We are driven to service of our neighbor through the paradoxical love of the cross, the love that is demanding, sacrificial and also unconditional, going out to all people irrespective of their moral or social status. And if we truly love we will be passionately concerned that our hearers come into a right relationship with Jesus Christ. We should let our light shine so that people "may give praise" to the "Father in heaven" (Mt 5:16 REB). To let our light shine does not mean to parade our virtues but to hold up Christ before others.

John the Baptist is often celebrated in church tradition as a model of holiness, as a "burning and shining lamp" (Jn 5:35). He was not himself the light, but he came to bear witness to the light (Jn 1:8). His testimony is inscribed in the memory of the church: "He must increase, but I must decrease" (Jn 3:30).

This self-effacing spirit, so alien to the current cultural ethos that upholds personal satisfaction and fulfillment as the goal of human existence, is the salient mark of discipleship and holiness. Our mandate is not to make something of ourselves but to wear ourselves out for Jesus Christ. Mother Teresa has rightly observed that we are called not to success but to fidelity to the One who has redeemed us. Or as Barth put it: "The temporal holiness of the saints is the service that they render to the eternal holiness of God."[81]

We should strive to be rich in good works not to merit salvation, not to win the admiration of others, not to gain self-esteem, but to demonstrate our gratefulness for Christ's gift of salvation. The Heidelberg Catechism rightly declares that the motivation for good works is gratitude to God for what he has done for us in Christ (Question 86).[82] Gratitude is not the only motivation in Christian service, but it should always be the crowning element.

Our task as believers is to take up the cross and follow Christ in order to make known to others the boundlessness of his love. We should endeavor to be salt and light so that people might come to know the love and mercy of God and give glory to the Father in heaven. By losing ourselves for the sake of the kingdom, we will find ourselves, realizing our true destiny as sons and daughters of the living God. By placing the welfare of others above our own happiness, we will come to know true happiness in the end—the joy of salvation.

Our peace and confidence are to be found not in our empirical holiness, not in our progress toward perfection, but in the alien righteousness of Jesus Christ that covers our sinfulness and alone makes us acceptable before a holy God. In the words of the Puritan luminary Samuel Bolton: "The foundation of our Christian peace is not in us but in Christ, not in our holiness but in His righteousness, not in our walking but in His blood and suffering."[83] By being exposed to the holiness and love of God we are led to imitate God (Eph 5:1) and thereby give concrete testimony to our indebtedness to God. The foundation of our holiness is not in our doing but rather in our being grasped by Christ and incorporated into his body. Once we are in communion with Christ we will want to do good works—to show our joy and gratitude to him. But our works do not sanctify us; they provide the evidence that we are being sanctified by the Spirit of Christ.[84] The call of the Christian is to be a sign and witness to the holy love of God, a love that must never be confounded with human virtue but creates within us the will to be virtuous, to be loving and holy. To be in the presence of Christ arouses within us a burning desire to please Christ and to walk in his ways.

·SEVEN·

THE MYSTERY
OF THE TRINITY

Go therefore and make disciples of all nations,
baptizing them in the name of the Father and of the Son
and of the Holy Spirit.
MATTHEW 28:19

The grace of the Lord Jesus Christ, the love of God
and the fellowship of the Holy Spirit be with you all.
2 CORINTHIANS 13:13 NJB

How much greater is the power of the blood of Christ;
through the eternal Spirit he offered himself without blemish to God.
HEBREWS 9:14 REB

When I say God, I mean Father, Son, and Holy Spirit.
GREGORY OF NAZIANZUS

The Son is in reality neither less than, nor inferior to,
the Essence of the Father.
JOHN CHRYSOSTOM

The Trinity is without qualification *the* mystery of faith.
WALTER KASPER

T he doctrine of the Trinity signifies the culmination of biblical and
apostolic reflection on the nature and activity of the living God.
It is implied in the biblical witness and articulated by the fathers
of the early church. It is neither an appendix nor a prolegomenon to
theology but the apex and goal of theology. We do not deduce the
doctrine of the Trinity from a general concept of God but draw out the
idea of the Trinity from the total biblical and apostolic witness concern-

ing God. A commitment to the Trinity is already apparent in the early sections of this volume,[1] but now is the appropriate time to define the Trinity and ponder its implications. I am here following the pattern of sacred history, which begins with God's self-revelation to the people of Israel and then leads to the incarnation of God in human flesh and the subsequent outpouring of the Holy Spirit on the church. The full impact of these events on the theologians of the patristic church is manifested in the early creeds, especially that of Nicaea (325) and of Chalcedon (451).

While the theologians of the church were willing to make the attempt to define the Trinity, they were unanimous in acknowledging the Trinity as a mystery that eludes rational comprehension.[2] The Trinity can be stated in paradoxical and symbolic language, but it cannot be resolved into a rational system. It reminds us that the mysteries of faith stand above reason though not necessarily against reason. Once accepted they make sense of the experience of faith, but they cannot provide a viable rationale for the decision of faith. Faith can reflect upon these mysteries, but it cannot furnish a rational framework that circumscribes them. Reason cannot penetrate these mysteries, but it can respect them and try to make them intelligible.

The doctrine of the Trinity is both an analytical development of the central facts of divine revelation (as Barth maintained) and a synthetic construction drawn from the church's reflection upon this revelation. We do not project upon God the human experience of interpersonal relationships, but we find in God the perfection of personal interaction as this is mirrored in the self-revelation of the Father in the Son and through the power of the Spirit.

In the historical development of the doctrine of the Trinity the churches of the East and West took two different courses. The theologians of Eastern Orthodoxy generally began with the three persons of the Trinity and then proceeded to affirm the unity and coinherence of these persons. The Western theologians, following the lead of Augustine, generally began with the idea of a single divine substance and then reasoned their way toward a recognition of ontological distinctions within this one substance or being.

The Biblical Basis

While the doctrine of the Trinity is not found as such in the Bible, it is the immediate implication of the fact, form and content of the biblical revelation (Barth). It is the product of a developing understanding of the significance of God's redeeming action in human history and how this action mirrors the inner life of God. One can say that in the New Testament there is "a fundamental trinitarian awareness, expressed in many triadic formulas."[3]

The roots of the doctrine of the Trinity can be traced to the plural titles that are often used of God in the Old Testament. This plurality in designation is not always evident in the English translation of the Hebrew text. A strictly literal rendering of Ecclesiastes 12:1 would read "your Creators" instead of "your Creator." Genesis 1:26 employs plural pronouns to describe God: "Let us make man in our image" (cf. Gen 3:22; 11:7; Is 6:8). The Hebrew word *Elohim* is a plural name used of God and is the most frequent name for God in the Old Testament. *Adonai* (meaning "Lord") also comes under what scholars call a "plural of majesty," indicating diversity within oneness.[4] This evidence attests that the God of revelation was conceived from the very beginning as a composite rather than a solitary unity.

While it would be inappropriate to perceive God as a trinity of persons in Old Testament history, three subjectivities are alluded to in Isaiah 48:16 and 63:7-10.[5] The wider biblical witness attributes the creation of the world to the Father (Ps 102:25), to the Son (Col 1:16; Heb 1:10) and to the Spirit (Gen 1:2; Ps 104:30). The New Testament associates three persons with deity: the Father is called God (Mt 11:25-27; Jn 6:27; Rom 1:7); the Son is referred to in this way (Jn 1:1, 14; Tit 2:13; Heb 1:8) and also the Holy Spirit (Acts 5:3-9; cf. Is 63:7-14). Each of these persons is depicted as omniscient—the Father (Rom 11:33), the Son (Rev 2:23) and the Holy Spirit (1 Cor 2:11). Each is presented as being equal to the others (Mt 28:19; Jn 10:30; 2 Cor 13:14; Eph 4:4-6). The Son's being seated at the right hand of God the Father (Acts 2:33; Col 3:1; Heb 1:3; 8:1) connotes equality.

At the same time, the equality of the three subjectivities that compose the Godhead is only implied in the Bible. I agree with Barth that there is no clear statement of equality in the New Testament. In his view the church in positing the equality of the three persons went beyond the Bible, but it was fully in accord with the intention of the Bible.[6]

A searching student must also seriously consider passages that denote the subordination of the Son to the Father (Jn 5:26; Phil 2:6, 7). Occasionally the inequality of the Son and Father is suggested (Prov 8:22-31; Jn 14:28, 31; 1 Cor 8:6; Phil 2:6). Conversely, John 5:22 seems to indicate a parallel subordination of the Father to the Son. John 5:18 can be interpreted as affirming equality between the Father and Son. A subordination of both Son and Spirit to God the Father can be gleaned from Hebrews 9:14. In John 15:26 the Spirit is said to proceed from the Father.

A fairly clear statement by Jesus on the trinitarian Godhead is in John 14, where Jesus speaks of the Father sending in the Son's name the Comforter, the Holy Spirit, who will guide the church into all truth (vv. 16, 17, 26). Jesus assures his disciples that in the eschatological denouement of history Jesus will be in the Father and the Father in him (v. 20; cf. 10:38). This is not an explicit designation of three persons, but it is a proleptic recognition that God exists in three modes of being, that there is a vibrancy and diversity in the divine life.

The threefoldness of God is definitely affirmed in the baptism of Jesus (Mt 3:16, 17; Mk 1:9-11; Lk 3:21, 22; Jn 1:32-34). The Spirit of God descends on Jesus like a dove, and a voice from heaven says, "This is my Son, the Beloved, with whom I am well pleased" (Mt 3:17 NRSV). A comparable threefoldness is indicated in Romans 15:30, where Paul exhorts his fellow believers to join him in earnest prayer to God through the power of Christ and the love of the Spirit.

An even clearer witness to the threefold unity of God is found in the

Great Commission of our Lord: "Go therefore and make disciples of all nations, baptizing them in the name of the Father and of the Son and of the Holy Spirit" (Mt 28:19 NRSV). An equally forthright witness is given in 2 Corinthians 13:14; Ephesians 4:4-6; 1 Peter 1:2; and Jude 20, 21.

The doctrine of the Trinity becomes explicit in 1 John 5:7 (KJV): "There are three that bear record in heaven, the Father, the Word, and the Holy Ghost: and these three are one." This verse, however, is not found in the earliest manuscripts and indicates not the witness of the original apostles but the mind of the early church as it reflected on the relation of Father, Son and Spirit. As such it is still theologically significant though not part of the inspired canon.

It is not simply the allusions to three modes of God's being and activity that furnish the foundation for the doctrine of the Trinity but certain underlying motifs that run through the apostolic testimony. One of these is the preexistent Word, the fact that the Word of God existed before the incarnation in unity with the Father. This is already hinted at in the Old Testament: "Your word, O Lord, will last forever; it is eternal in heaven" (Ps 119:89 GNB). Proverbs 8 pictures Wisdom as a master worker who stood beside God in the formation of the world (vv. 23-31). What is pointed to in the Old Testament is given explicit articulation in the fourth Gospel: "In the beginning was the Word, and the Word was with God, and the Word was God. He was in the beginning with God; all things were made through him" (Jn 1:1-3). The identification of the preexistent Word with Jesus Christ and also with the Son of God and the Son of Man provides the basis for the doctrines of the preexistent Christ and the deity of Christ. These in turn supply the groundwork for the doctrine of the Trinity. The equation of the Spirit of Christ with the Holy Spirit served further to explicate the mystery of the Trinity. The Holy Spirit came to be seen as the power of God, God in action.

The precise relation between Christ and God proved to be a festering problem in the early church. The deity of Christ is definitely affirmed in the apostolic witness (particularly Jn 1:18; 8:42; Gal 4:4; Phil 2:5-7; 2 Cor 8:9). But how is "the only Son, who is in the bosom of the Father" (Jn

1:18), related to the Father in eternity? It is stated that Christ "proceeded and came forth from God" (Jn 8:42), but does this imply subordination and inequality between Father and Son? The nature of this relationship was defined at the Council of Nicaea (325) and at the Council of Constantinople (381).

Historical Development

The dogma of the Trinity emerged in the church only through a continuing struggle with heresy. It was because misunderstandings of the faith infiltrated the very bastions of the church that theologians were compelled to articulate the wider implications of the threefold nature of God.

One of the most formidable heresies was Arianism, which taught that the Son is an intermediate being between God and the world. He was not God in himself, yet he was divine. He was not the highest god but a demigod. It was said that the Logos is "preexistent but not eternal." Arius (fourth century) declared, "He was that which was not"; "There was when He was not"; "He was made of things that were not." The Logos was "alien and unlike in all respects to the essence and selfhood of the Father."[7] In Arianism "God was interpreted deistically, man moralistically, and Christ mythologically."[8] The semi-Arians, who tried to accommodate to the traditional notion of the deity of Christ, contended that Christ is like the Father (homoios) but still different from the Father.

The orthodox party in the church, led by Athanasius, stressed that Christ was of one substance with the Father (homoousios). He was not only a mediator between God and humanity but God himself in human flesh. The Nicene Creed sided with Athanasius. The creed stated plainly that he was "begotten, not made" and that Christ was "of one substance with the Father."[9] Nicaea also asserted that both the Son and the Holy Spirit proceed from the Father. At the Western Council of Toledo (589) it was affirmed that the Holy Spirit proceeds from the Father and the Son. This formulation was not accepted by the Eastern Church, which held that both Son and Spirit proceed from the Father.

Sabellianism (after Sabellius in the third century) argued that God was a monad, a single person viewed under three different forms. The three persons were simply faces or masks of the one God. Also known as modalism or modalistic monarchianism, this heresy taught that the Trinity is three successive roles played by God or three successive phases of his being. The divinity of Christ was merged into the essence of the Father. The Sabellians recognized no independent personality of Christ and saw the incarnation as a mode of existence or manifestation of the Father. Father, Son and Spirit are distinctions that pertain to God in relation to us. The modalists could affirm the economic trinity (a threefoldness in God in relation to the world) but not the ontological or essential trinity (a threefoldness in the inner being of God). Sabellius was accused of patripassianism, which asserted that the Father was necessarily subject to the suffering of Christ, since there is ultimately no real distinction between them. In the modern period Schleiermacher veered toward the modalist position. Christ is God's *prosōpon* (the form in which God appears).[10]

Another heresy, dynamic monarchianism, held that Christ was the Son of God by adoption. Its most well-known representative was Paul of Samosata. For him the Logos existed in Jesus not personally or essentially but only as a quality. The personality of Jesus was entirely human. The Son was nonexistent before the Nativity. The union between Christ and God was not ontological but moral. The concern was to safeguard the monarchy of the Father, but it was done at the price of surrendering the deity of the Son.

The church also found itself challenged by Gnosticism, a syncretistic movement that drew upon various currents of spirituality in the ancient world, though it also appealed to the biblical corpus.[11] It taught that the problem that confronts humanity is its entanglement in the material world, and the only solution is to disengage ourselves from the material and rise into a purely spiritual realm. The deepest within the self is divine, and the promise of deliverance rests on our ability to discover and to cultivate this divine element. Salvation comes through knowledge of one's true self in a myth revealed by a Savior figure. Christ was the revealer of the unknown, high and all-perfect God. The Logos was not one with the Father but emanated from the Father. Against the Gnostics the church father Irenaeus stressed the eternal coexistence of the Logos with the Father. He also affirmed the essential goodness of creation, which the Gnostics identified with the Fall.

Subordinationism posed a more subtle danger to the Christian faith in view of a palpable subordinationist motif in the New Testament. Subordinationism holds that Christ was subordinate and inferior to God. The Father was the source of the Son and the Spirit. This was an attempt to preserve the monarchy within the Trinity. The apologists were generally subordinationist, since they considered the Godhead a triad rather than a Trinity, with the Son and Spirit totally subordinate to the Father. For Tertullian both Son and Spirit derive from the Father by emanation and thus are subordinate to him. In its wider sense this heresy includes Arianism, Monarchianism and even Gnosticism.

The most influential subordinationist in the early church was Origen. In his theology the Son or Logos, though entirely God, was a mediating organ within the Godhead lower in rank than God the Father. The Son represented one stage in the movement toward multiplicity and mutability and the Spirit signified a third stage, ranking after the Son and produced by the Son. Origen affirmed one Godhead but with grades within it. Only the Father is without origin *(autotheos),* for he is not even generated. At times Origen referred to the Father as the eternal One beyond all distinctions. One critic complains: "The mediatorial activity of Jesus Christ is not . . . a gracious and paradoxical self-giving into human history and human nature on the part of God, but a device within the Godhead for reducing itself sufficiently to be able to communicate with what was not God."[12] Even so, Origen was still basically orthodox, for he taught a subordination not of essence or nature but of existence or origin.[13] He urged that prayer be addressed only to the Father, the highest level within the Godhead and from whom all things come. Indeed, "The Father's will is wiser than the Son's; at creation the Son was the Father's servant, executing His commands."[14] Origen affirmed that the Father and Son are coeternal but not coequal.

Subordinationism and orthodoxy also coexisted in Athanasius and Novatian. Novatian (third century) held that the Son is less than the Father and was originated by the Father. Yet at the same time he contended that the Son is eternally in the Father. J. F. Bethune-Baker included Novatian within the heresy of Monarchianism.[15]

The Council of Nicaea was directed not only against Arianism but also against all forms of subordinationism. It asserted that Jesus Christ is "very God of very God," not less than the Father but one with the Father. The Second Ecumenical Council held at Constantinople (381) opposed the teaching that the Holy Spirit was subordinate to Father and Son. It taught that the Holy Spirit must be worshiped and glorified along with the Father and the Son.

The Athanasian Creed, which found wide acceptance in the Eastern and Western churches, though never becoming part of the Ecumenical Symbols, was aimed partly against subordinationism. Its authorship is unknown, though many scholars surmise that it originated in the fifth century. The creed states: "In this Trinity none is before, or after another: none is greater, or less than another."[16]

Against the subordinationists the church asserted that the concept of *homoousia* means identity of being and not merely similarity of being. For the subordinationists everything depended on preserving the unity and monarchy of God. In the developing orthodox teaching the three persons in the Trinity are coequal and coeternal with each other, although an order and distinction in the Godhead was duly acknowledged.

There is both an orthodox and a heretical form of subordinationism. One can say that the Son proceeds from the Father and the Spirit from the Father and the Son. It is in keeping with sacred tradition to affirm a subordination in function or activity but not in being. It is misleading to portray the Father as the "source" of the Son, though this language was used by the early church fathers and is still prevalent in Catholic and Orthodox circles. It is theologically more felicitous to affirm a relationship of dependence between the three persons in their mode of operation than to speak of subordination.

The dangers in subordinationism are polytheism and agnosticism. If we make Christ and the Spirit inferior to God the Father we are in danger of positing three different deities. If we make the Father the eternal abyss out of which the Son and Spirit emanate, we end with a God who is basically unknowable and unreachable.

Augustine in the West and John of Damascus in the East articulated or shaped the orthodox doctrine of the Trinity. Traces of subordination-ism remained in John of Damascus, who persisted in referring to the Father as the source of the Godhead. For Augustine the Father subsists in the Godhead in the mode of paternity, the Son in the mode of filiation or generation, and the Spirit in the mode of procession or spiration. Whereas the Greeks were inclined to explain the Trinity in terms of causal relations, Augustine offered another approach.

> For him, the one primordial God was not the Father, but the Trinity. The different persons found their cause not in some generation or procession, but in an inherently necessary interior relationship with each other. . . . The implications of this way of thinking were manifold and far-reaching. Causality was eventually replaced altogether by pure relations, existing of necessity in the very being of God.[17]

Subordinationism persisted in the church in the tradition of Christian mysticism, which was heavily influenced by Neoplatonism. Plotinus, the luminary of Neoplatonism, taught that ultimate reality lies beyond all temporal distinctions and that there are grades of the Godhead: the *Nous* (Reason) and the World-Soul emanate from the One and are there-fore less than the One. Dionysius the Pseudo-Areopagite (fifth-sixth century) affirmed the Trinity, but he understood it as a symbol for the God who is beyond numbers, beyond being. God is not the highest being but beyond any possible highest being. He is the superessential dark-ness, which transcends the reach of human cognition and imagination. According to Tillich, interpreting Dionysius, "even the problem of unity and trinity disappears in the abyss of God."[18] This tradition includes

Origen, who envisaged the Father as the eternal One beyond all finite realities. It also appears in John Scotus Erigena, who affirmed the Trinity but interpreted it along Neoplatonic lines. God is the ideal of motionless unity out of which all things emanate. The Absolute generates the Son, who enshrines the intelligible order of the universe, and the Son in turn generates the Spirit, who makes manifest the intelligible structure of all things. All theophanies are destined to return to the primal unity, which neither creates nor is created. Erigena skirted pantheism, but he tried (most scholars believe unsuccessfully) to maintain the qualitative difference between God and the creature.

Neoplatonic mysticism was conspicuous in the writings of the Rhineland mystics of the thirteenth and fourteenth centuries. Meister Eckhart was concerned with a "pure God" who transcends the distinctions of Father, Son and Spirit. This is the Eternal Rest, the Primal Unity, the Nameless Being, who is simply beyond human comprehension. Eckhart as well as Jan van Ruysbroeck and Henry Suso postulated an Abyss of Godhead underlying the Trinity. In the words of Ruysbroeck, "We can speak no more of Father, Son and Holy Spirit, nor of any creature, but only one Being, which is the very substance of the Divine Persons. There were we all one before our creation, for this is our super-essence. There the Godhead is in simple essence without activity."[19] All of these men taught that human beings can ascend through unitive knowledge beyond the triunity to the ultimate unity of the divine ground. We see in these mystics an attempt to get beyond the historical Christ to the ahistorical Godhead.

The Christian mystics sought to maintain the catholic doctrine of the Trinity, but by envisaging God in Neoplatonic terms as a motionless, undifferentiated unity they were not able to preserve the biblical conception of a God who actively works in history and identifies with our pain and sorrow. To find the pure God, they said, we need to rise above words and images, time and materiality, to the realm of pure spirit. The mystical ladder to heaven, which we ascend through works of purification, took the place of the ladder of free grace by which God descends to our level and meets us in the incarnate Christ.[20]

The legacy of Neoplatonism is discernible in Angelus Silesius, J. G. Fichte, Friedrich Schleiermacher, Paul Tillich, Thomas Merton, Simone Weil, George Maloney, Jürgen Moltmann and James Mackey,[21] among many others. This mystical-idealist tradition in the Christian faith stresses the continuity between God and humanity even while placing God beyond the compass of discursive reason. We find God by entering into ourselves and discovering the spark of divinity that links us to the eternal. Against this tradition I maintain that the historical Jesus is not simply a means to the ahistorical Godhead: we find God himself in the historical sign—the Jesus Christ of history. We do not proceed upward to God on a mystical ladder or stairway, but God proceeds downward to us and meets us not in a mystical experience in which human individuality disappears but in an I–Thou encounter in which human personhood is reaffirmed albeit on a new level.

Contemporary Reassessments

In recent times there have been new approaches to the doctrine of the Trinity. Some theologians have seen this doctrine as an attempt to reconcile discordant affirmations of the faith. For John Whale the Trinity succeeds in bringing together three apparently incompatible axioms: monotheism, belief in the divinity of Christ and the new experience of God in the Holy Spirit.[22] Emil Brunner regarded the Trinity as a defensive doctrine that does not form a part of the original New Testament witness and message, though it is valuable in preserving the church's self-identity.[23] Similarly Helmut Thielicke saw the Trinity as an effort on the part of the early church to confirm its intuitions with regard to the nature of God's self-revelation in Jesus Christ. It is "not the object of faith but the reflection of faith on its object."[24]

Cyril Richardson questioned the adequacy of the trinitarian formula, preferring to speak of God as a multiplicity rather than a Trinity.[25] Richardson referred to the members of the Godhead as "symbols" rather than "persons." Threeness, he maintained, is an arbitrary way of conceiving the richness and complexity of a dynamic God. He called the doctrine "an artificial threefoldness."

Tillich too had reservations regarding the way the trinitarian doctrine developed. Yet he also felt that this doctrine cannot be discarded.[26] It expresses the self-manifestation of the Divine Life to humanity. The three persons are symbols of this divine activity. For Tillich God is the ground of being, the infinite abyss and being-itself; God includes personality but is not a person. In his relation to the human creature God is personal. Tillich's position has affinities to the tradition of Christian mysticism going back to Origen that posits an eternal ground behind the manifestations of God as Son and Spirit. For him the God who is seen and adored in trinitarian symbolism and who is revealed preeminently in Jesus Christ "has not lost his freedom to manifest himself for other worlds in other ways."[27] Tillich made the Spirit the all-inclusive category, here reflecting the influence of Hegel. He often referred to God as the Divine Spirit and the Spiritual Presence. But Tillich also spoke of the God above God, the abyss of the Godhead, God in his abysmal nature who is sharply differentiated from God in his self-manifestation. According to Tillich trinitarian monotheism is concrete monotheism, an affirmation of the living God, in contrast to mystical monotheism in which everything concrete disappears in the infinite abyss.[28]

G. W. H. Lampe also proposed an ontology of the Spirit.[29] He suggested that Jesus was "inspired" to an exemplary degree by the Spirit who inspires all of creaturely life. He consistently denied a transcendent God who decisively intervenes in history and instead affirmed a God who is immanent in creation. For Lampe it is the Spirit, not the Logos, who is incarnate in Jesus Christ. The resurrection of Christ signifies the experience of the disciples of the creative activity of the Spirit, who was at work in the life and death of Jesus. According to Ray Anderson, Lampe's theology represents a return to the cosmological unitarianism that caused Arius to deny the eternal deity of Jesus Christ.[30]

Barth's explication of the Trinity was radically different.[31] He did not see the doctrine of the Trinity as a synthesis of unrelated elements in the apostolic witness but as an analytical development of the central fact of biblical revelation. The Trinity is not a revealed doctrine but is directly implied in the act and content of God's self-revelation in Jesus Christ as attested in Holy Scripture. Barth strongly affirmed the immanent or essential Trinity as preceding the economic Trinity; that is, the threefold way in which God interacts within himself is prior to the way he relates to the world. Barth preferred to speak of God as one person in three modes of being, though not in the sense of modalism, since the modes of being exist simultaneously, not successively. He recognized that the modern concept of person contains the notion of self-consciousness, and a three-person Trinity would then imply tritheism (three individuals) rather than monotheism. Barth saw a pattern of relationship exemplified in the concepts of Revealer, Revelation, Revealedness; Creator, Reconciler, Redeemer; holiness, mercy, love; Father, Son, Spirit. In each case there is a relation of dependence of the second on the first and of the third on the first and second. The oneness of God, said Barth, must not be confused with "singleness" or "aloneness." "God in Himself is not only existent. He is co-existent."[32]

Barth was adamant that the divine act cannot be separated from the divine being. The threefoldness indicated by the terms "Father," "Son," "Spirit" is a threefoldness in the structure or pattern of the one act of God in Christ and therefore the structure of the being of God. He saw an order of procession in the Trinity: generation—the Son from the Father, and spiration—the Holy Spirit from Father and Son. Barth affirmed one divine subject in three modes of existence. He spoke both of the persons of the Trinity and of God as "a divine Person." "God is really a person, really a free subject."[33] The unity of the triune Godhead lies in the lordship or rule of God. There is one Lord, one Name, one Thou.

Karl Rahner, the eminent contemporary Roman Catholic theologian, differed from Barth by identifying the economic Trinity and the immanent Trinity. Whereas for Barth the first reflects the second, in Rahner the second is absorbed into the first.[34] Rahner spoke of the Father as "the simply unoriginate God."[35] Christ and the Holy Spirit originated from the Father, but the Father has his origin from himself. Rahner was content with the word "person" because of its illustrious history in trinitarian theologizing, but he preferred to speak of "distinct manner of subsisting." Walter Kasper is critical of this substitute: "No one can invoke, adore and glorify a distinct manner of subsisting."[36] Whereas Barth posited a self-movement in God himself, Rahner affirmed the essential unchangeability of God, but God becomes subject to change in something else—that is, in the humanity of Christ.[37]

Much closer to Barth is Thomas F. Torrance, who sees the one being of God as "self-identifying personal being." God relates himself to the world not out of need but out of sheer love, the love that is characteristic of his inner life. Torrance is critical of the monarchy of the Father as used by Basil and Gregory of Nyssa and affirms the full equality of the members of the Trinity. He grounds the unity of the Trinity in the perichoresis (mutual relatedness) of the three persons rather than in the Father.[38]

Robert Jenson takes a similar approach, focusing on the Trinity as God rather than the Father as God.[39] For Jenson the Son and the Spirit are equally sources and principles with the Father. In his view there is not one name but three names, not one identity but three identities. Jenson uses the phrase "temporal infinity" to describe the unbounded futurity that characterizes the eternity of God. Instead of "person" or "mode of being" Jenson suggests "identity" as an apt description of the members of the Godhead.

Reflecting a Hegelian process understanding, Jürgen Moltmann envisages the Trinity not as a mutual fellowship within the Godhead, not as a closed ontological circle, but as "an eschatological process" open for people on earth.[40] God is an "event" that includes all other events in history. We do not pray to God but in God. God in his transcendent aspect is Father, in his immanent role he is Son, as Spirit he opens up the future of history.[41] "The trinitarian Persons *subsist* in the common divine nature; they *exist* in their relations to one another."[42] Moltmann breaks not only with patriarchal monotheism but with monotheism altogether, since his God is not one being but three movements or processes that converge and complement one another. In opposition to both Barth and Rahner, Moltmann envisages three subjects, three centers of consciousness in God. We have in the Trinity a community of persons rather than simply a commonality of a single vision. Again in contrast to Barth Moltmann holds that God needs to suffer in order to love. "While Barth carefully excluded *any* notion of necessity from both the immanent and economic trinity, Moltmann believes that the Father *necessarily* generates the Son."[43]

Another proponent of a social doctrine of the Trinity, Anglican theologian Leonard Hodgson, spoke of three persons in the highest kind of personal and social unity.[44] While Barth began with the oneness of God and then discovered a threeness within this oneness, Hodgson like Moltmann began with the threeness. He could refer to "the social life of the Blessed Trinity." God is a social organism inspired by mutual love. The question arises whether this kind of approach opens the door to polytheism.

Quite different is the Dutch Catholic theologian Piet Schoonenberg, who holds that God in himself is not tripersonal but becomes so in the incarnation.[45] The Word *becomes* the Son in the incarnation. The Spirit *becomes* the Paraclete at the glorification of our Lord. In his definition of "personal," Schoonenberg includes individuality. The Word is with God in the beginning, but not the Son. He refuses to speak of God except in his relationship to the creature. He challenges the notion of the "exclusive immutability" of God. It is inappropriate to speak of "the Father" until the incarnation, since this symbol has meaning only in reference to the Son. Schoonenberg can be criticized for failing to do justice to the transcendence of God, for being unwilling to affirm God's personhood apart from his relationship to the creature. One can detect the Neoplatonic notion of the One beyond the personal and differentiated. The Word is an expansion of the outgoing of God, revealed preeminently in Jesus.

One of the most innovative and provocative efforts to redefine the Trinity is that of Wolfhart Pannenberg, who sees history as the unfolding of the Trinity. He seeks to retain the monarchy of the Father, but not a monarchy independent of the Son and Spirit. God the Father has his kingdom in the Son and through the Spirit. "Through the work of the Son the kingdom or monarchy of the Father is established in creation, and through the work of the Spirit . . . the kingdom or monarchy of the Father in creation is consummated."[46] He affirms the mutuality and mutual dependence of the persons of the Trinity, but this does not mean that the monarchy of the Father is destroyed. Pannenberg contends that the perichoretic unity of the three persons is the basis and source of the monarchy of the Father.[47] God is personal "only through one or another of the three hypostases, not as a single ineffable entity."[48] Through his creation of the world God makes himself "dependent on this creation and on its history."[49] One critic comments: "For God to be identified with the divine rule, there needs to be a world that is ruled; and in this sense, God has chosen to become dependent upon his creation."[50]

In contrast to Barth, Pannenberg sees the three persons not as differing modes of being of the one divine subject but as "life processes" of converging centers of activity. The monarchy of the Father does not mean his superiority over the other persons of the Trinity but his Lordship over creation, one that is mediated by the Son and the Spirit. A subordinationist orientation is evident when Pannenberg contends that the content of the gospel lies in the Father alone, not in the Son. As Roger Olson observes, "In spite of his denials to the contrary, there would seem to be a subordinationist slant in his repeated assertions that the monarchy of the Father, who is the 'God' of the Old Testament, is the content of the salvation-historical unity of the three persons in their mutually interdependent relations."[51]

Ted Peters also closely relates the Trinity to the unfolding of the life processes of history.[52] He affirms Rahner's dictum that the immanent Trinity is the economic Trinity, which "permits the God of history to be the God of eternity."[53] God does not exist as a self-contained Absolute before history but as a creative process that animates history. The absoluteness of God lies in his "total relatedness" to everything else.[54] Peters opposes the current ideological distortion of the faith that substitutes a democratic, egalitarian God for a monarchial one. God must still be seen as King and Lord, but his lordship is a liberating rather than a domineering one. "To let God be king—to worship the lamb upon the throne—liberates us to work freely in a world wherein no individual or class or race or gender can claim transcendent rights for ruling over others."[55] He finds the unity of the Trinity not in the monarchy of the Father but in the mutual relatedness *(perichōrēsis)* that makes the Trinity a fellowship of love. Eternity is not a timeless eternal now, which separates God from human history, but the eschatological consummation of all things in the salvific trinitarian process in which the purposes of God come to fulfillment.

Roman Catholic scholar Catherine Mowry LaCugna also envisages the Trinity as a process of outgoing and return in which the creative initiative of God results in the transformation of the cosmos.[56] Each person of the Trinity is person-in-relationship. Instead of speaking of an immanent Trinity before creation she postulates one life in the triune God, and this life includes God's relation to us. She likens the movement of God into the world to an arrow beginning from the Father, descending through the Son and Spirit to the world, then ascending through the Spirit and the Son to the Father. There is one ecstatic movement of God "from whom all things originate and to whom all things return."[57] LaCugna's chiastic model of emanation and return echoes the legacy of Neoplatonic mysticism, which has left an indelible imprint on both Roman Catholic and Eastern Orthodox Christianity. God in his trinitarian movement remains ineffable mystery, and we can only begin to know as we are known by participating in this mystery through wonder and adoration.

A Catholic theologian who stands against the slide toward immanentism, unashamedly drawing upon Thomas Aquinas, is William J. Hill.[58] Hill defends the immanent Trinity as prior to the economic Trinity and therefore the transcendence of God over the creation. God is not an immutable, unfeeling Absolute, however, but a fellowship of persons who are equal and one "in their essential actions *ad intra* and in all actions *ad extra*."[59] The doctrine of the Trinity presupposes not only a sense of plurality within the Godhead but "some clue as to the distinctive identity of those who constitute it."[60] The persons in God, he says, "constitute a divine intersubjectivity: Father, Son and Spirit are three centers of consciousness in community, in mutual communication."[61] The members of the Trinity are "subjects and centers of one divine conscious life."[62] The Trinity is a divine koinonia: "Three who are conscious by way of one essential consciousness, constituting a divine reciprocity that is an interpersonal and intersubjective unity."[63] God does not simply lure the world toward a higher ideal (as in process thought), but he enters into the world in its sin and suffering and redeems it without himself becoming subject to the sin and discord that rule human life.[64]

Restating the Trinity

The doctrine of the Trinity does not contradict Hebraic monotheism but deepens and enriches it. The Christian too can confess the Hebrew *Shema* or creed: "Hear, O Israel: The Lord our God is one Lord; and you shall love the Lord your God with all your heart, and with all your soul, and with all your might" (Deut 6:4-5). This one supreme being, however, is not a solitary unity but a composite unity. He is not monochrome but multichrome.

A trinitarian monotheism asserts that God is one person in three modes of being or three persons in one being. Both of these articulations are acceptable depending on how "person" is defined. If we conceive of personhood in terms of independence, autonomy and self-consciousness, then we cannot speak of God as three persons. On the other hand, if we adhere to the original meaning of hypostasis as signifying an abiding mode of being or activity, then we can retain the classical formula.[65]

Father, Son and Holy Spirit are symbols that correspond not to inner feelings or experiences but to ontological realities. Their dominant reference is objective rather than subjective. The persons of the Holy Trinity connote agencies of relation rather than separate personalities. God in his essence is one, but the way he interacts within himself is threefold. In the Godhead there is one being but three modes of existence. There is one person but three agencies of relationship. There is one overarching consciousness but three foci of consciousness. There is one will but three acts of implementing this will. There is one intelligence but three operations of intelligence.

God does not simply act in a threefold way but exists within himself in a tripersonal relationship. The economic Trinity reflects the immanent Trinity, but it also follows it and is not to be equated with it. The doctrine of the Trinity asserts that there are distinctions within God himself, and these distinctions constitute a fellowship of subjectivities that in their perfect unity mirror one divine intellect and one divine will. There is a trinity of persons but a unity of essence. We can even speak of "the triunity of the essence" of God (Barth).

Because God is a Trinity he is a living and loving God. God is not lifeless but active and creative. He is not static and immovable but dynamic and mobile, though ever constant in his inmost being and purpose. We can attribute motion to God but not process in the sense that God grows or changes in his essential being.

To assert that there are three independent persons interacting with one another is to fall into the heresy of tritheism.[66] I agree with Brunner that we have the Father through the Son and in the Son but not alongside the Son.[67] Nor is the Spirit alongside the Son or the Father but is given through the Son and from the Father.

Denial of the Trinity finally leads to deism, pantheism, polytheism or agnosticism. In deism God is remote and detached, a solitary being who remains aloof from the suffering and travail of the world. In pantheism God is identical with the world, or in the form of panentheism God is inseparable from the world. The world is an emanation of the being of

God or an expression or manifestation of his all-encompassing unity. In polytheism God is no longer one, nor is he supreme. Father, Son and Spirit become separate gods rather than expressions of the one God. In a mystically tinged agnosticism God becomes an ineffable unity behind the world of phenomena, beyond the symbols of human imagination. He is the infinite abyss, the God above God, who remains essentially un-knowable.[68] He is not simply mysterious but sheer mystery impenetrable to the human mind, hidden even from the eyes of faith. One can also show that where the Trinity is denied, related doctrines such as the deity of Christ and his preexistence fall by the wayside.

The Trinity is indeed incomprehensible to human reason, but by no means unintelligible. It can be defined though not fully explained. It is not a logical absurdity but a paradox that can be grasped by reason only in the passion of faith. It does not wholly defy the imagination but transcends the reach of human perception and conception.

Sacred tradition has given ample testimony that the mystery of the Trinity can be illumined by analogies and metaphors drawn from human experience and nature. These do not prove the Trinity, but they show that the doctrine of the Trinity is not irrational. Anselm offered the illustration of the spring, the stream and the lake; Tertullian proposed the root, the tree and the fruit. In both of these a subordinationist element is apparent. I prefer to speak of one space with three dimensions— height, length and depth. We can see a trinity in matter: solids, liquids and gases. There is ice, water and steam—one substance (H_2O) but three subsistences. All can exist at the same time depending on the variations in temperature.[69] Augustine proposed lover, beloved and love itself. Also helpful is the analogy of the wax, the wick and the flame of a candle. Or we can think of one atom with three components: proton, neutron and electron. Or of one apple composed of the core, the flesh and the peel. Gregory of Nyssa likened the Trinity to three torches in which the light of the first passes to the second and is then relayed to the third.[70]

This brings us to the nature of the intertrinitarian fellowship.

The apologists of the early church really conceived of a triad rather than a trinity, since the Father was given preeminent ontological status and the Son and Spirit were clearly subordinate to the Father. A great number of the church fathers strongly adhered to the monarchy of the Father in that the Father was the principle of unity in the Trinity.

Standing in the Augustinian tradition I affirm the full equality of the Trinity but within this equality a differentiation in roles or activity. The Father does not have ontological superiority over the Son and the Spirit, but he does have an existential priority in that his existence is the presupposition of the existence of the Son and Spirit. In his operations the Father represents an originating source of his other modes of activity. In his essence Father, Son and Spirit are one. We can say that the Father is the initiator of action, the Son the culmination of action and the Spirit the power of action. The Father is an originating source not as a first cause in the sense of an efficient cause but as a presupposition or ground. The Father's initiation is not independent of the Son and Spirit but together with them. The Father represents the commencement of the creative activity that comes to fruition in the mutual love of the three persons of the Trinity. The Father is not over and above the Son and Spirit but in, with and for the Son and Spirit. He is, however, over and above the Son in the Son's incarnate state. I here agree with Claude Welch:

> Interpreting the problem of relations by recourse to the analogy of personal existence, we say that in the eternal divine self-differentiation, God's being the Father is ontologically the possibility and ground of his being the Son and the Holy Spirit. This does not mean . . . that there is any temporal priority, or that the Son and Holy Spirit are in any sense *less* than the Father. There can be no thought of diminution of deity here, for God is wholly existent in each of the modes of being.[71]

We must avoid the pitfall of Monarchianism, which depicts the Father as sole ruler and the source and origin of the other members of the

Godhead. Welch says rightly that "we cannot speak of origin in the literal sense of *communicatio essentiae* (or of the dictum *Pater est fons totius trinitatis,* which has the same connotation of an origination and trans-mitting of essence)."[72] The Father is not the fount or origin of the Trinity but the ontological ground and initiator of fellowship in the Trinity. It is a profound mistake to contend (as does Origen) that the fullness of being is in the Father alone, and in the Son and Spirit only derivative being. The fullness of being is in the Trinity itself, and each member of the Trinity shares in this fullness equally. The unity of the Trinity is to be found in the perichoresis, the mutual indwelling of the members of the Trinity.

Yet we must not slip in the other direction of denying an order of procession within the Trinity. The Son is not only loved by the Father but also born of the Father. The Spirit is not only the power of love in the Trinity but the receiver of love from the Father and the Son. There is a unity in being but an order in procession or action. There is an order in the Godhead—but of modes of existence, not of higher or lesser degrees of being. There is a relationship of interdependence in the God-head but also of dependence. The Son is dependent on the Father and the Spirit on the Father and the Son.

Dependence does not connote subordination, however, for the Son and Spirit fully participate in the essence or being of God. They are not less than the Father but equal to the Father. I would not say with Greg-ory of Nazianzus that the Father is "greater" in the sense that "the equality and the being" of Son and Spirit came from him.[73] Nor would I contend that the Son simply receives from the Father, and the Spirit simply implements what has been decided by Father and Son. I concur with Robert Jenson that there is a reciprocity in the Trinity. The Son receives, but he also acts. The Father acts, but he also receives from both the Spirit and the Son. Moreover, each member of the Trinity participates in the actions of the others. This means that the Son and Spirit too are sources of creativity and not simply instruments of the Father's creative action. Jenson proposes the Father as the "unoriginated" and the Spirit as "unsurpassed," and just as the Father and Son "breathe" the Spirit, so the Spirit and Son "free" the Father.[74]

The biblical witness does not support an ontological subordination-ism, which makes the Father supreme over the Son and Spirit. In John 5:26 and 15:16 it seems that the Son is subordinate to the Father, but in 5:22 the Father appears to be subordinate to the Son. One could infer on the basis of Mark 1:12 and Matthew 4:1 that the Son is subordinate to the Spirit. Hebrews 9:14 suggests some dependence of the Son on the Spirit, and Revelation 21:23 suggests a priority of the Father to the Son. A subordination of Father to Son and Son to Father is indicated in Luke 10:22.

While it is preferable to speak of interdependence and an order of procession within the Trinity itself, we must speak of subordination in God's relation to the world. The Son and Spirit are clearly subordinate to the Father by bringing the fruits of Christ's victory to those elected by the Father in Christ. This is a voluntary subordination, however, not a necessary one. It is based not on the lesser being of the Son and Spirit but on the mutual consensus of the members of the Trinity. By subor-dinating himself to the will of the Father, Christ becomes our model as we take up the cross and follow him in the role of servants of the Word. Paul declares: "Let the same mind be in you that was in Christ Jesus, who, though he was in the form of God, did not regard equality with God as something to be exploited, but emptied himself, taking the form of a slave, being born in human likeness. And being found in human form, he humbled himself and became obedient to the point of death—even death on a cross" (Phil 2:5-8 NRSV). It was precisely in his humiliation and subordination that Christ was exalted, that his deity was revealed to the whole of creation. His essential lordship was established in his role of servanthood.

The current attempts to resymbolize God in order to speak more forcefully to the times in which we live are fraught with peril, for new symbols of deity prepare the way for new conceptions of deity. When God is referred to as Father-Mother (as in feminist theology) we no longer have trinitarianism but binitarianism.[75] When God is depicted as Heavenly Parent or Divine Providence, we introduce a deistic understanding in which God is no longer heavenly Father but providential Ruler. When God is portrayed as Eternal Spirit, which animates and encompasses all of reality, we are then in the ethos of pantheism or panentheism. When God is depicted as Creative Process or as the Life Force, a pantheistic worldview is again evident. God is no longer a person but now a process, albeit the process that enlivens and rejuvenates all of nature. When God is conceived of as Immanent Mother or as Womb of Being (as in feminist theology), we no longer have a transcendent Creator God but a God of the depths out of which all things emanate. When we portray the Spirit of God or Christ as predominantly feminine, we are perilously close to polytheism, for we now have divinities that are basically unlike one another. When the Virgin Mary is elevated to the status of co-redeemer with Christ (as in a pervasive strand within Catholicism), it would seem that we no longer have a trinity but a quaternity.

We need to bear in mind that God infinitely transcends gender and sexuality; at the same time God is the ground and source of gender. He is the creator of gender, and therefore it is possible to describe his actions in terms of gender. But when we do so we are speaking symbolically, not univocally. Nevertheless, we cannot afford to jettison the biblical imagery concerning God, which is predominantly masculine, for otherwise we fall into a radically different mindset. The sign and the thing signified cannot be separated—either in devotion or in theology. God relates himself to us in the form of the masculine, but he also contains the feminine within himself. He can be described as like a mother even though he is to be addressed as Father, Son and Spirit. It is theologically more felicitous to speak of masculine and feminine imagery concerning God rather than masculine or feminine attributes of God. God is not partly male and partly female, but he relates himself to us mainly as Father, Son and Lord; but in the church, the mystical body of Christ, the feminine side of the sacred again comes to the fore, for we are born in the womb of the church, which then functions as our mother.

Trinitarian Spirituality

Belief in the Trinity has far-reaching implications for the spiritual life. It means that the God we worship is not a solitary, detached being but a living, personal God who can enter into meaningful relations with us. If God were simply an abysmal silence or infinite depth of being, we could not pray to this God, though we could meditate upon God. But if God is a heavenly Father who adopts us into his family as sons and daughters and who lovingly cares for his children, we can converse with him, knowing that he answers prayer. Arius hardly ever referred to the love of God, but a trinitarian God experiences self-giving love within his own life and can therefore bring this love to others. To depict God as love does not mean that God is absorbed in himself (as in Aristotle) but that he is capable of sharing and giving to others.

Subordinationism taught that only the Father is God in the fullest sense, and therefore only the Father should be the object of our prayers. Origen held that we should pray not to Jesus but to God the Father alone. In our day Geoffrey Wainwright, though stoutly affirming the Trinity, contends that prayer should be directed to the Father through the Son and in the power of the Spirit.[76] But if we believe that the Son and Spirit are as fully God as the Father, then we can certainly pray to Christ, to the Spirit and even to Jesus. Prayers can also be directed to the Blessed Trinity, though this was a possibility made available to the church by the Spirit in postapostolic times. Some biblicists point out that in the New Testament prayers are normally directed to the Father, and this pattern should hold true for the church through the ages. But if we believe that the Spirit guides the church into a deeper perception of the mystery of God's self-revelation in Christ, we will then appreciate the witness of the fathers and doctors of the church catholic as well as the apostolic witness, though the latter should always have precedence. We should remember that the New Testament gives examples of prayers to

Jesus (Jn 20:28; Acts 7:59; 9:5; Rev 22:20) and to the exalted Christ (Rev 1:5-6). It also speaks of Christ encountering the believer in prayer (Mt 28:17-18; Acts 11:5-8; Rev 1:12-20). The Holy Spirit, too, is depicted as engaging in prayer with the believer (Acts 20:23; Rom 8:15-16, 26-27; 1 Cor 2:13; Rev 14:13; 22:17).

We should bear in mind that in the early church "Father" was applied not simply to the first *hypostasis* but to the *ousia* (the divine nature). For Augustine prayers to the heavenly Father were prayers to the Godhead. Augustine addressed prayers to God, the Creator, the Lord, Jesus Christ and Beauty.

A too-rigid adherence to the monarchy of the Father would cancel out the element of reciprocity in our relationship to God. The correct attitude would then simply be surrender and submission. But in biblical prayer we pour out our soul before God, we entreat him and beg him for his favor and mercy.[77] We do not merely bring our requests before God, but we struggle with God, even wrestle with God. God is over us and above us to be sure, but he is also within us and beside us. He is not only Lord and Master but Friend and Brother. A purely monarchial view of God is challenged by Jesus: "No longer do I call you servants . . . but I have called you friends" (Jn 15:15; cf. Ex 33:11; Jer 3:4).

In both public and private prayer a trinitarian Christian will include an invocation in the name of the Father, the Son and the Holy Spirit or in the name of God the Father and the Lord Jesus Christ, or something similar (cf. Rom 1:7; 1 Cor 1:3; 2 Cor 1:2; Gal 1:3-5). The early church quickly came to the conclusion that the baptismal rite should be performed in the trinitarian name of God (Mt 28:19), even though among some New Testament Christians people were baptized solely in the name of Jesus (Acts 19:5).

In the mystical tradition of the church, prayer invariably takes the form of meditation and contemplation, and these begin to supplant petition in the life of the Christian. In the new mysticism of the earth, prayer becomes an affirmation and celebration of life rather than importunate pleading with God and intercession for the world. The older mystics never abandoned the biblical pattern of prayer, but they sought to go beyond it—praying not only to God but in God.

If we move toward tritheism as opposed to trinitarianism, we become prone to think of the members of the Trinity as varying in their responses to our requests. If we receive no answer to our prayers from one person of the Trinity, the temptation is then to solicit the favor of another. In popular Catholic piety toward the end of the Middle Ages, prayers were often directed to Jesus or the Son rather than to the Father because the Father was thought of as too distant and was associated with judgment more than with mercy. In some circles even Christ was considered too intimidating, and prayers were then directed to the Virgin Mary or to the saints. Mary effectively became the comforter and healer and in this respect usurped the role of the Holy Spirit.[78]

We do not pray to the Father over the Son or to the Son and Spirit apart from the Father, for this again is to verge toward tritheism. We pray to the Father in the Son and through the power of the Spirit. We pray to Christ who proceeds from the Father and who is made available to us by the Spirit. We pray to the Spirit through the intercession of Christ and by the grace given to us by the Father. Because of the perichoresis (mutual indwelling), each member of the Trinity is fully present in the being and acts of the others. A prayer to Christ is also a prayer to the Father and vice versa.

The question naturally arises: Why not direct our prayers simply to God or to the Father? The answer is that God chooses to relate himself to us in different ways and under different names. If we pray to God the Father exclusively, we might then lapse into a patriarchal monotheism, which often serves as a screen to enhance male domination and keep women in subjection. If we pray only to Jesus, we might come to see God primarily as a suffering companion and no longer as Lord and Master. If we address our prayers exclusively to Christ as Elder Brother, we might begin to align the faith with the ideology of democratic egalitarianism. Prayers directed to Father-Mother or simply Mother might result in supplanting monotheism by a nature mysticism or pantheism in which faith is sacrificed at the altar of environmentalism. If we address our prayers only to the Spirit or the Spiritual Presence (à la Tillich), we might lose sight of the personal nature of God and reduce God to a creative force in nature, an élan vital.

We need to vary our prayers to the living God and even be willing on occasion to address God by metaphors that have biblical support—such as Rock, Fortress, Sun, Light and Fire. But in our prayer life we must finally return to the name by which God discloses himself to us in his revelation—Father, Son and Spirit. Our invocations and benedictions should always include this name (or at least one of the names within this name), but in the prayer conversation itself we should use the freedom God has given to us to call upon him in ways that speak to our deepest needs and concerns. Our spiritual life must be controlled by biblical norms, but this does not abrogate the possibility of using language about God that deepens rather than subtracts from his Lordship and Fatherhood. We can here learn from the mystics who despite their penchant for suprapersonal metaphors for God nevertheless often had a rich prayer life precisely because they laid hold of the freedom given by the Spirit to probe more deeply into the God-human relationships and express their love for God in multiform ways. The trinitarian formula—Father, Son and Spirit—must never become an idol that directs us only to words and rites as opposed to the reality that encompasses this name. On the other hand, the trinitarian definition will always be the ruling criterion that regulates the life of worship and prayer, one that keeps us on the biblical path and prevents us from projecting on God our own vision of what God should be like. We are free to draw from cultural resouces in explicating the nature and activity of God, but we must never be led by the spirit of the culture (Zeitgeist), which will invariably controvert the claims of biblical and apostolic faith.

Appendix A: Modern Forms of Unitarianism

Modern Unitarianism has its roots in Arianism, Monarchianism and Neoplatonic mysticism. As a religious movement within Christianity it is associated with Laelius Socinus (1525–1562), Faustus Socinus (1539–1604) and the Racovian Catechism (1605). Faustus Socinus denied the three persons of the Trinity and held that worship should be directed only to God the Father. At the same time, he had a deep respect for Jesus and accepted many of Jesus' miracles. He held Holy Scripture in high regard, but this was based on rational and historical grounds rather than on the inward testimony of the Holy Spirit.

Jakob Boehme (1575–1624) reflected the abiding influence of Neo-platonism within Christianity. Boehme spoke of an Abyss or *Ungrund,* the undifferentiated Absolute that is neither light nor darkness, love nor wrath. The "eternal generation of the Trinity" occurs because the *Ungrund* contains a will to self-intuition. This will (the Father) finds itself as the "heart" (the Son) and emanating from these is the "moving life" (the Spirit). While Boehme saw a trinitarian movement in God, he also posited a God above God, the infinite abyss.

A unitarian thrust is also found in Friedrich Schleiermacher (1768–1834), though he gave lip service to the Trinity. The Father refers to the unity of the Divine Essence rather than one of the supposed distinctions within this essence. The divine is essentially the ground of all finite being as it comes to self-consciousness in human nature. To ascribe personality to the Universal Source of Being would reduce it to the level of finitude. The Holy Spirit is merely "the common Spirit of the Christian society."[79] For Schleiermacher God became a Trinity in time just as he became Creator and Redeemer in time.

William Blake (1757–1827) depicted the Godhead as unfolding itself in a universal kenotic process of redemption resulting in the divinization of humanity. He had only contempt for God the Father and Lawgiver but affirmed Christ as the creative power within humanity. Blake equated the God of historical Christianity with Satan, who died so that the spirit of Jesus could live on in the hearts of men and women. Thomas Altizer hails him as the first Christian atheist, since he affirmed the death of God in the passion and death of Jesus.[80] Blake spoke of a universal generation of the Son from the Father of which the historical Jesus is the supreme epiphany.

The philosopher G. W. F. Hegel (1770-1831) affirmed an economic Trinity but not the immanent Trinity of classical Christian faith, which portrays God as a trinitarian fellowship apart from and before the world of creation. Hegel spoke of the Absolute Spirit separating from itself (the Logos) and returning to itself (the Holy Spirit). There is only one God— the Absolute Spirit *(Geist)* in various manifestations. The Son in Hegel's philosophy refers to the incarnation and immanence of God in the phenomenal world. The Holy Spirit signifies the return of the finite to the infinite, of variety into simplicity. H. R. Mackintosh makes this perceptive observation: "Such a Trinity, clearly, represents that which is in no sense eternal but only coming to be; it has no meaning, or even existence, apart from the finite world. It is a dialectical triad, not Father, Son and Spirit in any sense in which the Christian faith has ever pronounced the three-fold Name."[81]

For Gerald Heard (1889-1971), as for his friend and colleague Aldous Huxley, the ultimate unity of the Divine Ground lies beyond the Trinity. It is possible to apprehend this unity by direct intuition. God is not Father, Son and Holy Spirit but "Supreme, Eternal and Ever-Free Consciousness."[82] Jesus is not God incarnate in time but the paradigm of sainthood, the one who reveals the indwelling reality of God in all of humanity. Heard drew upon Neoplatonic mysticism and the modern theory of evolution in delineating a post-Christian mysticism. He also betrayed a gnostic thrust, affirming a fall from divinity into the world of temporality and materiality.

Similarly, Paul Tillich, already discussed in this chapter, displayed a this-worldly mysticism. His conception of the three persons as symbols of God's self-movement toward the world reinforces unitarianism rather than trinitarianism. As in Hegel, deity is reduced to Spirit or Spiritual Presence. Christ becomes a revelation of all-encompassing Spirit. While affirming the trinitarian formula, Tillich reinterpreted it in the light of the mystical heritage of the church and modern evolutionary theory. God becomes the power of being in all finite being rather than a trinitarian fellowship who exists prior to all created being.

A different kind of unitarianism is found in Count Zinzendorf (1700–1760), who verged on Christomonism. Christ is Creator and Sustainer of the Universe and Lord of history as well as Redeemer. Zinzendorf referred to the Trinity in functional terms—Father, Mother, Son; the Mother is the Holy Spirit. He asserted that God becomes our Father only through faith in Christ. Thus God is our Father indirectly rather than directly or immediately. We are related to God the Father as to a father-in-law or even a grandfather.[83]

Unitarianism is also prevalent among the sects and cults, which have found the doctrine of the Trinity an insuperable obstacle in spirituality. Many of these movements stand in the Platonic-mystical tradition; others manifest kinship to ancient Monarchianism and deism. The Unitarian Church, as it was originally constituted, affirms the eternal God but not the eternal Son. Jesus becomes the supreme revelation of the one God. God is distant and removed from the world of the created order.[84] "The Way," founded by Victor Paul Wierwille, also promulgates a unitarianism of the first person. The Father alone is God. Similarly, the Jehovah's Witnesses, who openly appeal to Arius, affirm the sole deity of the Father; the Son is an intermediary being who points us to God.

Some cults and sects teach a unitarianism of the second person. The Jesus Only movement in Pentecostalism, which includes the United Pentecostal Church, identifies Jesus of the New Testament with Jehovah of the Old Testament. The Father and Spirit are not absorbed into the Son, but the Son is the one divine person who is elsewhere called Father and Holy Spirit. There is one God in three manifestations, but not three persons. Swedenborgians also teach a unitarianism of the second person. For Emanuel Swedenborg, Father, Son and Holy Spirit are "three Modes of manifestation" or "three essentials of the one God." Before the creation of the world, the Trinity did not exist. When God became incarnate, it was then possible to speak of a Trinity. In his *True Christian Religion* Swedenborg identified God as "Jesus Christ, who is the Lord Jehovah, from eternity the Creator, in time the Redeemer, and to eternity the Regenerator."[85] It would perhaps be more accurate to label this position a trinal monism.

A unitarianism of the third person is conspicuous in many aberrant Christian and post-Christian movements. The Doukhobors, who trace their lineage to Russian dissenters, taught that the Spirit alone is God, but he manifests himself through various Messiahs or Christs.[86] In Quakerism one often finds the idea that there is only one God but in various manifestations or modes. One can frequently detect a tendency to absolutize Spirit. Elias Hicks, an early American Quaker, denied the Trinity. Nonetheless, a significant number of Quakers are evangelical and adhere strongly to the classical doctrines of the divinity of Christ and the triune Godhead. The Bible Way movement within Pentecostalism envisages God as the Eternal Spirit who is everywhere present. Jesus, in whom the Spirit dwelt, is acknowledged as the Son of God.

A binitarianism is evident in many of the cult groups. Mother Ann Lee, founder of the Shakers, taught that God is not triune but dual—male and female.[87] Just as Christ came in the form of a man at his first epiphany, so he will manifest himself in the form of a woman at his second coming. Radical feminism today continues this gnostic thrust that depicts God as a biunity, having a masculine and a feminine side. An androgynous God is not the trinitarian God of traditional Christian faith, though God's movements can indeed be described by masculine and feminine imagery. In the Shaker–feminist perspective God is a dyad rather than a trinity. Some radical feminists embrace a Unitarianism of the third person and elevate Spirit to preeminence.

Mormonism can be interpreted as both unitarianism and polytheism. Mormon theology posits one eternal God—the Father, who begets many spirit children, including Christ the Son. God the Father was originally a man who became god, just as we are men and women on the way to becoming deity. Deity signifies the perfection rather than the transcendence of humanity. Mormons believe that "both the Father and the Son are in form and stature perfect men; each of them possesses a tangible body, infinitely pure and perfect and attended by transcendent glory, nevertheless a body of flesh and bones."[88]

Radically different is Christian Science, which envisions God as spirit rather than matter, as universal truth rather than an absolute individual. Mary Baker Eddy decried all anthropomorphism and deified Mind or Idea. God is not heavenly Father but Infinite Mind. She occasionally referred to God as "Father–Mother," but only as a metaphor or symbol of an indescribable, all-encompassing reality. Eddy defined the Holy Spirit as "Divine Science"—"the development of Life, Truth and Love."[89]

The hallmark of a cult movement is to appeal to private illuminations, empirical evidences or logical deductions rather than to the living Word of God, Jesus Christ, as he speaks through the Scriptures and to the church in every age. Many cults will affirm the authority, even the inerrancy, of Scripture, but they divorce Scripture from the sacred tradition of the church universal, which is not of itself infallible but which mediates the truth of Scripture by the power of the Spirit to every generation. The denial of the ontological Trinity is a potent indication that a religious movement is probably a cult or aberrant sect rather than a branch of the one holy, catholic and apostolic church.

Appendix B: Subordination and Equality

My position on this matter can be clarified by comparing a number of models, some of which overlap.

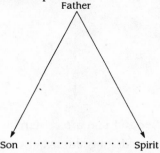

Father

Son ·············· Spirit

In model 1 we see the Spirit proceeding from the Father alone just as in the case of the Son. The Father is the source, the fountainhead or the unoriginated. There is a marked dependence of the Son and Spirit on the Father, but all are deemed equally God. This represents an important emphasis in the Eastern church.

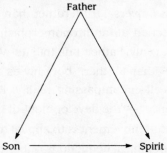

Model 2 depicts the Son proceeding from the Father and the Spirit proceeding from the Father and the Son.[90] The Father begets, the Son is begotten and the Spirit is breathed. Both the Father and the Son breathe the Spirit and also "send" the Spirit. This schema reflects some of the concerns of the Western church. The difficulty lies in the apparent absence of reciprocity between Father and Son and between both and the Spirit. If we envisage the Spirit as an interactive agency linking Father and Son (as in model 6) then there is a measure of reciprocity, for the Spirit now represents the breathing out of the love of Father and Son for each other.

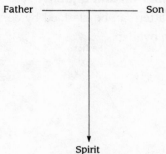

In model 3 the Father and Son are coeternal and equal in glory, but the Spirit is assigned a mediating status between divinity and the creaturely world. In some of the theologians who stood against Arianism the boundary between divinity and the creaturely world was located not in the Logos but in the Holy Spirit.[91]

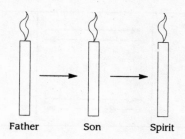

Father   Son   Spirit

In model 4 (proposed by Gregory of Nyssa) the light originates with the Father and is passed through the Son to the Spirit. The second torch is lit by the first, and the third by the second. This is not a temporal succession but an eternal reality. This view is deeply rooted in church tradition—both East and West.

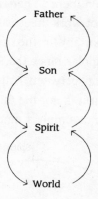

Model 5 is a schema that we often encounter in Christian mysticism adapted from Neoplatonism. In the Neoplatonic version the One goes out of itself into the Nous (or Reason), then into the World-Soul, and finally into human souls and the world. The Son, the Spirit and the world are emanations from God. In returning to the One (the Father) the soul loses its individual identity and becomes part of the primal unity. In Christian mysticism the One becomes the Father, the Nous the Son and the World-Soul the Spirit. The Holy Spirit prepares us for the Son, and the Son leads us back to the Father. The subordinationist bent is conspicuous.

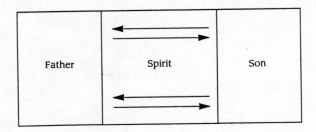

Model 6, offered by David N. Bell, reflects Augustine's emphasis on the double procession in which the Holy Spirit proceeds not simply from the Father *through* the Son but from the Father *and* the Son.[92] Bell likens the trinitarian relationship to an electric battery in which the Father is the positive pole and the Son the negative; the Spirit is "the current flowing and flashing between them." There is only one substance, electricity, but the battery cannot work unless all three realities are present. Both poles are equally important for the operation. This analogy tends to be bipolar rather than tripolar, since the Spirit appears to be reduced to the reciprocal interaction between Father and Son.[93] This idea is prominent in Augustine, but it is not the full picture in the Augustinian system. He gave the Spirit not simply a functional but also an ontological status.

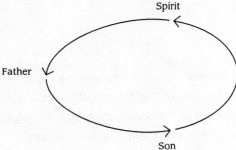

Model 7, the one that I favor, shows the mutual self-giving and fundamental equality among the persons of the Trinity.[94] Here we see not subordination but interdependence. The Son and Spirit proceed from the Father, but they also return to the Father. The Spirit returns with the Son and the Son through the Spirit. There is not only initiation of action by the Father but also active response by the Son and Spirit. This circular action pertains to the inner life of the Trinity and not simply to God in his relationship to the world (as in Neoplatonism). The return to the Father indicates not a propensity to blend into the Father but a loving response to the Father, who receives as well as directs and invites. This diagram resonates with themes in Athanasius, Augustine, Barth and Torrance.

It should be kept in mind that no member of the Trinity acts without the cooperation of the others. For example, the Father does not act unilaterally; his activity is anchored in the power that comes from the Spirit in unity with the Son. The Father can intend an action, but he cannot carry it through without the active collaboration of Spirit and Son. Similarly, the Son and the Spirit act through the impetus provided by the Father. No person of the Trinity is the underlying principle that sustains and undergirds the others. No person can exist by itself in splendid isolation from the others.[95] Yet there is still an order of succession within the Trinity. The Father has a certain priority in that his creative action anticipates the creative and receptive activity of both Son and Spirit. The Father is not the source of the creative energy that constitutes the divine, but he is the first of three expressions of this energy.[96] While the Son and Spirit are not ontologically inferior to the Father, they are dependent on the Father for their identity, but the Father too is dependent on them in order to realize his purposes.[97]

In the current charismatic movement within the mainline denominations the Spirit is sometimes depicted as the unifying or undergirding principle of the Trinity.[98] At their best, charismatics view the Spirit as "person" rather than impersonal force, but we must insist that the Spirit is person only in relationship to the Father and the Son. He should indeed be revered as the Lord and Giver of life (2 Cor 3:17-18; Gal 6:8), but he gives life always through the Son and under the direction of the Father (Eph 1:13-14; 2:18). The Spirit gives life by calling those who are dead in sin to faith in Jesus Christ (Rom 8:1-17). The baptism in the Spirit is at the same time baptism into the body of Christ (1 Cor 12:12-13; Eph

4:1-5). Like creation and reconciliation, regeneration involves all three persons of the Trinity, who act together as well as in their distinctive ways to radiate the glory that is in God to the whole of humanity.

EIGHT

THE BIBLICAL–
CLASSICAL
SYNTHESIS

We must not measure the Divine nature by the limitations
of [our] own, but gauge God's assertions concerning Himself
by the scale of His own glorious self-revelation.
HILARY OF POITIERS

When all is said, it still must be maintained that the net result
of Augustine's philosophical speculation was to achieve
a platonic understanding of the Christian Revelation.
ÉTIENNE GILSON

Fundamentally irreconcilable with the Biblical concept
of creation *ex nihilo,* Platonism had been the greatest temptation
for Eastern Christian thought from the time of Origen.
JOHN MEYENDORFF

There is but one living and true God, everlasting,
without body, parts or passions.
THE THIRTY-NINE ARTICLES
OF RELIGION

A compelling case can be made that the history of Christian thought shows the unmistakable imprint of a biblical–classical synthesis in which the ontological categories of Greco-Roman philosophy have been united with the personal-dramatic categories of biblical faith.[1] The attempt at synthesis began already with the early apologists, who sought to vindicate the claims of Christianity to the pagan culture of their time. The Hellenizing of Christian faith was particularly apparent in Clement and Origen, who introduced "elements of religious speculation and intellectualistic spirituality belonging to a world altogether different from that of the Gospel."[2] The synthesis with classical thought was also conspicuous in Augustine, John Scotus Erigena and later Catholic scholastic orthodoxy, including Thomas Aquinas.

In the twentieth century Reinhold Niebuhr has been one of the foremost critics of synthetic theology, drawing a sharp distinction between the classical and biblical views of life and the world.[3] Niebuhr recognized that the Bible is not simply the unfolding of a drama of God's interaction with his people in a particular history but also a story that contains metaphysical truth claims, although these are not elucidated in a systematic manner. Wherever God or humanity becomes subject to an ontological necessity, the freedom of both God and humanity is denied and the biblical ethos is thereby compromised.[4] According to Niebuhr the central affirmations of biblical faith elude assimilation into a rational system of meaning. Mystery and paradox belong to the very core of biblical faith and thus prevent theology from developing into a finalized system of truth. For Niebuhr paradox does not mean a logical contradiction but a confrontation with a reality that defies human imagination while at the same time providing illumination of the human condition.

The Jewish theologian Abraham Joshua Heschel also questioned the adequacy of Hellenistic philosophy to uncover the mystery of prophetic faith:

> The God of the philosophers is all indifference, too sublime to possess a heart or to cast a glance at our world. His wisdom consists in being conscious of Himself and oblivious to the world. In contrast, the God of the prophets is all concern, too merciful to remain aloof to His creation. He not only rules the world in the majesty of His might; He is personally concerned and even stirred by the conduct and fate of man.[5]

Paul Tillich demonstrated far more openness to the harmonizing of

Hebraic and Hellenistic traditions, trying to show that despite an admitted dissonance between them they are not necessarily in contradiction.[6] He rejected synthesis as an amalgamation of Christian faith and cultural thought, but he supported synthesis in the sense of a unified structure of meaning in which the questions of the culture find their fulfillment in Christian revelation. His goal was a vital relationship in which philosophy and theology coexist not in terms of an upper and lower story (as in Thomism) but in terms of quest and fulfillment. He endeavored to bring philosophy and theology, Christ and culture together in a higher unity in which the probings and concerns of culture are assimilated into a theonomous picture of reality. Although Tillich's theology probably comes closer to a biblical-modern synthesis than to a synthesis with classical thought, there is ample evidence that Platonism and Neoplatonism figure prominently in his speculation.[7]

One should keep in mind that the revelation of the mystery of God's love in Jesus Christ contravenes not only the Greek conception of God but also the Jewish expectation of the Messiah. The Messiah who came was not the triumphal Messiah of popular Jewish imagination but the suffering Messiah whose kingdom was not of this world. The God who manifested himself in Jesus was not the unchangeable deity of Hellenistic speculation but the God of boundless love who demonstrates his power by undergoing suffering and death on a cross. Indeed, "there is no mystery in heaven or earth so great as this—a suffering Deity, an Almighty Saviour nailed to the Cross."[8] The gospel cannot be reconciled with either Hebraic triumphalism or Greek otherworldliness, but we are certainly free to use both the imagery of the biblical prophets and the ontological concepts of Greek philosophers to clarify the central claims of Christian faith. Only we must not allow these images and concepts to dilute or to compromise the gospel affirmation that the Word became flesh in Jesus of Nazareth and that this Word took upon himself the suffering and pain of a condemned human race so that all who believe might be liberated from bondage to sin, death and the devil.

The Living God and the Eternal Now

When the church confronted the wisdom of the ancient world, its doctrine of God was sharply challenged and in the end drastically modified. The God of the Hellenistic ethos was the self-contained Absolute who had no lack or deficiency within himself and was consequently radically independent of temporality and materiality *(autarkeia)*. The God of the Bible is also radically transcendent over nature and history, but he willed to enter human history in order to direct it to superhistorical ends. The God of Hellenism was characterized by imperturbability and impassibility. The God of the Bible is not sublimely removed from the created order but actively involved in it. While not subject to the pain and tribulation that mars his creation, he freely makes himself vulnerable to the responses of his people and identifies with their joys and sorrows. The God of Hellenism was static and timeless; the God of biblical faith is ever-active and ever-willing. The God of Hellenism was the Eternal Now—"an unqualified now with everything in full manifestation."[9] The God of biblical religion is also eternal, but with an eternity "understood as everlastingness, as reality with an unlimited future."[10]

Not surprisingly the apologists and church fathers drew freely upon the conceptuality provided by the creative thinkers of their time in order to render the message of faith intellectually respectable and credible. The rationalism of Plato and Aristotle and the mysticism of Plotinus and Proclus helped to shape the development of theology in the early church and throughout the Middle Ages. The apologists identified Christ with the Logos of contemporary Middle Platonism, but the Holy Spirit was "left to hover uncertainly in the background."[11] Tillich had these astute comments on Justin Martyr: "All the characteristics which Parmenides attributed to Being are here attributed to God—eternal, without beginning, needing nothing, beyond passions, indestructible, unchangeable, and invisible."[12] Tillich pointed out, however, that Justin broke decisively with the Platonic worldview when he affirmed God as almighty Creator.

Augustine maintained an enduring commitment to the biblical vision of God, but he often interpreted this God through the eyes of Platonism and Neoplatonism. He conceived of God as both omniscient and immutable, meaning that God is not affected by anything outside himself, that "there can be no increase in the content of the divine knowledge."[13] Augustine referred to God as "the Absolute Form," "the Selfsame" and "the Supreme Substance," but he did not regard these designations as substitutes for the personal names of God given in Holy Scripture. At times he appeared to envision God as a supermind in which the category of knowledge is determinative in unfolding the mystery of God's inner being.[14]

In the ninth century John Scotus Erigena sought to reconcile the Christian idea of creation and the Greek idea of emanation, but the latter proved more determinative than the former. He interpreted the biblical creation of everything out of nothing as a creation by God out of himself.[15] This meant that God was basically continuous with his creation: God became the ground of being rather than the creator and lord of being. Against this position Wolfhart Pannenberg contends that "God, as the origin, is never merely the invisible ground of present reality, but the free, creative source of the ever new and unforeseen."[16]

The main problem confronting the intellectuals in the early church and continuing into the medieval and modern periods was how the Absolute could under any circumstances come into contact with the world of change, decay and death. The very doctrine of the incarnation was at stake in this discussion, since the church maintained against pagan philosophy that the timeless, unchangeable God entered into time, assumed the garb of human flesh, and suffered and died on the cross in the person of his Son. The church fathers, followed by the medieval and Reformation theologians, insisted that God remains impassible even in the incarnation. The human nature of Jesus suffers and dies, but the divine nature is unaffected. According to Anselm, when we speak of God as enduring any humiliation, "we do not refer to the majesty of that nature, which cannot suffer; but to the feebleness of the human constitution which he assumed."[17] The medieval mystic Meister Eckhart considered it impossible "that the Son of God should suffer in eternity." Therefore "the heavenly Father sent him into time to become human and suffer."[18] Indeed, "when the Son in the Godhead willed to be human and became so, suffering martyrdom, the immovable disinterest of God was affected as little as if the Son had never become human at all."[19] The Greek idea of divine impassibility was also reflected in the nineteenth-century Anglican theologian Frederick William Robertson: God "is not affected by our mutability; our changes do not alter Him. When we are restless, He remains serene and calm; when we are low, selfish, mean, or dispirited, He is still the unalterable I AM."[20] It can also be seen in the nineteenth-century American Presbyterian theologian Archibald Alexander Hodge: "God is absolutely unchangeable in his states and moods, as well as in his essence."[21]

As I have discussed elsewhere, it is important to maintain the consensus of the early church that God in himself is indestructible, eternal and unchangeable, for this idea has firm biblical support.[22] Yet we must also insist that God is free, and in his freedom he makes himself vulnerable to pain and suffering. He is essentially independent, but he freely enters into reciprocal relations with his people. The God of the Bible is not the Eternal Absolute divorced from time but the God of uncompromising integrity who remains faithful throughout time. Whereas the God of mysticism and rationalistic idealism rests in sublime detachment, the God of biblical religion actively involves himself in his creation.

In a mysticism that is no longer regulated by the dogma of the church (as in Gerald Heard and Aldous Huxley), the incarnation is reduced to a broken reflection or fleeting manifestation of the God who remains essentially unknowable and indescribable.[23] I hold to the contrary that the divine presence incarnate in Jesus was neither some emanation or energy flowing from God nor some spark of divine fire inherent in humanity, but God himself in all of his majesty and splendor. Jesus was not simply transparent to God in a superlative degree: he was God incarnate in human flesh, a God who enters into concrete relationships with his people while still remaining true to the integrity of his being and steadfast in his purposes for humanity.

The sun that shines unfailingly on both good and evil (Mt 5:45) describes one side of God's nature. But the angel who wrestles with Jacob and who allows himself to be mastered by Jacob (Gen 32:22–32) describes another side. God is unchangeable and unswerving in his will and purpose for humanity, but he makes himself vulnerable for the sake of our redemption. The biblical God is one who is both transcendent and immanent, unchanging and open to change, ever at rest and ever active. As theologians of the church we are allowed to draw on the wisdom and creative insights of pagan philosophers so long as we subordinate them to the revealed gospel of God. We cannot have a pure conception of God divorced from the culture and history in which faith is transmitted, but we must not allow culture and history to determine faith's content. We should resist both the Hellenizing and the Judaizing of the faith without abandoning its Hellenistic matrix and Judaic roots.

Modern theology, both liberal and conservative, has been hampered by its uncritical assimilation of the idea of perfection inherited from the Hellenistic ethos. If perfection means the summation of all possible value in pure being, then the idea of any change or novelty in the experience of God would be highly questionable. Following Plato, Carl Henry says, "God is perfect and, if perfect, can only change for the worse."[24] A refreshingly different evangelical voice, James Oliver Buswell Jr., urges the church to "shake off the static ideology which has come into Christian theology from non-Biblical sources."[25] We need to see perfection in terms of an indomitable love that overcomes the world rather than a beatitude that towers above the world and remains basically unaffected by human suffering and dereliction. This love is constant in its purpose and fidelity but ever new in its responsiveness to human need and petition.

Providence and Fate

Christianity sharply challenged the pervasive belief in fate that cast a shadow over the ancient world. Fate is an external, inexorable force that controls all events and thereby makes human striving meaningless.[26] In fate "the future is independent of what the individual can will or not will."[27] The action of fate is "blind, arbitrary, relentless. It moves inexorably onwards, effecting the most terrible catastrophes, impressing us with a feeling of helpless consternation, and harrowing our moral sense."[28] Fate can include contingency if we mean by the latter a happening by unforeseen causes. It rules out absolute contingency, but not unpredictability.

Stoicism sought to counter the harsh aspects of fatalism by identifying fate with providence and nature. Fate was reinterpreted as a continuous chain of causation, but this was determinism, not fatalism. "Fatalism is the belief that a definite event will take place, whatever happens."[29] The Stoics advocated resignation to the law of nature; yet this was a rational law that guaranteed meaning and purpose in a world that the fatalists believed was capricious and irrational.

The Greek tragedians perceived fate as the primary adversary of humanity, and heroism as the noble though futile defiance of the power of fate. Aeschylus confessed that "against necessity, against its strength, no one can fight and win."[30] Christian faith speaks of the law of retribution that is not irreversible but inevitable if repentance is lacking. The Greek tragedians referred to the nemesis that invariably follows hubris, an ordeal heightened rather than lessened when accompanied by an open acknowledgment of our personal implication in the tragic unfolding of events.

Christian faith asserts against fatalism that all events are controlled by the providential hand of God, which does not override human freedom but establishes it.[31] Providence is the divine direction of human destiny to new possibilities, not the sealing of human destiny to an unforeseen doom. One can make a case that Christianity inserted hope and optimism into the ancient Greco-Roman world, which was under the spell of fatalism. In contradistinction to the cultural ethos of that time, Christianity insisted that God is superior to fate, that consequently our destinies can be changed by outside intervention.

Regrettably in their attempt to penetrate the bastions of paganism, theologians tended to blur the distinction between fate and providence; both became identified with the law of nature. Divine ordering became divine determinism, and the biblical view of the future as partly open was irremediably compromised. Pannenberg astutely perceives that "even in the metaphysics of providence, the divine ground of the world was understood not as acting contingently but rather as the law of the world."[32] When God becomes the personification of an immutable law, natural or ethical, there may well be a reversion to the ancient idea of fate.[33]

I have already noted the partial synthesis with classical thought achieved by Tillich, who preferred to speak of destiny rather than fate.[34] Whereas fate is meaningless, destiny is "necessity united with meaning."[35] Whereas fate happens to us, we contribute to our destiny. Yet Tillich's emphasis was on the ontological fall rather than the historical fall, on ontological fate rather than historical guilt. The core of the human dilemma is not the deliberate misuse of our freedom but the subjection of our freedom to the fate of mortality. Reinhold Niebuhr observed cogently that Tillich spoke more of the fatefulness of sin than of human responsibility in precipitating the fall into sin.[36] For Tillich the fall of Adam is not a historical but an ontological symbol depicting the transition from essence to existence. Tillich could not escape the thought-world of Neoplatonism, which sees humanity descending from an original unity with the primal force and returning to a restored unity. Yet to his credit he recognized the abiding tensions between the Christian concept of providence and the ancient idea of fate that paralyzes the human will, though he failed to see God actively involved in human history reversing human fortune and enabling humans to rise above the power of sin and death, at least to a degree.[37]

Truth as Event and Idea

As Christianity penetrated the centers of learning and power in the ancient world, the biblical notion of truth was time and again obscured in the often well-meaning attempts to demonstrate the validity of the

Christian message in terms that pagans could understand. Truth in biblical religion refers to God's self-disclosure in biblical history.[38] Truth is something that happens, and as a happening it also impresses itself upon the human mind. Yet it never becomes totally assimilated by the mind because it remains God's unique possession. It is meaning that shines through mystery rather than mystery reduced to logic (as in rationalism). In the Hellenistic view truth is the manifestation of an eternal idea or ideal or simply the unveiling of primordial being. Platonism posited an underlying continuity between the human soul and the eternal God. Truth is discovered by introspection, finding the point of identity between God and humanity within the self. By contrast, biblical faith insists that truth confronts us from without. Truth is being addressed by the living God rather than a discovery of the eternal presence of God within the depths of one's own being.

A synthesis of biblical and classical ideas is evident in Augustine, who accepted the Greek notion that "truth is that by which being is made manifest."[39] Yet Augustine contended that Christ, who is the source and origin of all existing unity, allows being to be made manifest.[40] Faith in Christ is the pathway to a bona fide understanding of truth.

In Thomas Aquinas the truths of reason are supplemented by the suprarational truths of faith. Faith illumines a realm of mystery that transcends the limits of human perceptivity. God's existence is known by reason, but only faith apprehends God as a Trinity. The true dimensions of selfhood lie beyond the purely rational self. They are to be understood as a *donum superadditum,* a gift that is added on to created human nature. Reinhold Niebuhr observed:

> Whenever one touches the Thomistic scheme, one finds a perfectly coherent world, a perfectly understood self, a perfectly possible virtue and justice. This coherent world has superimposed upon it an aura of mystery and meaning in which the limitless possibilities of man's and God's freedom find expression. It is a two-story world with a classical base and a Christian second story.[41]

According to Niebuhr, in the synthetic theology of the past "the eternal and divine element in man is abstracted from the conditions of finite-ness in history."[42] Truth is established not merely in principle but in fact in the hearts of those who have accepted Christ. By contrast, Niebuhr contended (and I agree) that "the truth, as it is contained in the Christian revelation, includes the recognition that it is neither possible for man to know the truth fully nor to avoid the error of pretending that he does. It is recognized that 'grace' always remains in partial contradiction to 'nature,' and is not merely its fulfillment."[43] The Christian is always in the position of "having and not having" the truth, since reason cannot pene-trate the paradox of God becoming human in Jesus Christ. Christian rationalists too simply "equate meaning . . . with rationality and thereby inevitably obscure some of the profoundest incongruities, tragic antin-omies, and depth of meaning on the edge of the mysteries in human life and history."[44]

Commendably, Niebuhr was alert to the peril of a premature synthesis with non–Christian thought in his own position. By comparing the bib-lical view with the classical and modern views one is tempted to reduce the first to yet another philosophy—more profound than the others because "it embodies heights and depths which are not comprehended in the others."[45]

We say we take historical facts seriously but not literally; but that may be on the way of not taking them as historical facts at all. Thus we reject the myth of the fall of man as a historical fact. With that rejection we can dispose of all nonsense about a biologically inher-ited corruption of sin. But we also easily interpret human evil as an inevitable condition of human finiteness and stand on the edge of Platonism, or, by rejecting the end of the world as a literal event, we easily obscure the eternity at the end of time and have only an eter-nity over time left, again a movement toward Platonism.[46]

Niebuhr consciously sought a synthesis of Renaissance and Reformation insights and thereby opened himself to a Platonism mediated by histor-ical consciousness as well as to the modern idea of a dynamic and open universe in which human initiative and creativity take precedence over divine predestination. He definitely preferred the Renaissance notion of infinite human possibilities to the Reformation notion of the total help-lessness of humanity by virtue of being in bondage to sin. Yet Niebuhr critiqued both the classical and modern ideas in the light of the biblical revelation and reaffirmed the doctrine of original sin—understood now not as an inherited taint but as the inevitable product of the anxiety of finitude, which is part of the human condition.[47]

Revelation and Reason

Whereas Hebraic religion appealed to a divine self-disclosure in history, Hellenistic philosophy endeavored to penetrate ultimate reality by the power of the human intellect. Against the anthropomorphism of mytho-poetic thought, Plato contended that we reach universal truth by means of a rational dialectic. It is not a mystical transcending of the self but an unfolding of the truth already latent within the self that sets us on the pathway to true knowledge. Both Plato and Aristotle preferred con-ceptual over mythopoetic language in describing God and the nature of things, though the former sometimes used myth to articulate concep-tual truth. Plotinus and Neoplatonism confessed the inability of concepts to grasp ultimate truth, but the process of abstraction can take us to the very limits of reason, where we confront the abyss of reason.

In rationalistic philosophy, revelation becomes rational insight or an intuitive grasp of the whole. In biblical religion, revelation is personal address in which God remains hidden in the I–Thou encounter. Human reason is not an extension of divine reason (as in the Greek philosophi-cal tradition) but a faculty within humanity that corresponds with and reflects divine reason. Its relationship to the divine reason is not univo-cal but analogical (as Thomas Aquinas duly recognized).

The fathers of the early church and their successors in the medieval church sought to employ the ontological categories of Greek philosophy in explicating the drama of the biblical revelation, but too often the content of faith was altered by metaphysical speculation. Gregory of Nyssa defined the image of God in humanity as "mind" and "word." The soul finds its perfection in what is intellectual and rational. For Thomas Aquinas the image of God is "primarily intellectual" in nature. For John Scotus Erigena true authority is "simply the truth discovered by the power of reason and entrusted to writing by the holy fathers."[48] He regarded the faith that moved Peter to confess the Messiahship of Christ as lower than contemplative wisdom, which rises above the corruptibility of the flesh.

In the mystical heritage of the church we see a synthesis of Hellenistic idealism and biblical religion, with the latter often subordinated to the former. The mystics spoke of the *Logos spermatikos,* which is in the human soul and accounts for the truths of the universe known even to pagans. This divine spark or light within the human self provides the point of contact with the biblical revelation. For the mystics we mount up to God by negating everything positive that reason can adduce regarding God and thereby end in a pure abstraction in which God remains basically unknowable. For some mystics God totally transcends the rational (Dionysius), whereas for others God fully encompasses the rational (Eckhart).

Bonaventure (thirteenth century) reveals his dependence on the Platonic tradition in delineating his epistemology:

That we may arrive at an understanding of the First Principle, which is most spiritual and eternal and above us, we ought to proceed through the traces which are corporeal and temporal and outside us; and this is to be led into the way of God. We ought next to enter into our minds, which are the eternal image of God, spiritual and internal; and this is to walk in the truth of God. We ought finally to pass over into that which is eternal, most spiritual and above us, looking to the First Principle; and this is to rejoice in the knowledge of God and in the reverence of His majesty.[49]

Hegel typifies the attempt to unite idealism and Christianity in the modern period. Both Hegel and Plato taught the identity of the knowing subject and the object known. Truth is a comprehensive grasp of the whole of reality rather than an incomparable revelation of God in a human person in history. For Hegel reason and revelation have the same content; Christianity and idealism are not only harmonious but identical.[50]

Rationalism took an evangelical turn in Benjamin Warfield, who believed that rational validation of the claims of faith sets the stage for the decision of faith. Christianity will overcome modern challenges to the faith by the force of logical persuasion. Christianity "has come into the world clothed with the mission to *reason* its way to its dominion. Other religions may appeal to the sword, or seek some other way to propagate themselves. Christianity makes its appeal to right reason, and stands out among all religions, therefore, as distinctively 'the Apologetic religion.' "[51]

Happily, many theologians have resisted the lure of rational support for the claims of faith. In the early church Athanasius declared that we do not prove "in plausible words of Greek wisdom; but we persuade by the faith that clearly precedes . . . argumentation."[52] The Reformers Luther and Calvin harbored deep misgivings toward any form of natural theology, though they did not deny that all people are inescapably related to God and thereby have some intimation of his presence and will. Pascal in the seventeenth century and Kierkegaard in the nineteenth century pointed to the grave limitations of reason in discerning the things of God.

In the twentieth century Reinhold Niebuhr has been one of the most avid critics of rationalistic religion, though, as we have seen, he too was attracted to a synthesis of biblical and philosophical thought. Niebuhr endeavored to steer theology between the Charybdis of mysticism, in which rationality is dissolved into mystery, and the Scylla of rationalism, in which mystery is swallowed up in logic. He claimed that a religion of revelation is to be distinguished from both "merely poetic appreciations of mystery" and "philosophies of religion which find the idea of revelation meaningless."[53] Revelation can have no real place in a purely rational religion because it approaches "the mystery of life with the certainty that human reason can at length entirely resolve the mystery."[54]

Yet Niebuhr rejected the idea that revelation is self-validating and sought a rational validation of the claims of faith by correlating the truth of the gospel with "truths about life and history, gained generally in experience."[55] Such a correlation "comprehends all of life's antinomies and contradictions into a system of meaning and is conducive to a renewal of life."[56] This sounds reminiscent of Hegel, though Niebuhr insisted that the truth of God can never be assimilated into a rational system and is found only at the limits of reason. A Platonic thrust is also apparent in Niebuhr. He spoke of rising above the flux of history in moments of prayerful transcendence. But does not Christian faith speak of God descending into the midst of history and creating faith within repentant sinners?

Agape and Eros

Since I have already delineated the cardinal differences between agape and eros,[57] I intend in this section to discuss some attempts to unite these two disparate types of love. Can agape, the paradoxical love of the cross, be brought into unity or even dialectical relationship with eros, the universal quest for self-realization? Can selfless love coexist with self-regarding love (the classical ideal)?

The mystical tradition of the church has given a prominent role to eros, despite the fact that the New Testament speaks primarily of agape and not at all of eros. Origen came to the conclusion that agape and eros are identical, but the eros motif proved dominant in his theology, for love is essentially the desire for communion with God. Augustine's *caritas* proved to be the spiritual form of eros, but the agape motif is prominent in his concept of grace. Unlike Plato and Plotinus, Augustine maintained that we cannot make the upward ascent to God unless we are assisted by divine grace. While for Plato love (eros) is a mediator between God and humanity, for Plotinus and the Christian mystics who followed him God is eros in that he is engaged in the contemplation of his own perfection. Dionysius called God eros because "he is the one who in the whole world attracts eros to himself."[58] According to Maximus the Confessor, if we call God love, then God must also be eros, since eros is the perfect expression of love.[59]

Whereas the movement in agape is primarily downward and outward, eros is exclusively an upward movement, since its goal is union with God. Thomas à Kempis put it this way: "Love wishes to rise, and not to be held back by anything beneath. Love wishes to be free and apart from every worldly affection, lest its inner vision be hindered. . . . Love is born of God, and cannot find rest save in God above all created things."[60] In the New Testament view agape also includes an upward thrust, but this is sharing with God our joy over the gift of undeserved salvation, not the desire to possess the greatest good.

One of the problems in Christian mysticism was how a God devoid of passion and insensible to pain and suffering could still be described as love. John Scotus Erigena, who was firmly wedded to the Neoplatonic notion of a God who neither acts nor suffers, finally had to deny that God loves in any realistic sense. If we call God love, then this can only be a metaphorical way of speaking. Erigena defined love as "a laudable desire for that immateriality which surpasses all reason and under-standing."[61]

Although because of their Christian commitment the mystics encour-aged service to the lowly and despised of the world, they found it difficult to reconcile this theoretically with the eros that aspires to a perfection beyond this world. The love directed to one's neighbor was reinterpreted to indicate a love directed to the God reflected in a broken and torn humanity. We love not the sinner as such but the pearl of divine right-eousness resident within the sinner. Ernst Troeltsch, who drew on the mystical tradition, explained that love for other persons is in the last resort not love for others "but love for God which loves that in man which is divine and not the poor confused creature as such."[62]

The mystics did make a place for friendship *(philia)*, though friendship is not the unconditional love of agape that goes out to all people indis-criminately but a mutual love contingent on the response of the person loved. Similarly to eros, friendship proceeds out of need and seeks the fulfillment of something lacking within the self. According to Schleier-macher, who stands in the mystical–idealist tradition, "Every man most tenderly loves the person who seems to supply all that he lacks to form his own humanity."[63] Friendship, like eros, is egocentric, whereas agape is unmotivated in the sense that it is not based on personal need or on the value or merit of the one loved.

In his critique of process theology the Dominican theologian William Hill renders a real service to theology by underlining the gulf between agape and eros.[64] In his opinion eros is not selfish love but the love that has self-fulfillment as its underlying motive.[65] By contrast, agape "is a love unknown to men and women in any exploration of their own innate impulses to love, and becomes manifest only in the words and conduct of Jesus as God's self-revelation."[66] Eros in the Hellenistic sense is foreign to Christian experience and was imported into the church only to clarify the human capacity for love.[67] Hill can be faulted for failing to see that eros love was also used by many of the mystics to describe God's own love for himself and for humankind.

Paul Tillich is perhaps the most striking but by no means the only example in modern times of the attempt to synthesize eros and agape. For Tillich love is the desire for reunion with the infinite ground of all being. It is the return of the soul to the undivided unity with the source of all existence. If eros and agape cannot be united, then there can be no place for agape toward God.[68] But if we are already in communion with God through faith in Jesus Christ, we do not need to aspire to such communion but simply praise God for the gift of communion and manifest our gratefulness in lives of self-giving service.

Blessedness and Happiness

Another manifestation of the biblical–classical synthesis is the confounding of the biblical concept of blessedness and the Hellenistic notion of *eudaimonia*. As used by Plato and Aristotle, *eudaimonia* indicates perfect well-being demonstrated in the subordination of the passions to reason. *Eudaimonia* is self-realization through possession of the greatest good. Blessedness, as understood in Scripture, is the state of being favored by God and also of being at peace with God. One of the key words for "blessed" in the New Testament is *makarios,* which means being full of God, being filled with his love and radiance. This word has a mythological background, referring to the sublime contentment of the gods. It is interesting to note that Mary is called blessed in Luke 1:42 and 1:48. She is both uniquely favored and full of grace.[69] In Romans 4:8 Paul calls blessed those who know God's forgiveness. Blessedness is also closely related to *shalom,* the wholeness and peace that come through a right relationship with God and our neighbor.

The concept of *beatitudo* as it developed in Catholic theology signified an attempt to reconcile the Hellenistic and biblical notions of happiness. To be blessed or happy meant not simply to have a well-ordered soul but a deeply committed life. Blessedness is not so much the discovery of the idea of the Good as being sought and found by the living God. The happiness of the blessed is not simply attaining moral well-being but dwelling with God, possessing the highest good—eternal life with God. The highest happiness is not the contemplation of the good but the vision of God.[70]

While the theologians of the church always pointed to the higher happiness that lies beyond the attainment of earthly well-being, they accepted the egocentric motivation of classical humanism: our chief end is to gain true happiness. Peter Kreeft contends that because our greatest good is happiness, seeking our own happiness is therefore something praiseworthy.[71] But he avers that our true happiness is to be found not in worldly peace and security but in the beatitude of being united with God. As the Roman Catechism puts it, "Supreme and absolute happiness . . . consists in the possession of God; for what can he lack to consummate his happiness who possesses the God of all goodness and perfection?"[72]

In biblical religion the goal in life is not the attainment of happiness but service to the kingdom of God. By being willing to let go of our desire for happiness and security, we will find our true solace in the end (Mt

6:31-33; 10:39). The blessed are those who hunger and thirst for the righteousness of the kingdom (5:6), those who try to make peace between their neighbors without any thought of gaining anything in return (5:9). They are those who seek to live out their vocations with single-mindedness of devotion or purity in heart; such persons will eventually see God (5:8). They are those who mourn for their own sins and for the sins of others (5:4). They are those who are persecuted for the sake of bearing witness to Jesus Christ and his kingdom (5:10). They rejoice when people revile them for upholding the claims of the gospel, for great will be their reward in heaven (5:11-12). But their reward is not what motivates them to do good works; what motivates them is unconditional love for their neighbor and zeal for the faith. They let their light shine so that others may see their good works and give glory to the Father in heaven (5:14-16).

Entirely different is the understanding of blessedness in idealistic philosophy with its heritage in Platonism and Neoplatonism. According to Fichte, "Blessedness is to rest and remain in the One. Misery is to be dispersed into multiplicity and differentiation. Therefore the condition of becoming blessed is the withdrawal of our love from the Many back to the One."[73] But in the New Testament blessedness is to deny oneself and take up the cross and follow Christ into the grime and agony of the world (Mt 10:38; Lk 14:27). Blessedness lies in the imitation of God (Eph 5:1), who descended into the depths of worldly affliction out of compassion for the lost. Idealists like Fichte could also speak of the imitation of God, but their God exists in sublime detachment from the world, impassible and imperturbable.

Our hope is for eternal happiness, but our goal is holiness—being separated by God for service to the world. It is not the desire to "satisfy" our "instinctive craving for self-realization"[74] that spurs us to do works of mercy but the grace that instills in us a love for our fellow human beings for whom Christ died. The pathway to true happiness lies in discipleship under the cross, and the motivation is simply to give glory to God, surely not to accumulate merits for ourselves or to gain a higher place in the kingdom of heaven. We should even be willing to be damned for the glory of God (cf. Ex 32:32; Rom 9:3) if this is what God should demand, but this very willingness indicates the conquest of self through submission to the will of the Father in heaven. Although holy living will bring us many blessings, our aim is not to gain blessings but to make the high and holy God visible in our lives and knowable through our words. Holy living may very well involve the loss of peace and security as the world understands this. It may even entail brokenness and despair rather than emotional or psychic well-being, but this despair will always be accompanied by a joy that is not dependent on the circumstances of life, the joy of knowing that nothing can separate us from the love of Christ—not even death itself (Rom 8:39).

Grace and Merit

In their espousal of salvation by free grace, the theologians of the church had to battle against nomistic Judaism as well as Hellenism. While God's undeserved grace to sinners is a prominent theme in the Old Testament, the idea of merit looms much more significant in Rabbinic Judaism—the idea that we can earn our spiritual status before God by obeying the demands of the law.[75] In Hellenism the noblest person is the one "who has raised himself by his own merit to a higher station" (Cicero).[76] Aristotle taught that the way to become virtuous is by the practice of virtue. For the Stoics the way to wisdom is the way of self-mastery.

The classical world entertained a concept of grace, though this was not the personal favor of a living God toward repentant sinners (as in the Christian view) but "a supernatural potency, sometimes as a divine elixir poured out on the forms of natural life, sometimes as a light that gilds with lustre even the inanimate."[77] In Hellenistic Greek and in Philo grace was understood in a semiphysical sense, as a power detached from God lying behind the natural endowments of humanity.

The apologists and church fathers sought to bring together the classical and Judaic idea of merit and the Christian message of free grace. For Clement of Rome the Christian would not be able to attain to love or salvation without God's grace, yet grace is given only to those who keep the commandments of God.[78] In *The Shepherd of Hermas* "remission does not come immediately in answer to repentance, but only after the believer has humbled, punished, and tortured his soul, suffering many afflictions. Then when God sees that the heart is clean from evil deeds, He will heal."[79] Athanasius saw no reason to be afraid of hearing about virtue, "for it is not distant from us, nor does it stand external to us, but its realization lies in us, and the task is easy if only we shall will it."[80] The apostolic fathers transposed the gospel into a new law, and grace became God's assistance in our obedience rather than the act of redemption of humanity through the incarnation and the atoning work of Christ on the cross.

The synthesis between grace and merit became part of the mystical heritage of the church. For John Cassian, God is reluctant to confer his gifts "on one who is asleep or relaxed in sluggish ease" but looks for some effort on the part of the sinner to will the good.[81] If we really wish to please God, said Macarius, we ought first of all to force ourselves "to cultivate all the virtues which are commanded," even against our natural inclinations.[82] Isaac the Syrian was convinced that "humility even without efforts gains forgiveness for many trespasses; but without humility even efforts are vain and may lead to much harm."[83] According to Bonaventure, as soon as the soul has mastered purgation, illumination and perfective union, "it becomes holy, and its merits increase in the measure of its completion of them."[84] Jean-Pierre de Caussade concluded that while we cannot merit the prayer of recollection, we can dispose ourselves to receive this gift by removing obstacles to spiritual growth, for example, by purifying our conscience.[85]

Augustine boldly challenged the idea that we can induce God to give us grace by acts of contrition and obedience. Because of sin the human will has become seriously impaired and cannot on its own take even the smallest step toward salvation. In his controversy with Pelagius, who believed that through our natural free will we can open the door to communion with God, Augustine was adamant that we are hopelessly lost in sin until God's justifying grace is infused in us through faith in Jesus Christ. Yet Augustine also held that once grace is given to us we can then merit an increase of grace by doing works of virtue. Nevertheless, we are to regard our merits as gifts of God's grace, since we can do meritorious works only with the assistance of grace.

In his earlier writings Thomas Aquinas held that if sinners do what lies within their own power *(facere quod in se est),* they can merit God's grace *de congruo*—in accord with what is fitting. In his mature work, he maintained that fallen humanity cannot do anything meritorious apart from the free gift of God's grace.[86] Once having received grace, however, we can then merit future graces *de condigno*—in the sense of deserving God's blessings.[87] The Augustinian synthesis, adopted though modified by Thomas and other medieval theologians, was apparent in the Council of Trent, which affirmed that even before the grace of justification the human will can prepare itself to receive this grace, albeit never to the point of meriting it and not without God's prevenient help. Final salvation or the fulfillment of justification can be merited, however, since the Christian in the power of grace can do much to insure God's continued assistance.

It remained for the Protestant Reformers, Luther and Calvin, to reaffirm the biblical theme of salvation by grace alone *(sola gratia).*[88] In their view justification is exclusively a work of God on the human soul, and our task is simply to receive this gift in faith. But faith is not a theological virtue that can merit grace—it is an empty vessel waiting to be filled. Once justified we can do works that attest God's blessing upon us through the sanctifying power of the Holy Spirit, but these works can never merit salvation because they are always accompanied by the perverse inclinations of the heart that are countered by grace but not eradicated.

Whereas Augustine had conceived of justification as imparted righteousness, Luther and Calvin depicted it as imputed righteousness—accounted to us by virtue of Christ's perfect sacrifice on the cross, provided that we have faith. As Luther phrased it, "Our righteousness is not by the Law and good works but by the death and resurrection of Christ."[89] Free will does not need to be assisted by grace: it must be turned around by grace. Our salvation is a result of a liberated will, not the outcome of a cooperative endeavor between grace and natural free will. Augustine could describe the Christian as partly righteous and partly sinful insofar as the reborn person now has infused righteousness as his or her peculiar possession. Against this view Luther held that the Christian is altogether sinful and righteous at the same time: we are extrinsically righteous because the alien righteousness of Christ is imputed to us, and we are intrinsically sinful because sin continues to pervade all our thoughts and actions, though sin is no longer outside our control. Because Calvin believed that we can make real moral progress in the Christian life though we can never escape the presence of sin, his position seems to be that the earnest Christian is increasingly righteous and decreasingly sinful. Calvin is here closer to the Augustinian synthesis, but still ruling out any claim to merit or extraordinary virtue on the part of the saints of God.[90]

Closely related to the synthesis between grace and virtue was the blending of the Greek ideal of heroism and the New Testament ideal of sainthood. In the Hellenistic ethos the hero is the one who defies the gods by exceeding human limitations in order to perform some feat that will redound to the good of humanity. The saint, on the other hand, submits to the will of God and conquers the powers of darkness by faith and perseverance in the truth of the gospel. The hero is focused on the heights of humanity's possibilities; the saint is concerned to serve in the depths of humanity's afflictions. The hero manifests the classical virtues of courage, fortitude and justice; the saint manifests the Christian graces of faith, hope and love.

In Christian history the saints came to be identified with those who did extraordinary feats of asceticism rather than with the little flock of the fainthearted who simply trust in the grace of God (Lk 12:32). Eventually it was held that the saints with the assistance of grace could do works of supererogation, beyond what was required for their salvation, and these merits could be transferred to those less worthy at the discretion of the clerics of the church.

Protestantism too allowed the Hellenistic ideal of heroism to usurp the biblical call to discipleship under the cross. In both Pietism and liberalism the notion of Christian heroism, which summoned men and women to scale the heights of human virtue, preempted the saintly ideal of selfless service in virtual obscurity. The Congregationalist theologian Henry Ward Beecher, who combined evangelical and liberal currents, commended heroism as the sacrifice of oneself for a moral ideal. "It is . . . the sacrifice of our lower life for the sake of evincing our faith in our higher life. There is no such thing as heroism which runs from good to bad. Heroism must always run from the lower toward the higher."[91]

Heroism celebrates human virtue; sainthood witnesses to divine grace. Heroism calls people to achieve their maximum potential; sainthood asks that people simply do what is required of them by God, even if this means being content with leading lives of humdrum existence outside the limelight. Heroism has a natural affinity with a theology of merit; sainthood in the biblical sense can be truly appreciated only in a theology of grace.

Sin and Ignorance

The gulf between biblical and classical thought is particularly obvious in their divergent attitudes toward evil. In the biblical view evil is a surd in God's creation and is to be traced to a tragic misuse of creaturely freedom.[92] In the classical view evil has its source in the privation of being. The material world is regarded as a prison house of the spirit; the aim in life is to disengage ourselves from the passions of the flesh and to be reunited with the unchanging world of pure being. The way to overcome evil is through knowledge of our fall from being. Once we know the good, we will do it (Plato). In the biblical view ignorance is not the seat of our misery but a manifestation of the hardness of the human heart, which uses ignorance as an excuse for disobeying God's commands.

In Hellenistic philosophy the tragic flaw is variously described as ignorance, fleshly passion, fate and hubris. According to Plato, people do wrong when they follow their appetites and passions rather than their intellect. In the biblical view people deliberately choose to do wrong, and their appetites consequently become disordered. Augustine reflected the biblical emphasis when he contended that "it is by sin that we die, and not by death that we sin."[93] The Greek tragedians in their conception of hubris perhaps come closer to the biblical understanding, but hubris is not prideful exaltation so much as immoderation, exceeding limitations imposed on us by fate and thereby suffering nemesis or retribution. The tragic hero does not aspire to be god but to be superhuman, and so disrupts the moral order of the universe.

The impact of Hellenistic speculation on Christian thought has been considerable. For Gregory of Nyssa, because the divine nature is altogether impassible, "a man who is always entangled in passions is debarred from union with God."[94] Clement of Alexandria traced the plight of humanity primarily to "the weakness of matter" and "the random impulses of ignorance."[95] Justin Martyr associated evil with ignorance and error. A later mystic, the author of the *Theologia Germanica*, regarded sin as "nothing but a turning away on the part of the creature from the unchangeable Good toward the changeable."[96] In more recent times Albrecht Ritschl defined sin as ignorance with respect to its origin and selfishness with regard to its content.[97] In a more biblically oriented theology ignorance is simply a sign of our unbelief and stubbornness. It therefore needs to be expiated, for it is not excusable.

Perhaps more than any other theologian of our time, Reinhold Niebuhr has been alert to the misunderstandings of the idea of sin in Christian theology because of its heavy dependence on Hellenistic philosophy. According to Niebuhr the root of sin is neither a defect in human nature nor ignorance of our original relatedness to God but the willful misuse of our freedom. Sin should be understood as "a self-contradiction, made possible by the fact of [our] freedom but not following necessarily from it."[98] For Niebuhr, Adam is the paradigm of the human person standing at the abyss of unfreedom threatened by the anxiety of finitude. The dizziness of freedom creates the condition for sin, but it is not by itself sufficient to induce sin. Sin is inevitable but not necessary because there is nothing within our created nature that compels us to sin. Reflecting his Augustinian roots, Niebuhr sees a bias toward sin before the act of sin, though he seeks to maintain human responsibility for our implication in sin. He interprets the story of the fall in Genesis as symbolic of the human condition rather than as an event in past history. The question is whether this story symbolizes a passage from anxiety to prideful self-affirmation (as Niebuhr contends) or a passage from communion with God to a break in this communion (as Ellul contends).[99]

We need to steer clear of the opposite perils of Pelagianism and Manichaeism. Against the first we should recognize that we come into the world already inclined to evil because our wills are subject to the gravitational pull of what theologians call original sin. Against Manichaeism we must insist that the evil within us is not part of our nature but the outcome of deliberate human choice. We are responsible for sin because we assent to it, but we assent to it partly because we are predisposed in this direction by virtue of our solidarity with our first parents. We want to do what is ultimately injurious to us. The paradox of human responsibility for sin and sinful inevitability eludes human comprehension, but we need to affirm this paradox in the face of misunderstandings that either make humans victims of a predetermined fate or masters of their own destinies.

In Ephesians 4:18 the apostle claims that we are alienated from God because of our "ignorance" and "hardness of heart." It is made clear, however, that our ignorance is "the consequence of closed minds" (NJB). The only solution is to put off the old nature (which is not our physical flesh but our self-centered orientation) and put on the new nature (a God-centered orientation, Eph 4:22-24). Yet this is not a decision available to us when we are caught up in our contumacy and pride but a decision made inevitable when the grace of God breaks into our lives and moves our will to do the good revealed in God's moral law and even more in his incomparable act of redemption in Jesus Christ.

Prayer and Contemplation

The accommodation of Christian thought to the Hellenistic ethos is strikingly apparent in the area of spirituality. For the Neoplatonists prayer is meditation and contemplation directed to the infinite ground and source of being rather than petition to a personal God who is intimately involved in the concerns and trials of his human creatures. For Plotinus "the only way truly to pray is to approach alone the One who is Alone. To contemplate that One, we must withdraw into the inner soul, as into a temple, and be still."[100] This idea is also expressed by the Protestant mystic and hymn writer Gerhard Tersteegen: because "God is a tranquil Being, and abides in a tranquil eternity," therefore the human spirit must "become a tranquil and clear little pool, wherein the serene light of God can be mirrored."[101] By contrast, in the biblical view prayer is the pouring out of the soul to a God who hears and acts. Prayer is crying out to God in our anguish and being set free when he answers (Ps 118:5 NIV; cf. Ps 116:1-8).

In Platonism and Neoplatonism God is beyond images and concepts. He is also beyond names, and therefore to invoke him by a name could lead to idolatry. For Philo, a first-century Jewish philosopher heavily influenced by Platonism, the best way to pray is simply to praise God rather than to ask for things from God. The tradition of *hēsychia* or inner prayer in the Eastern church taught that one should "abstain from thoughts" as much as possible when engaged in prayer.[102] In the biblical or evangelical view prayer is not so much perpetual communion with God as lively conversation with God. It is not so much gazing on the beauty and wonder of God as struggling with God. It is not withdrawal from the world but active intercession for the world. While recognizing that the living God transcends human imaging and conceptualizing, the biblical Christian insists that God enters into images and concepts and remolds them. The Spirit of God does not take us beyond words but pours new meaning into our words. There can be no communication with God that is not at least partly conceptual. We are told to pray with "mind awake and thankful heart" (Col 4:2 NEB). By contrast, the mystics hold up the ideal of imageless prayer—prayer that consists in ecstatic awareness of the unconditional.

The mystical tradition of the church that effectively united biblical and Neoplatonic themes made an important place for silence in the life of prayer. Isaac of Nineveh advised, "If you love truth, be a lover of silence. Silence like the sunlight will illuminate you in God and will deliver you from the phantoms of ignorance. Silence will unite you to God himself."[103] Thomas Merton, whose spiritual writings have had a noticeable impact on both modern Catholic and Protestant spirituality, urged us to wait on the Word of God in silence, and when we are answered it is not so much by "a word that bursts into" our silence as by our silence itself "suddenly, inexplicably revealing itself" to us as "a word of great power, full of the voice of God."[104]

Although the tradition of biblical or prophetic religion also holds silence in high esteem, it never excludes the spoken Word of God. Silence is to be used not to take us beyond the Word (as in Neoplatonism) but to enable us to hear the Word. It is not silence itself but the Word that breaks into our silence that brings us true knowledge and freedom.

The Christian mystics did not draw on the Platonic and Neoplatonic traditions uncritically, and for the most part they tried to relate their insights to the Bible. Because biblical faith so clearly regards the petitionary element in prayer as fundamental even when it takes the form of adoration and thanksgiving, the mystics had to make room for petition and confession. Augustine allowed for petition for beginners in prayer, but when we make progress in the spiritual life petition can be set aside as we go on to meditation and contemplation. In the Eastern church the Jesus prayer, which became prominent from the sixth century onward, is petitionary in form, but its goal is the transcendence of words and concepts to a state of constant openness to the eternal.[105] According to John Tauler, one of the Rhineland mystics of the fourteenth century, verbal prayer is not the essence of prayer but its clothing. True prayer is being "totally subjected to God in loving desire."[106]

While the mystics advocated spiritual exercises to prepare the way for the prayer of the heart, they generally acknowledged that contemplation is a gift from God and cannot be induced by human effort alone. Macarius the Great declared, "To pray often is in our will, but to pray truly is a gift of grace."[107] This note is not likely to be found in the Hellenistic philosophical world. We should also recognize that the naive realistic prayer of biblical faith could reappear even when one was raised to the heights of contemplation.

In the twentieth century the mystical tradition, anchored as it is in the biblical–classical synthesis, is represented by Tillich, who defined prayer as "the spiritual longing of a finite being to return to its origin."[108] This definition mirrors the Neoplatonic vision of the reunion of the soul with the eternal through disentanglement from the bonds of the flesh.[109] Prayer in this tradition is discovering the divine will and conforming ourselves to it. By contrast, P. T. Forsyth could speak of prayer as wrestling with God, challenging God, seeking to change the will of God but also submitting to this will after we have made our needs and petitions known to him.[110]

One's understanding of prayer is indeed correlative with one's doctrine of God.[111] If we envisage a world of higher spirits (daemons) who are superior to mortals but limited in power, then prayer might well take the form of trying to cajole or control these higher beings (as in primitive religion). If we conceive of God as the architect of the universe or a providential ruler sublimely detached from the created order, then prayer would probably be limited to resignation and thanksgiving (as in idealistic philosophy). If God is envisaged as a supreme being who is infinite in power but also merciful and just, then prayer could assume prescribed forms that do not bend the will of God but discipline the human mind to be receptive to God's providential ordering and leading (as in ritualistic religion). If God is portrayed as the infinite ground and depth of all created being, the uncreated center of the soul, then prayer could assume the role of introspection, meditation and contemplation. If God is envisaged as the all-powerful and all-loving heavenly Father—infinitely concerned with the well-being of his sons and daughters—then prayer could express itself in heartfelt supplication, intercession and confession (as in biblical religion).

Justification and Deification

The theme of justification runs throughout Scripture, but it was articulated in a systematic way by Paul the apostle. For Paul justification or righteousness *(dikaiosynē)* was primarily a legal concept indicating a judicial act by which the status of the sinner is altered in the sight of God. Justification is a writ of pardon procured for us by Christ on the cross. Christ "was delivered over to death for our sins and was raised to life for our justification" (Rom 4:25 NIV). Through faith we are accounted righteous by virtue of the perfect righteousness of Christ, our representative and substitute. Justification is being covered by the righteousness of Christ, though we still need to struggle against actual sin in our daily existence. These notes were given prominence in the Protestant Reformation, which set forth the idea of extrinsic and forensic justification in opposition to the Catholic concept of infused grace whereby we are actually made righteous before God. In the Reformation view faith is an empty vessel that simply receives the gift of divine justification. In the Catholic view faith is a meritorious act that insures that the grace of justification will continue in our lives. Faith must also be completed by love to be wholly effective. In the Reformation view love is the fruit but not the ground of justifying grace.

The differences in soteriology between Protestants on the one hand and Catholics and Orthodox on the other must be partly attributed to the confounding of justification and deification *(theōsis)* in the early church. Deification or divinization (I use these terms synonymously) has its roots in Greek philosophy and the mystery religions. Plato held that we could be assimilated to God by the practice of virtue. For Philo divinization means that the soul at the time of death becomes incorporeal and is thereby raised above the constrictions of the material world.[112] Philo did not hold to any ultimate absorption into God as in the Platonic view. In Gnosticism we are deified through knowledge of the heavens.

The temptation among the fathers and doctors of the medieval church was to interpret salvation in terms of deification, thereby losing sight of the New Testament meaning of justification. For Origen salvation was the attainment of the gift of divinity, which is already mirrored in the depths of one's being. Athanasius, who was alert to the dangers of compromise with Greek thought, nevertheless consistently "took Christian salvation to mean deification."[113] Moreover, the evil that deification remedied "was not the sin of personal guilt deserving divine punishment but rather the sin of personal passion and finitude requiring divine cure."[114] In Dionysius deification became the climax of the process of purification, illumination and union. Maximus the Confessor, a century later, claimed that "we may be by grace all that God is by nature," though this is possible not through self-effort (as in Platonism) but through God's self-emptying in the incarnation.[115] Augustine had interpreted justification as primarily an inward purifying process and thereby in effect subsumed it under deification. In the developing Catholic view deification is fully realized only after death when those who believe enjoy the beatific vision of God. We become divinized by gaining "a perfect knowledge" of God.[116] Those who have this knowledge "assume a certain admirable and almost divine form, so as to seem gods rather than men."[117]

While Luther staunchly contended for the extrinsic and forensic character of justification, he nevertheless believed that God's justifying grace must make experiential contact with the sinful human being. Regeneration is therefore correlative with justification, and indeed might be regarded as the subjective pole of justification. For Calvin justification and regeneration constitute a twofold blessing. Christ for us must be held in tension with Christ in us. Although we are justified while we are still in our sins, God does not leave us in our sins but works purification within us, though this is a lifelong process.

The concept of deification reappeared in Luther's perception of the Christian as a bearer of divine love. When divine love is poured into us by the Holy Spirit we become "gods" and "saviors," since we are then literally conduits of divine energy. Luther was careful to specify that this deifying work is an act of God's grace and that we are only instruments. One critic nevertheless suggests that the distance between Plotinus and Luther may not be so great after all.[118]

One should note that the church fathers did not adopt the language of deification uncritically but were always quick to emphasize that the purifying work that brings us into the likeness of God rests fully on God's grace.[119] They also were firm in contending that deification does not mean absorption into God but transformation in the image of God. The fathers remind us that the final consummation is more than a restoration: it is an elevation in which we are made to radiate the glory and splendor of the living God. But deification can be stressed in such a way as to obscure the gospel of free, justifying grace that goes out not to the righteous but to sinners (cf. Mk 2:17; Lk 19:10; Rom 5:6-8; 1 Tim 1:15), and this note was sadly diminished among many of the Christian mystics.

Reconciliation and Reunion
Closely related is the polarity of reconciliation and reunion. Whereas biblical religion emphasizes the first, the Hellenistic tradition accentuates the second. Those who sought to bring together the two traditions in a higher synthesis were inclined to reinterpret reconciliation as the restoration of the soul to harmony with its divine core or center.

The Greek mystical tradition explained the plight of humanity as the fall of the soul from its heavenly origin. To be saved is to be reunited with the realm of pure being from which we have been severed. The Gnostics referred to the return of the soul as "the restoration to the Pleroma."[120]

The compromise with the classical worldview can be seen in Augustine, who affirmed both reconciliation to a holy God and the return of the soul to its divine origin. Augustine was enough of a biblical Christian to recognize that the cleft between God and humanity is made by sin, not finitude. Yet in describing the mystical ascent to God, he reintroduced the Neoplatonic, mystical theme of reunion and return: "We fear not that there shall be no place of return because we fell from it. However long we are away, our home falls not to ruin. It is your eternity."[121]

The Neoplatonic view has had an unmistakable impact on the history of both theology and philosophy in the West. The mystical philosopher Jan van Ruysbroeck believed that the "essential union of our spirit with God does not exist in itself, but it dwells in God, and it flows forth from God, and it depends upon God, and it returns to God as to its Eternal Origin. And in this wise it has never been, nor ever shall be, separated from God."[122] The Anabaptist theologian Hans Denck was speaking in Platonic terms when he longed to "cry aloud to the whole world that God, the all-highest, is in the deepest abyss within us and is waiting for us to return to Him."[123] The same is true of Angelus Silesius: "If you, my soul, return to what has been your source, You'll be what you have been, that which you honor and love."[124] And according to the French mystic Madame Guyon, "This spirit which went forth from God, returns back unto God; this being its sole end."[125] In Schelling's philosophy "history appears as the story of the return to God of fallen humanity, of man alienated from the true centre of his being."[126] For Hegel salvation is the return to our essential identity with God. While he made a prominent place for reconciliation, it meant no more than entering into a higher unity. I have already alluded to Tillich's commitment to the mystical idea of the outgoing and return of the soul to divinity.[127]

Once again Reinhold Niebuhr is helpful in his analysis of the havoc that the biblical-classical synthesis has wrought in theology and philosophy.

When Hellenic concepts of "being" are substituted for the idea of a "creator," and of the mystery of creation as the ontological anchor for the historic revelation, the emphasis is invariably shifted from the content of the revelation, which is, according to the Bible, the reconciliation between God and man on the divine initiative. The "Incarnation" becomes instead the revelation of the eternal in the temporal and the dramatic account of the reconciliation between God and man is obscured.[128]

The Hellenistic tradition has also penetrated the bastions of Christian orthodoxy, which sometimes depicts reconciliation as affecting humanity but not God.[129] God, who is impassible, unchangeable and the summit of all perfection, does not need to be reconciled, for he remains above the discord and defectiveness of human history. It is the fallen human creature that needs reconciliation, and this occurs when through repentance and faith we bring our wills into harmony with the unalterable will of the almighty God.

In the more authentically biblical view God is both the reconciler and the reconciled. He reconciles fallen humanity to himself by taking upon himself in the person of his Son our guilt and shame, thereby allowing us to enter into fellowship with him. Our conversion indicates not a return to an undivided unity with the ground of our being but a restoration to fellowship with God that was broken by sin. As God reconciles us to himself, so God in turn is reconciled with us, for the demands of his holy law have now been satisfied. His wrath against human perfidy and ignominy has been placated but only because his love broke through the intransigence of the human heart and enabled us to repent, believe and trust. Through faith and repentance sinners are reunited with their loving heavenly Father (as was the prodigal son), not by entering into the depths of themselves but by being set in a new relationship with the One from whom they have been estranged.[130]

Resurrection and Immortality

Whereas early Hebraic thought was agnostic concerning human immortality, Greek thought staunchly affirmed the inherent immortality of the soul, since the soul is connatural with God. What is immortal is not our bodily but our spiritual nature. Death brings about a separation of the soul from the body, thereby enabling the soul to return to its eternal home. The Platonic *meditatio mortis* ("meditation on death") stressed the baseness of the body and the hope of transcending the material world. Both Plato and Plotinus taught the preexistence as well as the reincarnation of the soul,[131] ideas that left an imprint on Origen and that reappear in the New Age movement.

In Hebraic thought the idea of a glorified body evolved slowly. Those who had extraordinary virtue were granted the privilege of being assumed body and soul into heaven (Enoch, Elijah). Two late Old Testament passages taught the resurrection of the body—Isaiah 26:19 and Daniel 12:2. At the time of Jesus the Pharisees strongly adhered to an eschatological resurrection of the body, whereas the Sadducees rejected the idea of resurrection as unscriptural.

In Hellenized Judaism the Greek idea of the immortality of the soul became increasingly prominent. The Wisdom of Solomon asserts that giving heed to the laws of wisdom brings "assurance of immortality, and immortality brings one near to God" (6:18, 19). The idea of the soul's preexistence is suggested in Wisdom of Solomon 8:19, 20: "I had received a good soul as my lot, or rather, being good, I had entered an undefiled body" (NJB).

In the New Testament immortality belongs to God alone (1 Tim 6:16), but we can participate in his immortality through faith in Christ. Paul argued for the deliverance of the body from corruption, not the deliverance of the soul from the body. The soul does not persist apart from the body, but the body is the vehicle of the soul, and at death we will be given a new body—glorious, incorruptible, immortal, although this transformation will not be completed until the second advent (1 Cor 15:20-23, 51-53; 1 Thess 4:14-17). We are promised a resurrection body like that of Jesus at his second coming (Phil 3:21).

For the Platonists and Neoplatonists death is the great liberator, for we are then free to return to our eternal origin. In the New Testament death is the last enemy, but we are assured of victory over death because of Christ's resurrection from the dead. Jesus approached his death with considerable distress, but he had the underlying assurance that he would never be abandoned by the Father. For fallen mortals death is the penalty for sin, but we can be confident that nothing can separate us from the love of Christ, even death (Rom 8:38–39). What is immortal is not the preexistent soul but our relationship to Jesus Christ, which is not temporary but eternal.

Among the church fathers and doctors of the medieval church and even the Reformers, the Greek idea of immortality was combined with the biblical view of resurrection. Origen held that the natural body will return to dust, but a spiritual body will be raised. For Tertullian the soul is "inherently immortal and death unnatural, yet the same body will be raised."[132] Basil urged his followers to "despise the flesh, for it passes away," and to be "solicitous for your soul which will never die."[133] According to Calvin the souls of the righteous departed are translated to an intermediate state where they wait to be clothed with the resurrected body on the last day.[134]

In the twentieth century Oscar Cullmann stressed the incongruity of the biblical and Greek ideas: "The *teaching* of the great philosophers Socrates and Plato can in no way be brought into consonance with that of the New Testament."[135] Cullmann rejected the idea of an intermediate state and spoke only of the resurrection of the body in the eschaton. However, he appears to have neglected many passages that suggest a present communion between the church triumphant and the church militant (cf. Mt 17:3; 27:52-53; Gal 4:26; Heb 12:1, 22-24; Rev 2:1; 8:3-4). There is no inherent immortality of the soul, but is there not an indissoluble relationship between Christ and his people that endures beyond death and that is corporeal as well as spiritual? Cullmann betrays the penchant in modern Protestantism to see fulfillment only at the end of history and not also above history in the fellowship of the blessed who have departed this life, a fellowship that extends to the pilgrim saints still struggling on earth.

• N I N E •

THE BIBLICAL –
MODERN
SYNTHESIS

Another type of faith is coming to challenge the old
traditional faith . . . in a Transcendent, lying above: it is a new faith,
a human faith in some Immanent, lying ahead.
PIERRE TEILHARD DE CHARDIN

It is not God who will save us—it is we who will save God,
by battling, by creating and by transmuting matter into spirit.
NIKOS KAZANTZAKIS

The world as a whole is a matter of chance.
CHARLES HARTSHORNE

Don't look up for God, look around. The finite is all there is.
LARRY RASMUSSEN

A God who is constantly changing is not a God whom we can worship:
He is a mythological being for whom we can only feel sorry.
EMIL BRUNNER

Whereas the biblical–classical synthesis was endemic to a significant part of Christian theology in the past, since the dawning of the Renaissance theologians have been tempted to accommodate the faith to modernity. A common distinction today is between modernity and postmodernity, and while it is true that universal laws and norms have been more or less shelved by an emergent historicism and relativism, the modern emphasis on autonomy and freedom persists.[1] One critic sees much of postmodernism "as *hyper-modern*" rather than "postmodern." "It is largely another attempt to carry out the old Enlightenment program of demolishing tradition, ritual, cult and historical narrative, except now without the Enlightenment's faith that reason and technology can assume their place. . . . Postmodernism is simply the Enlightenment once more with feeling—combining the worst excesses of rationalism and romanticism."[2]

While I shall use "modern" in the broad sense to include the upsurging relativism and nihilism, I acknowledge that modernity is entering a new phase. The new mood is biocentric (centered in life) rather than logo-centric (centered in abstract reasoning). Trust is now rooted in the will and passions more than in the intellect. Naturalism is supplanting idealism as the dominant worldview, though this is a vitalistic rather than a mechanistic naturalism.[3] Leading figures in this new spirituality include Friedrich von Schelling, G. W. F. Hegel, Friedrich Nietzsche, D. H. Lawrence, William James, Ralph Waldo Emerson, Nikos Kazantzakis, Carl Jung, Henri Bergson, Alfred North Whitehead, Charles Hartshorne, Samuel Alexander, Joseph Campbell and Pierre Teilhard de Chardin. Among theologians who show the impact of this spiritual revolution are Friedrich Schleiermacher, Paul Tillich, Henry Nelson Wieman, Ernst Troeltsch, Rudolf Bultmann, John Cobb, Bernard Meland, Peter Hodgson, Jay McDaniel, Rosemary Radford Ruether, Elisabeth Schüssler Fiorenza, Sallie McFague, Naomi Goldenberg, Morton Kelsey and Matthew Fox.

Authority and Truth

In the new worldview authority is rooted in the self (autonomy) rather than in an external creed or institution (heteronomy) or a transcendent God (theonomy). Here we see the continuity between the classical view and the modern view, but what makes the latter distinctive, especially in its postmodern phase, is the distrust of discursive reason and the celebration of imagination.

Truth is no longer an objective datum but "a creative discovery" (Nicolas Berdyaev).[4] It is a stream of experience that revivifies rather than an abstract concept that illuminates. Truth is what leads us into whole-ness and authenticity rather than a universal standard that reason sim-ply needs to acknowledge. Even a cursory reading of process theolo-gians will show how this new concept of truth has entered Christian thought and experience.

Whereas modernity in its idealistic strand located the source of truth in ideas that shape history, modernity in its naturalistic phase sees truth emerging in history. The goal is not to rise above nature and history but to penetrate more deeply into natural and empirical reality. It is in the vital impulses that animate nature that we make contact with ultimate reality.

One can speak of the rise of a new mysticism, a mysticism of the earth rather than a transcendental mysticism. Karl Rahner referred to "the mysticism of everyday life, the discovery of God in all things."[5] We find God not in a spiritual realm above nature and history but in the move-ment of nature and history. Moreover, nature is not dead or inert but alive and pulsating. The new worldview is naturalistic because it accepts only that reality that is accessible to sight and experience; and it is hylozoistic because it regards everything that exists as alive. It is also a form of panpsychism because it regards nature as filled with mind and purpose.

Miracles are not occasions when God intervenes in history but won-ders that excite the imagination yet are always open to natural expla-nation. Moreover, miracles can be induced through techniques rooted in human ingenuity. We create our own miracles as we build our own worlds and thereby shape the course of human history.

The naturalistic strand in modernity appeals to Heraclitus and the pre-Socratics more than to Plato and Aristotle.[6] It also manifests an affinity to Stoicism, which portrays God as physical as well as spiritual—as the animating fire of the universe. When Sallie McFague describes the world as God's body, she is simply expressing a kind of monism already anticipated in Stoicism.[7] Modernity is closer to Epicurus than to the Stoics, however, in its preference for an open universe governed by chance rather than a closed universe determined by fate.

God, Humanity and the World

In the new worldview God is essentially immanent rather than transcendent. He is neither a supernatural being above nature and history nor an eternal idea that guides the movement of history but the life force that moves history[8] or the infinite pulsating ground that sustains the world order. Because God is life and not merely being, God has a fate or destiny and is thereby subject to suffering and becoming (Schelling). Fichte, whose philosophy signified a union of idealistic and naturalistic strands, described God as "an endlessly self-developing life which always advances towards a higher self-realization in a never-ending stream of time."[9] For Schelling the creation is not an emanation (as in Neoplatonism) but a begetting or generation. The creative possibility actualizes itself by going out of itself.

God is not static, unmovable being but dynamic becoming. Nor is God the summation of all possibilities but the realization of ever new possibilities in an evolutionary ascent. Whereas the older philosophy and theology explained the world as a creation of God, the new view, already present in the Renaissance, envisages the world as the history of God (Hegel). The world is not a kind of emanation (from the perfect to the imperfect) but the product of evolution (the imperfect to the perfect). The process theologian Henry Nelson Wieman equated God with creativity. God cannot be a person because creativity has ontological priority over personality.[10]

Another hallmark of the modern worldview is finding darkness as well as light in God. The late Renaissance mystic Jakob Boehme saw within God a dynamic process with the potentiality for conflict. According to Tillich, who was greatly influenced by Boehme, God contains nonbeing within himself, which God continually resists and overcomes.[11] For Alan Watts, God is the "total energy-field of the universe, including both its positive and negative aspects, and in which every discernible part or process is a sort of microcosm or hologram."[12] Whitehead envisioned an ultimate harmony of opposites in which pain and joy would be fused in an all-encompassing superconsciousness.

The idea of a finite God is also a part of the modern worldview. God does not exist in sublime isolation, removed and detached from the universe, but God is the vital force of the universe struggling to realize itself. Nikos Kazantzakis informs us, "My God is not Almighty. He struggles, for he is in peril every moment. . . . He is defeated incessantly, but rises again, full of blood and earth, to throw himself into battle once more."[13] While Schleiermacher retained the idea of omnipotence, he regarded God as the Infinite in the finite, not as beyond or before the finite.[14] For Whitehead, God and humanity are co-creators, and this means that God depends partly on the efforts of humans for his growth in meaning; just as God helps to create humanity, so humanity in turn helps to create God.[15] In Jürgen Moltmann's theology God cannot overcome suffering, since "suffering itself is the *principle* which encompasses his very being and love."[16] To suggest that God must suffer in order to be God is to place a significant limitation on God's power as it has traditionally been understood.

It is fashionable in the new worldview to locate transcendence in the future. Nietzsche urged his contemporaries not only to remain true to the earth but also to look to the sky, the symbol of the future, and to build a new world.[17] In process philosophy and theology (Whitehead, Wieman, Meland, Cobb) both God and the world are moving toward infinity in an ever expanding and open universe. Moltmann and Pannenberg could describe God as "the power of the future." Bultmann depicted God as "the Uncertainty of the Future" and "the Darkness of the Future."[18]

In the modern worldview and in modern theology in general a panentheistic orientation supplants both pantheism and theism. In panentheism God and the world are considered inseparable but not identical. There is a relationship of mutual dependence rather than subordination. Theism has not been eclipsed, but it has been drastically modified. Peter Hodgson expresses the new mood when he describes the world as "a moment within the divine life." He speaks not of God's directing but rather of "God's 'luring' and 'shaping.' "[19] For the Russian existentialist Lev Shestov, God is not a superintelligence who directs the world according to eternal laws but "absolute freedom" who creates truths rather than embodies truths.[20]

The New Spirituality

The synthesis of religious tradition with modern romanticism and naturalism has produced a new spirituality, which one could describe as a post-Christian mysticism, though many of its votaries prefer to maintain a semblance of Christian identity. People of faith are no longer sheep sent out among wolves (Mt 10:16) but warriors who transmute matter into spirit. We are now called to discover the "tiger" within us and to develop our heroic potential to the fullest (Joseph Campbell). A tragic heroism takes the place of discipleship under the cross in which we simply follow rather than lead. In the new spirituality life is considered tragic because it entails loss and pain as well as growth and joy. Love is neither self-giving service (agape) nor desire for the highest good (eros) but the will to life and power *(epithymia).*

Faith too is drastically reinterpreted. No longer simple trust in the mercy of God, it is now a venture into the unknown without any guarantees of final success. With Kierkegaard, Shestov describes faith as "a mad struggle for possibility. For only possibility opens the way to salvation."[21] John Baillie illustrates how Christian theology is altered by this new understanding: "The faith which Jesus required of men was neither credal adherence nor mystic ecstasy so much as the faith that is in some sort native to every pure and gentle heart—the faith in man, the faith in life, the faith in the power of love, the faith in the Unseen Love of God."[22]

Prayer is no longer petition to a personal God (as in prophetic religion) nor contemplation of the beauty and wonder of God (as in the older mysticism) but reaching out to the possibilities of an unknown future. Neither the flight of the alone to the alone (Plotinus) nor the elevation of the mind to the realm of spirit (Christian mysticism), prayer is now descending into the depths where we make contact with the power of creative transformation.

Worship becomes an adventure into novelty (Whitehead) or a voyage of discovery (Gerald Heard). It is not a grateful response to God's mighty acts of creation and redemption but a celebration of human potentiality and dignity. Worship is not bowing in submission but marching in defiance of the fates and powers that conspire to bind humanity to outmoded rites and traditions.

The fall of humanity is interpreted as an upward ascent on the evolutionary path freeing humanity from servile dependence on a higher power. Or it is portrayed as the fall into patriarchy from an original harmony and unity between the sexes (Matthew Fox). We should speak not of the bondage of the will but only of the glorious opportunity to test the waters of life, to expand the human horizon to the utmost.

In contrast to the monism of Platonic tradition, the new age celebrates pluralism in which ultimate reality is pictured in terms of infinite complexity rather than cosmic uniformity (William James). Cultural pluralism is also vigorously affirmed, since it is duly recognized that every person is shaped by both biological inheritance and historical context. God's absoluteness is redefined as absolute relatedness (Hartshorne). Time is no longer the antithesis of eternity but the unfolding of an eternity yet to be fully realized.

The cross in the perspective of the new theology is "the symbol of shared sorrow" (Hartshorne) in which God takes our pain and transmutes it into an inner joy.[23] Life for Hartshorne and various other process philosophers is not a battle between two cosmic forces but an "art of creation, with God the eminent but not the sole creator."[24] In biblical faith, by contrast, life is a battleground between the forces of light and darkness, and the cross is a symbol of victory over the powers of darkness.

Multiculturalism is another facet of the new spirituality in which ethnic and racial distinctives are celebrated rather than sacrificed for a universal or cosmopolitan orientation that characterizes "the world come of age."[25] The universal norms of the Enlightenment are supplanted by the norms of tribal consciousness, as in Romanticism and its offshoots. For Schleiermacher the superiority of Christianity lies only in its freedom from exclusiveness rather than in its anchorage in an authoritative revelation of God in world history.[26]

Worldviews in Conflict

The drastic changes in Christian theology today are integrally related to the emergence of a new worldview that calls into question the supernaturalism of Christian tradition. The new worldview is naturalistic and vitalistic. God is an emergent reality rather than an impassible Absolute removed from nature and history. Whereas biblical faith speaks of creation and Neoplatonism of emanation, the new naturalism absolutizes evolution. God himself is caught up in the evolutionary process, though at the same time he gives shape to evolution by guiding emergent possibilities toward the ideals of truth, beauty and goodness (Whitehead).

While classical culture emphasized fate and biblical religion stressed providence, the modern view upholds chance.[27] Hartshorne could declare: "The world as a whole is a matter of chance."[28] Charles Darwin explained the evolutionary process as based on natural selection without any overarching purpose or design. One observer claims that Darwinism "replaces the old God with an even more incredible deity—omnipotent chance."[29] Nietzsche, the prophet of nihilism, cherished the "blessed security" that he discovered in the fact that all things prefer "*to dance* on the feet of chance."[30]

The three worldviews (classical, biblical, modern) also radically diverge on the problem of evil. In the classical view the tragic flaw is ignorance or fate. In the biblical view it is sin—understood as rebellion against a holy God. In the modern or postmodern view it is instability or imbalance. The discord in life is explained as resistance to change—intractability and obstinacy. For the prophets of biblical religion the plight of humanity lies in being overcome by an antigod force—the power of sin, death and the devil.

Salvation is understood in the classical or mystical view as reunion with the ground or source of all being. In the biblical view it is depicted as forgiveness or justification by a wholly righteous and ever-loving God. In the modern view it is liberation from everything that hinders humanity in its quest for a richer and fuller life.

The kingdom of God in classical Christian mysticism is a spiritual realm that towers above the material and temporal. In the biblical view the kingdom of God is God's new creation in the midst of human suffering, pain and death. In the modern view it is a new society that celebrates human freedom and dignity. We are the agents in the delivery of this kingdom (Hegel) rather than the elect people of God who inherit a kingdom prepared for us from the foundation of the world (cf. Col 1:13).

As Reinhold Niebuhr has amply documented, the idea of inevitable progress has indelibly shaped the understanding of moderns.[31] Even the prophet of postmodernism, Nietzsche, pinned his hopes on a new world order that would be inaugurated by a superhumanity manifesting greatness in soul and glorying in the will to power. The movement of history is not cyclical, as in the Greek view, but spiral. The evolutionary ascent includes an ascent of humanity from archaism and traditionalism to freedom from the taboos and constraints that have crippled society in the past.

The ethics of the classical view was the cultivation of virtue—courage, wisdom, prudence and justice. Biblical faith propounds an ethics of grace in which we receive not only commands from God but also the power to obey these commands. The ethics of the new spirituality is one of struggle for world mastery. It is an ethics of freedom—the freedom to explore and to create, not freedom for obedience (as in traditional Christian understanding).[32] It is the freedom "to follow one's bliss" (Joseph Campbell), not the freedom to serve the lowest and the poorest. Whereas Neoplatonism preached an ethics of self-denial and Christianity an ethics of self-giving love, the new worldview, rooted in the Renaissance and the Enlightenment, sounds the call to world affirmation and world conquest.

In classical mysticism life is to be perfected and transcended. In biblical Christianity it is to be enjoyed and redeemed. In the modern view it is to be celebrated and enhanced. Human life is not marred by the curse of original sin but is filled with infinite possibilities that need to be realized.

Pivotal symbols in the classical mystical view are the mountain of purgation, the ladder of love and the stairway of the saints. The biblical view associates the salvation experience with thunder and lightning, God's lightning striking on earth from the beyond. The modern view, especially in its Romanticist form, envisages divine power as a volcanic eruption from the depths of human existence.

Of course, not all theologians of the modern era have accommodated the faith to the new worldview. Many have sought to counter the new faith perspective by strenuously reaffirming the insights of biblical and prophetic religion. P. T. Forsyth voiced signal discomfort with modern naturalism and vitalism: "God's participation in man's affairs is much more than that of a fellow-sufferer on a divine scale, whose love can rise to a painless sympathy with pain. He not only perfectly understands our case and our problem, but He has morally, actively, finally solved it."[33]

On the Catholic side Peter Kreeft underscores the unique features of biblical religion:

As a man comes into a woman's body from without to impregnate her, God creates the universe from without, and performs miracles in it from without, and calls to Man from without, revealing Himself and His Law. He is not the Force, but the Face; not Earthspirit Rising, but the Heavenly Father descending; not the ideal construct of the human mind, but the Hound of Heaven.[34]

God and Futurity
A distinctive characteristic of the modern view is reading temporality

and futurity into the very nature of God. In contrast to the classical view, God is not removed from temporality but contains temporality within himself. This means that God as well as the world has a real future. For the Lutheran theologian Ted Peters God has "an unlimited future," and his eternity embraces a temporality with "a yet-open future."[35] God's eternity is not something already fully realized but is "gained through the victory of resurrection and transformation."[36]

Closely related is the question of whether God undergoes change—in any respect or in some respect. The new spirituality contends that God is affected by the world just as the world is affected by God (Whitehead, Hartshorne). For Norman Pittenger our deeds and prayers can actually enrich the life of God.[37] Somewhat surprisingly, Norman Geisler advances the view that while "God cannot grow essentially" he "can be enriched relationally. That is, He cannot attain any new attributes by interaction with the world, but He can and does acquire new relationships and activities."[38]

In my position God in himself does not look forward to any future, for the future is included in his all-encompassing vision. But God toward us, in his relationship to humanity, has a future in that he shares our hopes and fears and identifies with our sorrows and joys. Because God condescends to our level in Jesus Christ and becomes involved in our history, he awaits with us the outcome of this history, which he already knows but not as an experienced fact. God does not have a future in the sense that he could become someone other than he already is. But God does have a future in that he participates in our future. With Karl Barth I am not willing to speak of a cleft within the inner being of God, but I do acknowledge that God freely chooses to enter into a history of contradiction.

As mere mortals we cannot add to God's *intrinsic* glory, the splendor of his intertrinitarian life, but we can either accentuate or impede his *extrinsic* glory, the radiance of his presence in the world.[39] We can block the light of his glory from finding its goal in our lives, but we cannot extinguish this light (Jn 1:5). We can diminish the perception of God's glory through our contumacy and rebellion, but we cannot rob God of his glory. God will be glorified even in our damnation.

We cannot create glory for God, but we can reflect his glory and in this way carry forward his glory in the world. We can be conduits of his glory but not sources of his glory. We can please God, but we cannot enrich God, since God is the summit of all perfection.[40] Yet this perfection can be radiated and mirrored in the human creation.

God is not shut up within himself, impervious to the agonies and trials of his people. God delights in himself and in his works. He also agonizes over the pain and distress of his creation. God's delight in his work of creation as well as his determination to redeem the creation do not add to his glory but poignantly reveal his glory. God does not grow in value as he interacts with humanity, but his preeminent value is manifested in ever new ways. God does not gain new knowledge, for all things are held together in his comprehensive vision; yet his relationship to his creatures is constantly in flux depending on their reaction to his gracious initiative. The God of the Bible is a mighty river that is always flowing yet ever the same (cf. Ps 46:4-5; Rev 22:1-2).[41]

God is indeed immutable, but if he were only or wholly so he would be lifeless and distant. God is in movement, but if his very nature and disposition were subject to change he would be unstable and untrustworthy. A God who is unchangeable in both his inner being and purposes and yet who graciously enters the world of change in order to realize his purposes is alone worthy of worship and lifelong commitment.

God freely enters the world of human pain and despair; yet he is not brought down by despair but triumphs over it in the death and resurrection of his Son, Jesus Christ. Even while residing in the midst of our suffering and anguish, he rises above it and transforms it so that we can endure it and gain victory over it. Even while identifying with our afflictions, he foresees their overcoming in the dawning of the millennium and the coming of the new heaven and the new earth.

I find much to appreciate in the Dominican theologian William Hill, who argues that "the suffering which God truly experiences, and in the profoundest way, does not result in any qualitative change or diminution of God's nature."[42] It is possible to hold that God abides in impassible glory without subverting "the incredible truth of revelation that God wills to suffer in and through the suffering of his people."[43] Hill denies that God can suffer in his divinity but acknowledges that God "does suffer *in and through* the humanity he has made one with himself."[44] I prefer to say that God in himself does experience our pain and suffering, but this experience brings out the magnitude of his love rather than indicating a deficiency in his being. Our resistance to his love changes the way in which he loves but does not in the slightest alter his nature as the sublime unity of love and holiness.

God's knowledge encompasses the past, the present and the future, but he does not experience the future until it actually occurs. History is not a picture in the mind of God (as in idealistic philosophy) but a reality that God creates outside himself and with which he engages in real relations. God is unchangeable in his will and purpose, in the integrity of his being, but he freely wills to enter the world of change and decay in order to redeem and perfect it. His glory is not diminished by this action but instead illuminated and accentuated.[45] The whole world is the theater of his glory (Calvin), the field in which his salvation is enacted and completed. The world is not an obstacle to his glory but the means by which his glory becomes visible to all peoples.

In the classical view God is the transcendent ideal that moves all things toward itself by the magnetism of its beauty. In the spiritual perspective ascendant in modern times God is the infinite abyss, the bottomless depths, out of which all things emerge. In the biblical view God is the almighty Lord who creates and rules over all things. He is also the compassionate Savior who redeems fallen humankind and promises to transform the sinful world into a new creation that will redound to his glory and bring deliverance to his people.

In modern idealism God is "the Poet of the Universe" (Georgia Harkness),[46] and in modern naturalism God is "the growth of living connections of value in the universe" (Wieman).[47] In evangelical, biblical Christianity God is the creator and upholder of the universe, and though he presides over the growth of the universe, he is not part of the process. He is the Holy One before he is Cosmic Companion, he is Lord before he is Friend. God is not simply the source of ideals (such as truth, goodness and beauty) but a supernatural person, who not only inspires but also commands. He is not so much an organizing mind as a living Spirit who does not merely plan and construct but loves and embraces the world even as he judges it. The God of Abraham, Isaac and Jacob is not the God of the philosophers (Pascal), but a knowledge of the latter can help to clarify the former.

Appendix C: Open-View Theism

The attack on classical theism is coming not only from mainstream contemporary theology but also from the evangelical community. Calling themselves "open-view theists" or "freewill theists," five respected scholars in theology and philosophy of religion propose an alternative to classical theism that supposedly avoids the pitfalls of process theology. Their book, *The Openness of God,* is provocative and also timely, for it speaks directly to the unhappiness of many younger evangelical scholars with what they perceive to be the traditional picture of God— an almighty despot or domineering ruler.[48] This work will also find a ready hearing in the wider church, for ever since the Holocaust that devastated the Jewish people, it is indeed becoming more difficult to affirm a God who "has the whole world in his hands."[49]

The God of this distinctly modern brand of theism is still powerful but not all-powerful in that he is not in control of all happenings. He has immense knowledge but not complete knowledge, since he cannot know the future before it happens. He is not detached and self-sufficient (as in the older view) but open to the world and receptive to new experiences. Much of what they say resonates with what I call biblical theism, but there are important differences.

Open-view theists take strong exception to the traditional view that

God's omnipotence means that he determines all things. Omnipotence instead should be reconsidered as the power of God to deal with any new situation that arises (Clark Pinnock).[50] God does not impose his will on the human creation but directs the world toward beneficent ends by working with humanity. God challenges humans to heroic and noble acts that are consonant with his will and purpose for them. He works not so much by coercion as by persuasion, since he respects their dignity as genuinely free persons.

God has an ultimate goal for the world, but his progress toward this goal is dependent on how his creatures exercise their freedom. David Basinger can even say that "God voluntarily forfeits control over earthly affairs" when he allows humans to work out their destiny as free agents.[51] God does not always know "beforehand exactly how things *will* turn out in the future."[52] God does not even have "simple foreknowledge," for acts that spring from genuine freedom cannot be subsumed under a foreordained conceptual scheme.

While acknowledging that God is unchanging in his love and moral character, open-view theists hold that this does not apply to God's experience and knowledge. He is "impassible in nature but passible in his experience of the world."[53] He is "temporally everlasting" but not "timelessly eternal."[54] The future for both God and humanity is open, and this means that it is "not completely certain" (Pinnock).[55] The future will to a degree be shaped by our own decisions. "What God decides to do depends on what people decide to do" (Richard Rice).[56]

These scholars plot a middle way between process theism and classical theism, but they are closer in some respects to the first. Pinnock uses the language of process theology when he describes the world as "capable of genuine novelty, inexhaustible creativity, and real surprises."[57] God is located not "above and beyond history" but within the temporal passage, for that is where he makes contact with us. God's love "does not command but woos and transforms us" (Pinnock).[58] It is not God's aggressive action in the world but his receptivity to the world that characterizes the open-view position.[59] Both process theologians and open-view theologians allow for tragedy in the world—the real loss of positive good, the real thwarting of God's will. William Hasker's contention that God does not change in his "essential nature" but he does so in "his thoughts and deeds toward us and the rest of his creation"[60] reminds one of Whitehead's distinction between God's primordial nature, which is unchanging, and his consequent nature, in which he is affected by the changes in the world. Where open-view theists diverge from process theology is in their affirmation of a real, living God who existed before the creation of the world and who creates out of freedom, not necessity.[61]

The biblical side of these theologians is apparent in their strong endorsement of petitionary prayer. This kind of prayer, they say, makes sense only if God has not predetermined everything, if prayer requests can actually induce God to change his ways and even his intentions. At the same time, Basinger admits that petitionary prayer is limited because God will not ordinarily override the freedom of the person who is being prayed for, even if this expectation forms the content of one's prayer. He considers "prayers requesting even noncoercive divine influence in the lives of others" to be "very problematic."[62] I agree that petitionary prayer is logically undercut by classical theists because their God is basically unaffected by the changing world scene. But it is also undermined by open-view theists, since their God is not wholly sovereign over human activity. He guides us toward what is best for us, but he does not ensure that we will finally attain what is best. The emphasis is on what humans can do to create a better life and a better world. God assists us and guides us, but he allows us to determine our own destiny. "God does not as a general rule intervene in earthly affairs," and therefore "humanity bears primary responsibility for much of what occurs" (Basinger).[63] This is a far cry from the God of Calvin and Luther who is ever active in all things and events, steering everything toward a foreordained goal and purpose.

The core of the problem is the attempt to make the mystery of God's sovereign grace and providence compatible with the biblical affirmation of human responsibility and freedom.[64] Classical theism errs by reducing human freedom to a chimera and explaining everything in terms of divine causation, though a place is made for secondary causes in which humans play an instrumental role. Freewill theism errs by positing a freedom that cannot be reconciled with God's sovereignty over human affairs. The Bible does not present a rationally satisfying answer to this problem, but it does throw light upon God's dealings with humanity. God rules not by deterministic decree but by working in, through and sometimes over and against human decisions to bring about a world in keeping with his purposes. Predestination is not the foreordination of whatever comes to pass (as in scholastic Calvinism) but the mysterious working out of God's purposes in human history in conjunction with and through human actions, both good and evil. This position, which might be called biblical providentialism, differs qualitatively from both determinism and indeterminism because it seeks to hold together in paradoxical tension two seemingly contradictory realities—God's sovereign rule and human responsibility.[65]

The problem is exacerbated by the concept of freedom entertained by freewill theists. For them freedom is the ability to do good or evil, the opportunity to realize our potential as we see fit. But freedom as delineated in the New Testament is the subordination of human will and desire to God's will and plan. We are most free when we are in complete conformity to what God wills and desires. Christian freedom is freedom for obedience, not freedom "to do otherwise."[66] Freedom is finding one's true Master, not trying to be in command of one's destiny. There is no logical contradiction between this kind of freedom and God's predestinating will. To be sure, God allows us to fall into unfreedom, he permits us to abuse our freedom, but this too is within his overall plan and purpose for our lives and for the world. It seems that for the freewill theist both God and humanity are subject to a still higher force—anarchic or libertarian freedom, which is only another name for indeterminacy or chance.[67]

Open-view theism has far-reaching implications for the doctrine of salvation that are only intimated in the book under review. In classical evangelical theology we are saved by divine grace, not by human free will.[68] Basinger claims that the separation between God and humanity "can be bridged completely" only when we as humans "choose freely to enter into a relationship with God."[69] Yet the human dilemma is that the human will is not free but in bondage to powers beyond its control—sin, death and the devil. We cannot free ourselves through an exertion of the will but must be freed by the only power superior to sin and the devil—the grace of our Lord Jesus Christ. Christianity does not celebrate free will (as Augustine, Luther, Calvin and Barth all fully recognized), but instead upholds a liberated will—a will liberated by divine grace. The kingdom of God is not something we build or even help build but something we inherit as a free gift of God (cf. Mt 25:34; Lk 12:32; 1 Cor 6:9-10; Heb 6:12; Jas 2:5). Open-view theologians contend that our eternal destiny is determined by how we respond to the light within us.[70] The biblical Christian holds that our eternal destiny is determined by what God has already done for us in Jesus Christ and is doing now and will do through the power of the Holy Spirit to accomplish his purposes in Christ.

Open-view theists rightly object to the traditional conception of God as unrestrained power, but they too readily divorce the biblical concept of power from coercion. They fail to do justice to the biblical claim that an all-merciful God may sometimes employ coercive power to accomplish his purposes. One can only surmise that they would have considerable difficulty with Isaiah 25:1-2 (and many comparable passages): "I shall praise your name, for you have done wonderful things, long-planned, certain and sure. You have turned cities into heaps of ruin, fortified towns into rubble; every mansion in the cities is swept away, never to be rebuilt" (REB). The God of the Bible is not only a compassionate parent and suffering servant but also the warrior-king. He brings down one nation and exalts another. To be sure, his power is in the service of his love. He makes all things work together for good, but this remains a mystery that is not yet comprehensible to a suffering and tormented humanity. It does mean, however, that no evil is entirely gratuitous—without purpose or meaning (as in both process and open-view theology)—and that every evil can be overcome by God's all-conquering grace.[71]

The authors of this book have drawn attention to some neglected aspects of the biblical view of God: that God can make himself vulnerable and that God seeks to realize his purposes in and through the strivings of his people. Yet when they argue that God is still learning and that the coming of the kingdom finally depends on human cooperation, I must vigorously dissent. I can appreciate their emphasis that God is open to the yearnings and sufferings of humanity, but I wish to stress that this is an act of his freedom, not a necessary implication of his being (as in process thought).[72] God is also free *not* to be open to his creation, to withdraw his grace and to harden himself to the cries of his people (cf. 1 Sam 8:18; Is 1:15; Zech 7:13). While this second note is muted in this book if it appears at all, I think that a number of open-view theologians could concur with both of these affirmations, and just possibly through their probings a new and more biblical understanding of the being and action of God might result.

One of the strengths of freewill theists is their incisive critique of classical theism. They rightly show that traditional theology needs to be rethought if the biblical view of God is to be intelligible to searching people. But when they claim that their view is "superior" to all others in the sense that it is demonstrably the "most plausible, appealing conceptualization" of the complex relation between God and the world,[73] one must ask whether they have made logic or reason rather than biblical revelation the final criterion, despite their well-meaning attempts to relate their position to Scripture. Practical human wisdom and experience also weigh heavily in their deliberations, but experience can be very deceptive, and human wisdom is only relatively trustworthy because of both human sin and finitude.

In my view freewill theism is part of the legacy of evangelical rationalism, since it tries to make revealed mysteries too transparent.[74] At the same time, it provides a service to the wider church by reminding us that old truths need constant reformulation, that a too-heavy dependence on philosophy can be dangerous—even and especially in the task of clarifying the message of faith. But the dangers come not only from Hellenism; they also come from modern philosophies that envisage God as process rather than being, that see the universe as open rather than closed,[75] that regard human destiny as being in the hands of the creature rather than in the hands of the Creator. Modernity can be just as much of a snare as antiquity, and for many Christians today it is far more beguiling. Most freewill theists still belong to biblical Christianity, but they need to refurbish their position so that it becomes more thoroughly biblical and also more solidly evangelical.

EPIL○GUE

The theology I uphold is biblical-prophetic rather than modern, postmodern or premodern. I am not interested in returning to an earlier age, nor am I mesmerized by the present age; instead, I look forward to the coming of an entirely new order of existence—the kingdom of God—celebrated by people of faith in all ages. My critique of culture and religion is based on a culturally transcendent norm—divine revelation—mirrored primarily in the witness of the prophets and apostles in Scripture and secondarily in the witness of the fathers and doctors of the holy catholic church.

I think it unwise simply to attack or discard the signal contributions of either the mystical or rationalist traditions of the faith or to dismiss altogether what moderns and postmoderns are saying about God, life and the world. Their insights need to be integrated in a comprehensive vision of evangelical catholicity, which holds the Bible above both sacred tradition and the cultural ethos. A church that is truly catholic and evangelical will confront the world with the exclusive claims of the gospel, but it will also have a markedly inclusive thrust; its goal is to bring all peoples to a saving realization of what God has done for us and the whole world in Jesus Christ.

In addition to a penitential spirituality, which calls for repentance in the name of Christ, and a eucharistic spirituality, which celebrates the blessings of the sacrifice of Christ, I believe we need a spirituality of combativeness, which strives to bring down the entrenched forces of evil through the power of the Word and Spirit. Here the pivotal metaphor is neither the mountain of purgation (as in the mystical-medieval view) nor the mountain of evolution (as in the modern view) but the sword of the Spirit—the Word of God—by which we cast out devils (Eph 6:17). We are called not to be *heroes,* who strain the limits of human capacity in realizing a potential for greatness, but *saints*, who conquer through the word of the cross uttered in the power of the Spirit.

A catholic evangelical spirituality will espouse the living God of biblical-prophetic tradition rather than either the God of radical immanence (as in modern pantheism and panentheism) or the God of remote transcendence (as in Platonism and Neoplatonism). God is the initiator of change without himself being subject to change. He is the sole Creator without himself being in any way part of the creation. The God of Greek philosophy *cannot* change; the God of modern spirituality *must* change; the God of biblical religion *may* change, if he wills—not in the integrity of his being but in his interaction with his human creation.

Divine perfection in the biblical view lies in the ultimacy of his love rather than in the infinity of his being or the absoluteness of his power. As a God of unsurpassable love he is both changing and unchanging. His love is constant in its purpose and fidelity but ever new in its responsiveness to human need and petition.

The God of biblical faith is also a God of holiness. He does not overlook sin but abhors and condemns it. Yet in his gracious mercy and compassion he enters into our sinful world and takes the pain and guilt of our sin upon himself in the life, death and resurrection of his Son, Jesus Christ. He forgives, not because he is lenient or nonjudgmental but because he has dealt with the sin problem once for all in the atoning sacrifice of Jesus Christ. He has taken the retribution that sin carries with it upon himself through an act of love that at once satisfies the demands of his holiness and goes beyond these demands by not only remitting our sin but adopting us into his kingdom as his sons and daughters.

God is almighty, all holy and all compassionate at the same time. His power is demonstrated in his self-sacrificing love. His love is triumphant because it conquers even in its forbearance, it overcomes even when it relents. His holiness is manifested in his grace that embraces sinners but also slays those who persist in sin. This God of power, wisdom, holiness and love is the only true God, and it is this God alone who answers the yearnings and strivings of lost and broken human beings who need not only meaning and purpose in their lives but also, and above all, forgiveness and healing.

God can enter into fellowship with his subjects because he already exists as a fellowship of love within himself—as Father, Son and Holy Spirit. We cannot assume a dialectic in God in the sense of questioning and resolution of conflict. But we can presuppose a dialogue within the Godhead, which expresses the perfection of unity and harmony. The God of the Bible is not an abstract principle but a concrete absolute who is both personal and interpersonal. We can worship this God because of the majesty of his glory. We can love this God because he has chosen to meet us on our level and enter into personal relations with us. May we bow before God the Holy Trinity and acknowledge him as Savior and Lord of the universe—now and forever.

Notes

Preface

[1]See my further discussion on pp. 241-42. Postmodernism can paradoxically take the form of both a secular nihilism that cuts loose from all tradition and a romanticist return to the primal traditions that have shaped human culture from the beginning. It signals both the death of God and the rebirth of the gods.

[2]For a helpful discussion of both the continuity and discontinuity between modernity and postmodernity, see David F. Wells, *No Place for Truth: Or, Whatever Happened to Evangelical Theology?* (Grand Rapids: Eerdmans, 1993), pp. 60-67.

[3]I find some things in common with Lutheran clergyman Richard H. Bliese in his "Bonhoeffer and Modernity," *Lutheran Forum* 27, no. 3 (1993):24-27. He contends that biblical Christians will be both for and against modernity in that they will see the hand of God at work in cultural upheavals but also human hubris and rebellion that must be countered by a renewal of faith in the living God. His view that Bonhoeffer favored a reconciliation between Christianity and secularism is debatable.

[4]For my fuller discussion, see pp. 254-60, 311-13.

Chapter 1: Introduction

[1]Friedrich Schleiermacher, *On Religion: Speeches to Its Cultured Despisers,* trans. John Oman, introduction by Rudolf Otto (New York: Harper & Row, 1958), p. 237.

[2]See Satprem, "Oneness and the Teaching of Sri Aurobindo," in *What Is Enlightenment?* ed. John White (Los Angeles: Jeremy P. Tarcher, 1984), pp. 111-12.

[3]See Gordon Kaufman, *In Face of Mystery* (Cambridge: Harvard University Press, 1993), pp. 3-31, 322-40, 445-61.

[4]See Henri Bergson, *Creative Evolution,* trans. Arthur Mitchell (New York: Henry Holt, 1911), p. 248.

[5]Jürgen Moltmann, *The Trinity and the Kingdom,* trans. Margaret Kohl (San Francisco: Harper & Row, 1981), pp. 10-11, 164-65. Cf. Jürgen Moltmann, *The Spirit of Life,* trans. Margaret Kohl (Minneapolis: Fortress, 1992), pp. 272-73.

[6]Moltmann, *The Trinity and the Kingdom,* p. 197.

[7]Those who stand closer to Alfred North Whitehead stress the distinction between God in his primordial nature and the world of concrete actuality. But even for Whitehead God has no real existence apart from his participation in the ongoingness of nature and history.

[8] *The Empirical Theology of Henry Nelson Wieman,* ed. Robert W. Bretall (New York: Macmillan, 1963), p. 281.

[9] Pierre Teilhard de Chardin, *Science and Christ,* trans. René Hague (New York: Harper & Row, 1968), p. 180.

[10] See Charles Hartshorne, *Omnipotence and Other Theological Mistakes* (Albany: State University of New York Press, 1984), pp. 122-23.

[11] See John B. Cobb Jr., *God and the World* (Philadelphia: Westminster Press, 1969), p. 77.

[12] See Yong Wha Na, "A Theological Assessment of Korean Minjung Theology," *Concordia Journal* 14, no. 2 (1988):144. Also see David L. Smith, *A Handbook of Contemporary Theology* (Wheaton, Ill.: Victor Books, 1992), pp. 218-22.

[13] See Maxine Negri, "Age-Old Problems of the New Age Movement," *The Humanist* 48, no. 2 (1988):23-24.

[14] Jay B. McDaniel, *Earth, Sky, Gods & Mortals: Developing an Ecological Spirituality* (Mystic, Conn.: Twenty-Third Publications, 1990), p. 41.

[15] Ibid., p. 43.

[16] Matthew Fox, *Original Blessing* (Santa Fe, N.M.: Bear, 1983), p. 161.

[17] Meinrad Craighead, "Immanent Mother," in *The Feminist Mystic,* ed. Mary E. Giles (New York: Crossroad, 1982), p. 79.

[18] Hans Küng, *On Being A Christian,* trans. Edward Quinn (New York: Doubleday, 1976), p. 305.

[19] See Hans Küng, *Does God Exist?* trans. Edward Quinn (New York: Doubleday, 1980), pp. 129-30, 136, 166, 602.

[20] Paul Tillich, *Perspectives on 19th and 20th Century Protestant Theology,* ed. Carl E. Braaten (New York: Harper & Row, 1967), p. 192.

[21] Ibid.

[22] For Tillich's indebtedness to Platonism and Neoplatonism, see Adrian Thatcher, *The Ontology of Paul Tillich* (Oxford: Oxford University Press, 1978).

[23] Brian Wren, "Bring Many Names," in his *Bring Many Names* (Carol Stream, Ill.: Hope, 1989), p. 9.

[24] Tillich would undoubtedly take strong exception to this hymn, since he was insistent that being is not subordinated to becoming but vice versa. "To speak of a 'becoming' God disrupts the balance between dynamics and form and subjects God to a process which has the character of a fate or which is completely open to the future and has the character of an absolute accident." Paul Tillich, *Systematic Theology* (Chicago: University of Chicago Press, 1951), 1:247.

[25] Emil Brunner, *The Word and the World* (Lexington, Ky.: American Theological Library Association, 1965), p. 26.

[26] For a contemporary defense of classical theism, see H. P. Owen, *Concepts of Deity* (New York: Herder & Herder, 1971), and *Christian Theism* (Edinburgh:

T. & T. Clark, 1984). Also see Gerald Bray, *The Doctrine of God* (Downers Grove, Ill.: InterVarsity Press, 1993).

27Hegel, who is commonly regarded as an absolute idealist, is probably closer to panentheism than to pantheism. See Küng, *Does God Exist?* pp. 129-69, 182-86. Mary Baker Eddy, the founder of Christian Science, propounded a form of absolute idealism that more nearly approaches pantheism. See Charles S. Braden, *These Also Believe* (New York: Macmillan, 1949), pp. 189-209.

28According to Jantzen, citing Tillich: "Pantheism is the doctrine that God is the substance or essence of all things, not the meaningless assertion that God is the totality of all things." She includes among her mentors Meister Eckhart, Jakob Boehme and Spinoza. Grace Jantzen, *God's World, God's Body* (Philadelphia: Westminster Press, 1984). See esp. pp. 145-50. The process philosopher John R. Wilcox comes close to pantheism in "A Monistic Interpretation of Whitehead's Creativity," *Process Studies* 20, no. 3 (1991):162-74.

29Moltmann, *The Trinity and the Kingdom*, pp. 164-65. Moltmann upholds the ideal of "immanent transcendence"—"God in all things." In this perspective the adoration of God involves the veneration of nature, for divinity suffuses the whole of reality. Moltmann's shift toward panentheism is especially noticeable in his *Spirit of Life* (see pp. 31-38), though he only rarely uses the term *panentheism* to describe his position. While freely acknowledging an affinity to Whitehead and process philosophy (cf. *The Trinity and the Kingdom,* pp. 249-50; and *Spirit of Life,* p. 33), he sometimes expresses dissatisfaction with the process view. See Jürgen Moltmann, *God in Creation,* trans. Margaret Kohl (San Francisco: Harper & Row, 1985), pp. 78-79. Moltmann's theology owes far more to Hegelian than to Whiteheadian panentheism.

30Moltmann, *The Trinity and the Kingdom,* p. 53.

31T. Z. Lavine, *From Socrates to Sartre: The Philosophic Quest* (New York: Bantam, 1984), p. 117.

32Biblical religion also regards God as beyond the grasp of the human intellect and the reach of the senses but insists at the same time that God descends into the horizon of human meaning and experience, enabling us to apprehend what was hitherto hidden from us.

33Matthew Fox, ed., *Breakthrough: Meister Eckhart's Creation Spirituality in New Translation* (New York: Doubleday, 1980), p. 108.

34Ralph Waldo Emerson, *Works* (Boston: Jefferson, n.d.), 1:286.

35Emil Brunner, *The Christian Doctrine of God,* trans. Olive Wyon (1950; reprint, Philadelphia: Westminster Press, 1974), p. 148.

36Moltmann, *The Trinity and the Kingdom,* p. 164.

37Ibid., p. 71.

38Anna Case-Winters, *God's Power: Traditional Understandings and Contemporary Challenges* (Louisville: Westminster/John Knox Press, 1990), p. 195.

39Hartshorne, *Omnipotence and Other Theological Mistakes,* p. 58.

40Joseph Campbell, *The Power of Myth* (New York: Doubleday, 1991), p. 99.

41See my discussion in Donald G. Bloesch, *A Theology of Word and Spirit* (Downers Grove, Ill.: InterVarsity Press, 1992), pp. 85-94.

42Gordon D. Kaufman, "Doing Theology from a Liberal Christian Point of View," in *Doing Theology in Today's World,* ed. John D. Woodbridge and Thomas Edward McComiskey (Grand Rapids: Zondervan, 1991), p. 410.

43John E. Thiel, *Imagination and Authority* (Minneapolis: Fortress, 1991), p. 26. Thiel says that he is "committed to the broad, theological assumptions of the romantic paradigm."

44See Garrett Green, *Imagining God: Theology and the Religious Imagination* (San Francisco: Harper & Row, 1989), pp. 5, 28-40.

45Susan Thistlethwaite in *The Chicago Theological Seminary Catalog for Prospective Students* (Chicago: Chicago Theological Seminary, 1992), p. 35.

46Schubert M. Ogden, "Doing Theology Today," in *Doing Theology in Today's World,* ed. Woodbridge and McComiskey, p. 434.

47Jean-Luc Marion, *God Without Being,* trans. Thomas A. Carlson (Chicago: University of Chicago Press, 1991). See esp. pp. 1-24. Marion describes himself as postmodern and acknowledges his indebtedness to Jacques Derrida (p. xxi). At the same time Marion is radically Christian, holding that divine revelation can be the only valid basis for a theology worthy of its name. (See David Tracy's foreword, esp. p. xi.) Marion seeks to understand being in terms of God's reality as unconditional love rather than God's reality in terms of the metaphysical concept of being, and here I find much to appreciate. But Marion goes too far in breaking all ties between divine revelation and metaphysics. He readily grants that there is an affinity between his position and the Christian Platonist tradition, which includes Dionysius the Pseudo-Areopagite and Bonaventure.

48The message of faith must be positively related to ontology, but we must not allow ontology to determine the shape and content of this message. The gospel cannot be correlated with ontology, nor dare we build on ontology in order to reach the cultured despisers of religion. Ontological concepts can, however, be brought into the service of the gospel; in this new role they are transformed into metaphors that illumine faith but do not divest faith of its mystery.

49See chap. 2, n. 73.

Chapter 2: Theology's Attempt to Define God

1Despite his emphasis on the practical over the metaphysical, H. Richard Niebuhr in *Radical Monotheism and Western Culture* (New York: Harper & Row, 1960) betrays his dependence on idealist philosophy when he defines God as "the universe of being," "the realm of being" and "the principle of being." See pp. 33, 89.

[2]See Eric L. Mascall, *Existence and Analogy* (London: Longmans, Green, 1949), p. 52.

[3]John Macquarrie, *Thinking About God* (New York: Harper & Row, 1975), p. 106.

[4]Karl Barth, *Church Dogmatics*, trans. T. H. L. Parker et al., ed. G. W. Bromiley and T. F. Torrance (Edinburgh: T. & T. Clark, 1957), 2(1): 268.

[5]See Arthur C. Cochrane, *The Existentialists and God* (Philadelphia: Westminster Press, 1956), p. 122. Cf. Barth, *Church Dogmatics*, 2(1):306.

[6]Cochrane, *Existentialists and God*, p. 122.

[7]Emil Brunner, *The Christian Doctrine of God*, trans. Olive Wyon (1950; reprint, Philadelphia: Westminster Press, 1974), p. 145.

[8]See Barth, *Church Dogmatics*, 2(1):264.

[9]See Karl Barth, *The Göttingen Dogmatics: Instruction in the Christian Religion*, ed. Hannelotte Reiffen, trans. Geoffrey W. Bromiley (Grand Rapids: Eerdmans, 1991), 1:372.

[10]Ibid.

[11]See my discussion in Donald G. Bloesch, *A Theology of Word and Spirit* (Downers Grove, Ill.: InterVarsity Press, 1992), pp. 61-66.

[12]Thomas affirmed that while faith brings deeper insight into the mystery of the being of God, it falls drastically short of comprehending this mystery. One sympathetic scholar gives this interpretation of Thomas: "Theology, when it treats of God, can no more go beyond the oscillation of analogical knowledge between likeness and unlikeness than can pure metaphysics. Nor can any theologian explain definitively the nature of God as it is in itself, and therefore it is impossible to define what God is." Per Erik Persson, *Sacra Doctrina: Reason and Revelation in Aquinas*, trans. Ross Mackenzie (Philadelphia: Fortress, 1970), p. 270.

[13]Barth has these searing comments on the older Protestant definitions of God: "They show remarkably little concern for the . . . element . . . of personality. God is eternal mind for Melanchthon, infinite spiritual essence for Calov, Quenstedt, and König, self-subsistent spiritual being or independent spirit for Hollaz and Baier, independent essence for the Reformed Alsted. . . . We have to seek the personal element here in terms like 'mind' and 'spirit.' It was overlooked—unwittingly of course—that a term like 'spirit' does not necessarily carry with it the concept of personality." *Göttingen Dogmatics*, 1:373.

[14]Eberhard Jüngel, "Toward the Heart of the Matter" (trans. Paul E. Capetz), *Christian Century* 108, no. 7 (1991):232.

[15]Ibid., p. 233.

[16]According to Copleston, Heraclitus postulated the unity of One existing in the many, a concrete universal rather than a world composed only of particulars.

Frederick Copleston, *A History of Philosophy* (reprint, New York: Doubleday, 1985) 1:38–46.

[17]Karl Barth, *Protestant Thought: From Rousseau to Ritschl,* trans. Brian Cozens (New York: Harper & Row, 1959), p. 283.

[18]Thomas F. Torrance, *The Ground and Grammar of Theology* (Charlottesville: University Press of Virginia, 1980), p. 153.

[19]Quoted by Copleston, *History of Philosophy,* 7:81.

[20]Paul Tillich, *Systematic Theology* (Chicago: University of Chicago Press, 1951), 1:246. Tillich interprets *actus purus* to mean static being. But for Thomas Aquinas (according to Gilson) it means Pure Act as "the ceaselessly overflowing source of its effects." Étienne Gilson, *Being and Some Philosophers,* 2d ed. (Toronto: Pontifical Institute of Mediaeval Studies, 1952), p. 185.

[21]See Eberhard Jüngel, *The Doctrine of the Trinity: God's Being Is in Becoming,* trans. Horton Harris (Grand Rapids: Eerdmans, 1976), p. vii.

[22]Plato, *The Republic,* trans. B. Jowett (New York: Modern Library, n.d.), 6.509.

[23]The transcendence of the One over the Good was especially emphasized by Iamblichus of the Syrian school of Neoplatonism. See Copleston, *History of Philosophy,* 1:476.

[24]See Christopher Stead, *Divine Substance* (Oxford: Clarendon Press, 1977), p. 168.

[25]See Tillich, *Systematic Theology,* 1:237.

[26]Eberhard Jüngel, *God as the Mystery of the World,* trans. Darrell L. Guder (Grand Rapids: Eerdmans, 1983), p. 381.

[27]A God whose essence is to create *must* create, whereas the God of the Bible may create if he chooses. See the discussion in Étienne Gilson, *God and Philosophy* (New Haven: Yale University Press, 1941), pp. 86–89. With Descartes, "Instead of the self-sufficient and self-knowing Being of Thomas Aquinas, we now have a self-causing energy of existence" (pp. 86–87).

[28]See Augustine, *The Confessions of St. Augustine,* trans. and ed. John K. Ryan (New York: Doubleday Image, 1960), 13.37.52, p. 369.

[29]Heinrich Heppe, *Reformed Dogmatics,* ed. Ernst Bizer, trans. G. T. Thomson (London: Allen & Unwin, 1950), p. 57.

[30]Ibid., p. 58.

[31]Ibid., p. 57.

[32]Heinrich Schmid, *The Doctrinal Theology of the Evangelical Lutheran Church,* 3d ed., revised (Minneapolis: Augsburg, 1961), p. 117.

[33]Cochrane, *Existentialists and God,* p. 151.

[34]Friedrich Schleiermacher, *The Christian Faith,* ed. H. R. Mackintosh and J. S. Stewart (New York: Harper & Row, 1963), p. 194.

[35]Heppe, *Reformed Dogmatics,* p. 61.

[36]Ibid., pp. 63, 68.

37See Schmid, *Doctrinal Theology*, pp. 118–19.

38See Anders Nygren, *Agape and Eros,* trans. Philip S. Watson (Philadelphia: Westminster Press, 1953).

39Jüngel can say: "God is . . . the radiant event of love itself" (*God as the Mystery*, p. 327). I prefer to say that God is preeminently love but not exclusively love.

40For a penetrating critique of Ritschl, see H. R. Mackintosh, *Types of Modern Theology* (London: Nisbet, 1937), pp. 138–80.

41 *The Book of Confessions* (Louisville: Office of the General Assembly, Presbyterian Church U.S.A., 1991), 7.004.

42Cochrane, *Existentialists and God*, p. 120.

43Adrio König, *Here Am I!* (Grand Rapids: Eerdmans, 1982), p. 64.

44Carl F. H. Henry, *God, Revelation and Authority* (Waco, Tex.: Word, 1976), 2:179.

45Thomas Hopko, "Apophatic Theology and the Naming of God in Eastern Orthodox Tradition," in *Speaking the Christian God,* ed. Alvin F. Kimel Jr. (Grand Rapids: Eerdmans, 1992), p. 160.

46The God of the Bible, to be sure, is more than simply the summation of all value (Aristotle's god was this): he is also the creator of value. He gives value to the world in the form of outgoing love. His value is not dependent on what the world can give him.

47Arthur O. Lovejoy, *The Great Chain of Being* (1936; reprint, Cambridge: Harvard University Press, 1976), p. 52.

48Ibid., pp. 49–55.

49Ibid., p. 74.

50Ibid., pp. 73–79.

51Ibid., pp. 165–82. See esp. 172.

52Alfred North Whitehead, *Science and the Modern World* (New York: Macmillan, 1954), p. 257.

53See William James, *The Varieties of Religious Experience* (Cambridge: Harvard University Press, 1985); *The Will to Believe* (Cambridge: Harvard University Press, 1979); and *Pragmatism* (Buffalo, N.Y.: Prometheus, 1990).

54Barth, *Church Dogmatics,* 2(1):499.

55Ibid., p. 370.

56Ibid., pp. 301, 307, 343, 352.

57Copleston, *History of Philosophy,* 4:200.

58See James Daane, *The Freedom of God* (Grand Rapids: Eerdmans, 1973). See esp. 152–205.

59König, *Here Am I!* p. 219.

60Cochrane, *Existentialists and God,* p. 117.

61Ibid.

62Tillich, *Systematic Theology,* 1:236–37. Cf. Tillich, *The Protestant Era,* trans.

and ed. James Luther Adams (Chicago: University of Chicago Press, 1948), p. 82.

[63]Søren Kierkegaard, *Philosophical Fragments,* trans. David F. Swenson and Howard V. Hong, 2d ed. (Princeton: Princeton University Press, 1962), p. 94.

[64]Søren Kierkegaard, *Eighteen Upbuilding Discourses,* ed. and trans. Howard V. Hong and Edna H. Hong (Princeton: Princeton University Press, 1990), p. 393.

[65]See Barth, *Church Dogmatics,* 2(1):490.

[66]Ibid., p. 608.

[67]Ibid., p. 617.

[68]For my further discussion, see pp. 86–87.

[69]Barth, *Church Dogmatics,* 2(1):611.

[70]Ibid., p. 610.

[71]For my further discussion, see pp. 85–87.

[72]Barth, *Church Dogmatics,* 2(1):467.

[73]One remains in continuity with Reformed theology so long as one holds that the finite can receive, grasp and bear the infinite only through the power of the infinite. Because of the cleavage between the infinite God in the splendor of his holiness and mortals under the sway of sin, we cannot truly know or apprehend God until God makes himself known. But we can truly know and respond to God when God speaks and acts. The finite is capable of the infinite when and insofar as it is made so by the infinite.

[74]Copleston, *History of Philosophy,* 4:100.

[75]Jüngel, "Toward the Heart of the Matter," p. 233.

[76]Walter Rauschenbusch, *A Theology for the Social Gospel* (New York: Abingdon, 1945), p. 179.

[77]Edward Scribner Ames, *The Psychology of Religious Experience* (New York: Red Label Reprints, 1919), pp. 311–20, 396–98. For a fascinating discussion of how our images of God are linked to our social commitments, see David Nicholls, *Deity and Domination: Images of God and the State in the Nineteenth and Twentieth Centuries* (New York: Routledge, 1989). Nicholls gives an illuminating analysis of the older liberal theology, process theology and Barthian theology. His affinities are with those who favor a more democratic vision of God, though he does not want to abandon the traditional images.

[78]Jürgen Moltmann, *The Crucified God,* trans. R. A. Wilson and John Bowden (New York: Harper & Row, 1974), p. 223.

[79]Jürgen Moltmann, *The Trinity and the Kingdom,* trans. Margaret Kohl (San Francisco: Harper & Row, 1981), p. 56.

[80]Wolfhart Pannenberg, *The Idea of God and Human Freedom,* trans. R. A. Wilson (Philadelphia: Westminster Press, 1973), p. 108.

[81]Wolfhart Pannenberg, *Basic Questions in Theology,* trans. George H. Kehm (1971; reprint, Philadelphia: Westminster Press, 1983), 2:241.

⁸²For a critical but still appreciative appraisal of Pannenberg from the perspective of process theology, see David McKenzie, "Pannenberg on God and Freedom," *Journal of Religion* 60, no. 3 (1980):307–29.

⁸³Nikos Kazantzakis, *The Saviors of God: Spiritual Exercises,* trans. Kimon Friar (New York: Simon & Schuster, 1960), p. 116.

⁸⁴Ibid., p. 106.

⁸⁵See Anna Case-Winters, *God's Power: Traditional Understandings and Contemporary Challenges* (Louisville: Westminster/John Knox Press, 1990), pp. 201–32.

⁸⁶Brunner, *Christian Doctrine of God,* p. 247.

⁸⁷Ibid., p. 248.

⁸⁸Barth, *Church Dogmatics,* 2(1):528.

⁸⁹Thomas F. Torrance, *Theological Science* (London: Oxford University Press, 1969), p. 59; see pp. 60–65.

⁹⁰Daane, *Freedom of God,* pp. 66–67.

⁹¹Ibid., pp. 79–80.

⁹²Ibid., p. 78.

⁹³Ibid., p. 77.

Chapter 3: The Self-Revealing God

¹See pp. 63, 98.

²Eberhard Jüngel, *God as the Mystery of the World,* trans. Darrell L. Guder (Grand Rapids: Eerdmans, 1983), p. 255.

³Ibid., p. 256.

⁴Ibid., pp. 228–29.

⁵See Søren Kierkegaard, *Philosophical Fragments,* trans. David Swenson and Howard V. Hong, 2d ed. (Princeton: Princeton University Press, 1962), esp. pp. 16–45, 68–88.

⁶Jüngel, *God as the Mystery,* pp. 250–51.

⁷Ibid., p. 251.

⁸Ibid.

⁹Barth also calls it a "revealing mystery." Karl Barth, *The Göttingen Dogmatics: Instruction in the Christian Religion,* ed. Hannelotte Reiffen, trans. Geoffrey W. Bromiley (Grand Rapids: Eerdmans, 1991), 1:361.

¹⁰That our union with Christ is presently hidden from human perception is attested in Col 3:2–4, but we shall apprehend him directly when he is revealed in the eschatological fulfillment of history.

¹¹For an illuminating critique of Brunner's position, see John Dillenberger, *God Hidden and Revealed* (Philadelphia: Muhlenberg Press, 1953), pp. 100–117.

¹²Jüngel, *God as the Mystery,* p. 260.

¹³See Eberhard Jüngel, *The Doctrine of the Trinity,* trans. Harris Horton (Grand

Rapids: Eerdmans, 1976), pp. 47-60.

[14]See Rudolf Otto, *The Idea of the Holy,* trans. John W. Harvey (New York: Oxford University Press, 1958), pp. 12-30.

[15]Augustine, *The Confessions of St. Augustine,* trans. and ed. John K. Ryan (New York: Doubleday Image, 1960), 4.7.12, p. 100.

[16]Gregory of Nyssa, *On the Beatitudes,* Homily 6. See *From Glory to Glory: Texts from Gregory of Nyssa's Mystical Writings,* trans. and ed. Herbert Musurillo (New York: Charles Scribner's Sons, 1961), p. 98.

[17]Ibid.

[18]See *The Cloud of Unknowing,* ed. William Johnston (New York: Doubleday Image, 1973), esp. pp. 20-24.

[19]Jüngel, *God as the Mystery,* p. 245.

[20]Helmut Thielicke, *The Evangelical Faith,* trans. and ed. Geoffrey W. Bromiley (Grand Rapids: Eerdmans, 1974), 1:277-82.

[21]Victor Preller, *Divine Science and the Science of God: A Reformulation of Thomas Aquinas* (Princeton: Princeton University Press, 1967), p. 25.

[22]Ibid., p. 30.

[23]Ibid., p. 24.

[24]Thomas C. Oden, *The Living God* (San Francisco: Harper & Row, 1987), p. 138.

[25]Gregory of Nyssa, *The Life of Moses,* trans. and ed. Abraham J. Malherbe and Everett Ferguson (New York: Paulist, 1978), p. 93.

[26]Fernand van Steenberghen, *Hidden God: How Do We Know That God Exists?* trans. Theodore Crowley (St. Louis: Herder, 1966), p. 300. The author allows for the fact that human beings receive constant divine assistance in the pursuit of their destiny (p. 289).

[27]Cf. Luther: "God will not have thee thus ascend, but He comes to thee and has made a ladder, a way and a bridge to thee." Cited in *A History of Christian Doctrine,* ed. Hubert Cunliffe-Jones and Benjamin Drewery (Philadelphia: Fortress, 1980), p. 321.

[28]Irenaeus referred to the Word and Spirit as "the two hands of the Father." See Jürgen Moltmann, *The Spirit of Life,* trans. Margaret Kohl (Minneapolis: Fortress, 1992), p. 233.

[29]Thomas F. Torrance, *Theological Science* (London: Oxford University Press, 1969), pp. 51-52.

[30]Jürgen Moltmann, *God in Creation,* trans. Margaret Kohl (San Francisco: Harper & Row, 1985), p. 64.

[31]See James Daane, *The Freedom of God* (Grand Rapids: Eerdmans, 1973), pp. 14-33.

[32]In this discussion one should of course distinguish between the great theologians of faith (Luther, Calvin, Arminius, Barth, etc.), who did for the most part grasp the paradox of salvation, and their followers, who often failed to

maintain the delicate balance between the gift of grace and the decision of faith. Barth lapsed into objectivism in the later volumes of his *Church Dogmatics,* but in vol. 4(4) he attributed a more prominent role to the Holy Spirit in applying the fruits of Christ's salvation.

33Henry Ward Beecher, *Plymouth Pulpit: Sermons Preached in Plymouth Church, Brooklyn* (Boston: Pilgrim, 1875), 1:314–15. Cf.: "There is no other Being that labors with so much assiduity, and that so humbles himself, and so bows down under weakness, and so lifts up with his strength, and so wastes the unwasteable existence of the infinite, as God, in the plenary service of love." *The Sermons of Henry Ward Beecher* (New York: J. B. Ford, 1872), 6:62.

34Beecher, *Plymouth Pulpit: Sermons,* 1:92.

35Calvin and Edwards would have difficulty with Beecher's asseveration that every person "is competent to become better, wiser, stronger, nobler than he has been." Beecher, *Plymouth Pulpit: Sermons,* 3:73.

36*Sermons of Henry Ward Beecher,* 6:469.

37Beecher, *Plymouth Pulpit: Sermons,* 2:460.

38I hold that the Spirit does inhere in the preexistent Word and vice versa, but freely identifies with the word of his witnesses in the Bible and the church. There is a difference between the perichoresis in the trinitarian relations of God's being and the perichoresis in the ways by which God relates himself to his people. My position may here be closer to the Reformed theology of Francis Turretin than to some other strands of Protestant orthodoxy. According to Timothy Phillips, "Turretin explicitly denies that the Bible *per se* possesses an inherent power. For Scripture's proclamation is not efficacious without God's decision and action through the Holy Spirit." Phillips, *Francis Turretin's Idea of Theology and Its Bearing upon His Doctrine of Scripture* (Ann Arbor: University Microfilms International, 1986), p. 560.

39See Avery Dulles, "Pannenberg on Revelation and Faith," in *The Theology of Wolfhart Pannenberg,* ed. Carl E. Braaten and Philip Clayton (Minneapolis: Augsburg, 1988), pp. 180, 182.

40Ibid., p. 172. See *Revelation as History,* ed. Wolfhart Pannenberg, trans. David Granskou (New York: Macmillan, 1968), pp. 3–21, 125–58; and Wolfhart Pannenberg, *Basic Questions in Theology,* trans. George H. Kehm (1971; reprint, Philadelphia: Westminster Press, 1983), 1:15–80, esp. 62–66. Pannenberg claims an affinity between his position and Luther's on the openness of revelation. See *Basic Questions in Theology,* 1:61–66.

41*Revelation as History,* p. 137.

42See Daniel P. Fuller, "The Holy Spirit's Role in Biblical Interpretation," in *Scripture, Tradition and Interpretation,* ed. W. Ward Gasque and William Sanford LaSor (Grand Rapids: Eerdmans, 1978), pp. 189–98. For an insightful critique of Fuller's position, see Millard J. Erickson, *Evangelical Interpretation* (Grand

Rapids: Baker, 1993), pp. 33–54. Erickson too sees the meaning of revelation embedded in the text but believes that the Spirit helps to bring this meaning to light and does not merely make it possible for the reader to receive this meaning in faith.

[43]See Theodore W. Jennings Jr., *Loyalty to God: The Apostles' Creed in Life and Liturgy* (Nashville: Abingdon, 1992).

[44]On the meaning of dialectic in theology, see Donald G. Bloesch, *A Theology of Word and Spirit* (Downers Grove, Ill.: InterVarsity Press, 1992), pp. 76–81.

[45]*Zwingli and Bullinger,* trans. G. W. Bromiley, Library of Christian Classics 24 (Philadelphia: Westminster Press, 1953), p. 78.

[46]Ibid.

[47]Ibid., pp. 54–55. W. P. Stephens maintains that Zwingli gave priority to the Spirit in its dialectic with the Word, since the Spirit is God himself speaking in Scripture. Zwingli also made a place for the "mystical" sense of Scripture, which supplements and fulfills the natural or literal sense. He was not a spiritualist, however, for he insisted on the unity and congruence between Spirit and Scripture. See Stephens, *Zwingli: An Introduction to His Thought* (Oxford: Clarendon, 1992), pp. 35–42, 61–66.

[48]See Richard John Neuhaus, "Presbyterians: Where Have All the People Gone?" *First Things* no. 28 (1992):66–68.

[49]Ibid., p. 66.

[50]The New Testament gives examples of how an inspired text in the Old Testament is interpreted as the present voice of the Spirit of God: Acts 13:47; Heb 3:7-11.

[51]Thomas F. Torrance, "The Christian Apprehension of God the Father," in *Speaking the Christian God,* ed. Alvin F. Kimel Jr. (Grand Rapids: Eerdmans, 1992), p. 140.

[52]Donald M. Mathers, *The Word and the Way* (Toronto: United Church Publishing House, 1962), p. 95.

[53]This disjunction between Scripture as the prism of God's light and the divine light itself is stoutly affirmed by Luther: "God and the Scripture of God are two things, no less than the Creator and the creature are two things." *Luther's Works,* ed. Philip S. Watson (Philadelphia: Fortress, 1972), 33:25. While Protestant orthodoxy tended to blur the distinction between the divine light and Scripture as a book, it nevertheless maintained it, though not always with consistency. Francis Turretin could speak of the Bible as a "verbal revelation" of God, but at the same time he distinguished between the matter or content of Scripture—the supernatural mysteries, which wholly transcend reason— and the form—the writing or human record. He could quote approvingly from Jerome: "The gospel is not in words of the Scriptures, but in the sense, not on the surface, but in the marrow, not in the leaves of words, but in the root of

reason." Francis Turretin, *Institutes of Elenctic Theology,* trans. George Musgrave Giger, ed. James T. Dennison Jr. (Phillipsburg, N.J.: Presbyterian & Reformed, 1992), 1:51. See Jerome, *Commentariorum . . . ad Galatas* (on Gal 1:11, 12).

[54]See H. Richard Niebuhr, *The Meaning of Revelation* (New York: Macmillan, 1941), p. 109; cf. pp. 93, 138-39.

[55]Cf. Lk 24:45 (GNC): "He then went on to open up their minds so as to make them grasp the meaning of the scriptures."

[56]My position here converges with that of Gabriel Fackre, who holds that faith affirmations rather than metaphysical propositions best describe "the evocative and expressive nature of biblical truth claims." See his *Ecumenical Faith in Evangelical Perspective* (Grand Rapids: Eerdmans, 1993), pp. 52-53, 58, 108.

[57]Although Warfield set out to be an inductive theologian, his final recourse was to deductive logic. For a convincing and illuminating discussion of Warfield's theological method, see Jack B. Rogers and Donald K. McKim, *The Authority and Interpretation of the Bible* (San Francisco: Harper & Row, 1979), pp. 323-61. For my critique of the Rogers-McKim book, see Donald G. Bloesch, *Holy Scripture* (Downers Grove, Ill.: InterVarsity Press, 1994), pp. 131-40.

Chapter 4: Transcendence & Immanence

[1]See Paul V. Mankowski, "Old Testament Iconology and the Nature of God," in *The Politics of Prayer: Feminist Language and the Worship of God,* ed. Helen Hull Hitchcock (San Francisco: Ignatius Press, 1992), pp. 168-69.

[2]See Giovanni Filoramo, *A History of Gnosticism,* trans. Anthony Alcock (Cambridge, Mass.: Blackwell, 1990); Kurt Rudolph, *Gnosis,* trans. Peter Coxon et al., ed. Robert McLachlan Wilson (San Francisco: Harper & Row, 1983); and Ioan P. Couliano, *The Tree of Gnosis,* trans. H. S. Wiesner (San Francisco: HarperCollins, 1992). For my further discussion, see p. 110.

[3]See Jaroslav Pelikan, *The Christian Tradition* (Chicago: University of Chicago Press, 1974), 2:200, 247, 270; Pseudo-Dionysius, *The Complete Works,* trans. Colm Luibheid (New York: Paulist, 1987), pp. 133-41; and Matthew Fox, ed., *Breakthrough: Meister Eckhart's Creation Spirituality in New Translation* (New York: Doubleday, 1980), p. 175.

[4]Augustine, *The Confessions of St. Augustine,* trans. and ed. John K. Ryan (New York: Doubleday Image, 1960), 1.4.4, p. 45.

[5]While these were two separate movements in the history of Christian thought, they have come to be identified, since they both allow for suffering in the Godhead. See Geddes MacGregor, *Dictionary of Religion and Philosophy* (New York: Paragon House, 1989), pp. 469, 609.

[6]See Frederick Copleston, *A History of Philosophy* (reprint, New York: Doubleday, 1985), 3:231-47.

[7]Ibid., p. 260.

[8]Friedrich Schleiermacher, *On Religion: Speeches to Its Cultured Despisers,* trans. John Oman (New York: Harper & Row, 1958), p. 101.

[9]J. N. Findlay, *Hegel: A Re-examination* (London: Allen & Unwin, 1958), p. 143.

[10]Henry Ward Beecher, *Notes from Plymouth Pulpit,* ed. Augusta Moore (New York: Harper & Bros., 1865), p. 167.

[11]Ibid., p. 283.

[12]Søren Kierkegaard, *The Sickness unto Death,* trans. Walter Lowrie (Princeton: Princeton University Press, 1941), p. 207. Cf. "Between God and man there is and remains an eternal, essential, qualitative difference." Kierkegaard, *On Authority and Revelation,* trans. Walter Lowrie (Princeton: Princeton University Press, 1955), p. 112.

[13]Paul G. Lindhardt, *Grundtvig: An Introduction* (London: S.P.C.K., 1951), p. 16.

[14]On the marked divergences between Kierkegaard and Grundtvig, see John W. Elrod, *Kierkegaard and Christendom* (Princeton: Princeton University Press, 1981). See esp. pp. 14–32, 193–204.

[15]Barth derived this term from Rudolf Otto's *Idea of the Holy,* trans. John W. Harvey (New York: Oxford University Press, 1958).

[16]Karl Barth, *Church Dogmatics,* trans. T. H. L. Parker et al., ed. G. W. Bromiley and T. F. Torrance (Edinburgh: T. & T. Clark, 1957), 2(1):311.

[17]Emil Brunner, *Revelation and Reason,* trans. Olive Wyon (Philadelphia: Westminster Press, 1946), p. 43.

[18]Emil Brunner, *The Christian Doctrine of God,* trans. Olive Wyon (1950; reprint, Philadelphia: Westminster Press, 1974), p. 139.

[19]Ibid., p. 175.

[20]See A. W. Moore, *The Infinite* (New York: Routledge, 1990); and Timothy J. Pennings, "Infinity and the Absolute," *Christian Scholar's Review* 23, no. 2 (1993):159–80.

[21]Barth, *Church Dogmatics,* 2(1):468.

[22]Ibid., p. 467.

[23]See Paul. S. Fiddes, *The Creative Suffering of God* (New York: Oxford University Press, 1992), p. 103.

[24]For further discussion, see pp. 52, 285.

[25]Heinrich Heppe, *Reformed Dogmatics,* ed. Ernst Bizer, trans. G. T. Thomson (London: Allen & Unwin, 1950), p. 58.

[26]Barth, *Church Dogmatics,* 2(1):615.

[27]Brunner, *Christian Doctrine of God,* p. 270.

[28]Otto Weber, *Foundations of Dogmatics,* trans. Darrell L. Guder (Grand Rapids: Eerdmans, 1981), 1:459.

[29]Ibid.

[30]Ibid.

³¹Heppe, *Reformed Dogmatics,* pp. 65–66.

³²Hans Küng, *On Being a Christian,* trans. Edward Quinn (New York: Doubleday, 1976), p. 307.

³³Cited in Weber, *Foundations of Dogmatics,* 1:448.

³⁴Wolfhart Pannenberg, *Systematic Theology,* trans. Geoffrey W. Bromiley (Grand Rapids: Eerdmans, 1991), 1:410.

³⁵Barth, *Church Dogmatics,* 2(1):617.

³⁶Bultmann unwittingly gives support to the King James translation by maintaining that God is here depicted as "the miraculous being who deals wonderfully" with his people as opposed to an impersonal force called "spirit." See Rudolf Bultmann, *The Gospel of John,* trans. G. R. Beasley-Murray, ed. R. W. N. Hoare and J. K. Riches (Philadelphia: Westminster Press, 1971), p. 191.

³⁷See p. 49.

³⁸Cochrane, *The Existentialists and God* (Philadelphia: Westminster Press, 1956), p. 117.

³⁹Küng, *On Being a Christian,* p. 307.

⁴⁰Mormonism signifies a major deviation from classical Christian teaching by envisaging the Father and the Son as having "bodily parts" and "passions." See Anthony A. Hoekema, *The Four Major Cults* (Grand Rapids: Eerdmans, 1963), p. 35.

⁴¹Barth, *Church Dogmatics,* 2(1):445.

⁴²Ibid., p. 449.

⁴³Ibid.

⁴⁴For a helpful analysis of the concept of divine immutability in the fathers of the church, see Joseph M. Hallman, *The Descent of God: Divine Suffering in History and Theology* (Minneapolis: Fortress, 1991). Hallman sees promise in Whitehead's philosophy.

⁴⁵The Puritan divine Stephen Charnock is here typical of the later followers of the Reformation: "If God doth change, it must be either to a greater perfection than he had before, or to a less . . . if he changes to acquire a perfection he had not, then he was not before the most excellent Being." Stephen Charnock, *Discourses upon the Existence and Attributes of God* (Grand Rapids: Baker, 1979), 1:331. According to Charnock (1:460-61) God's knowledge is also unchangeable: "Though things pass into being and out of being, the knowledge of God doth not vary with them, for he knows them as well before they were, as when they are, and knows them as well when they are past, as when they are present." Yet Charnock displayed a more biblical side when he said with startling inconsistency that for our redemption "God must be made man, Eternity must suffer death, the Lord of angels must weep in a cradle, and the Creator of the world must hang like a slave" (1:261).

⁴⁶See his essay "Suffering and God" in Baron Friedrich von Hügel, *Essays and*

Addresses on the Philosophy of Religion (London: J. M. Dent & Sons, 1926), pp. 167–213, esp. 212.

[47]Ibid., p. 205.

[48]H. P. Owen, *Concepts of Deity* (New York: Herder & Herder, 1971), p. 24. See also Owen, *Christian Theism* (Edinburgh: T. & T. Clark, 1984). Another proponent of classical theism is Gerald Bray, who defends the traditional notion of God suffering only in the humanity of Jesus. See his *Doctrine of God* (Downers Grove, Ill.: InterVarsity Press, 1993), pp. 194–95.

[49]E. L. Mascall, *He Who Is: A Study in Traditional Theism* (1943; reprint, London: Longmans, Green, 1948), p. 111.

[50]Fiddes, *Creative Suffering of God*, pp. 58–59.

[51]Adrio König, *Here Am I!* (Grand Rapids: Eerdmans, 1982), pp. 68–70.

[52]Ibid., p. 70.

[53]Ibid.

[54]Cited in H. R. Mackintosh, *The Doctrine of the Person of Jesus Christ* (1913; reprint, Edinburgh: T. & T. Clark, 1962), pp. 233–34; see pp. 230–37.

[55]Paul Althaus, *The Theology of Martin Luther*, trans. Robert C. Schultz (Philadelphia: Fortress, 1966), p. 197.

[56]See Moltmann's discussion in *The Crucified God*, trans. R. A. Wilson and John Bowden (New York: Harper & Row, 1974), pp. 233–35.

[57]Barth, *Church Dogmatics*, 2(1):494.

[58]Ibid., p. 491.

[59]Barth, *Church Dogmatics*, trans. G. W. Bromiley et al., ed. Bromiley and T. F. Torrance (Edinburgh: T. & T. Clark, 1957), 2(2):163, 166. See the discussion in Fiddes, *Creative Suffering of God*, pp. 112–23.

[60]Barth, *Church Dogmatics*, 2(1):496. See my further comments on Barth's position in chap. 9, n. 44.

[61]Paul Tillich, *Systematic Theology* (Chicago: University of Chicago Press, 1963) 3:404–6.

[62]See Thomas C. Oden, *The Living God* (San Francisco: Harper & Row, 1987), pp. 110–14.

[63]Barth, *Church Dogmatics*, 2(1):496.

[64]Hans Küng, *Does God Exist?* trans. Edward Quinn (New York: Doubleday, 1980), p. 666.

[65]James I. Packer, "God," in *New Dictionary of Theology*, ed. Sinclair B. Ferguson, David F. Wright and J. I. Packer (Downers Grove, Ill.: InterVarsity Press, 1988), p. 277.

[66]I here agree with Berkouwer over Moltmann. See G. C. Berkouwer, *A Half Century of Theology*, trans. Lewis B. Smedes (Grand Rapids: Eerdmans, 1977), pp. 253–56.

[67]See Heppe, *Reformed Dogmatics*, p. 67. For a perceptive critique of immuta-

bility in the older theology (both Catholic and Protestant), see Isaak August Dorner, *Divine Immutability: A Critical Reconsideration,* trans. Robert R. Williams and Claude Welch, introduction by Robert R. Williams (Minneapolis: Fortress, 1994), pp. 82–119. Dorner (d. 1884) reconceived of immutability as enduring love rather than absolute timelessness. God "determines himself to enter into alteration and change, not in respect to his being, but in respect to the exercise of his constantly self-identical love" (p. 182). Note that Barth acknowledged his indebtedness to Dorner's provocative study on this subject. See Barth, *Church Dogmatics,* 2(1):493.

[68]See Frederick Sontag, *Divine Perfection* (New York: Harper & Bros., 1962), p. 58. Note that this is Sontag's interpretation of Nicholas of Cusa.

[69]See Arthur O. Lovejoy, *The Great Chain of Being* (1936; reprint, Cambridge: Harvard University Press, 1976).

[70]See J. A. T. Robinson, *Honest to God* (Philadelphia: Westminster Press, 1963), pp. 45–63.

[71]Küng, *Does God Exist?* p. 602.

[72]Jay B. McDaniel, *Earth, Sky, Gods & Mortals* (Mystic, Conn.: Twenty-Third Publications, 1990), p. 36.

[73]See the discussion in Fiddes, *Creative Suffering,* pp. 93–94.

[74]See David A. Pailin, *God and the Processes of Reality: Foundations of a Credible Theism* (London: Routledge, 1989), esp. pp. 152–53, 131–32.

[75]See Jürgen Moltmann, *Theology of Hope,* trans. James W. Leitch (New York: Harper & Row, 1967).

[76]Moltmann, *Crucified God,* p. 256.

[77]Ibid.

[78]Ronaldo Muñoz, *The God of Christians,* trans. Paul Burns (Maryknoll, N.Y.: Orbis, 1990), p. 80.

[79]For my critique of narrative theology, see Donald G. Bloesch, *Holy Scripture* (Downers Grove, Ill.: InterVarsity Press, 1994), pp. 208–18.

[80]Admittedly there are many different kinds of narrative theology. That espoused by Gabriel Fackre is much closer to the claims and concerns of traditional faith. See his *Ecumenical Faith in Evangelical Perspective* (Grand Rapids: Eerdmans, 1993), pp. 89–146. Also see Fackre, *The Christian Story,* 2 vols., rev. ed. (Grand Rapids: Eerdmans, 1984–1987). The danger in narrative theology is to subsume the gospel under narrative or reduce the gospel to narrative. We need to remember that the gospel is a divine Word from the beyond that breaks into the narrative history of the people of God and redirects and judges this history.

[81]See Thomas F. O'Dea, *The Mormons* (Chicago: University of Chicago Press, 1957), pp. 120–33.

[82]See G. W. Butterworth, *Spiritualism and Religion* (London: S.P.C.K., 1944); Jane

T. Stoddart, *The Case Against Spiritualism* (New York: Doran, n.d.); and Robert Laurence Moore, *In Search of White Crows: Spiritualism, Parapyschology and American Culture* (New York: Oxford University Press, 1977).

[83]See Karen Hoyt et al., *The New Age Rage* (Old Tappan, N.J.: Revell, 1987); Douglas R. Groothuis, *Unmasking the New Age* (Downers Grove, Ill.: InterVarsity Press, 1986); and Groothuis, *Confronting the New Age* (Downers Grove, Ill.: InterVarsity, 1988).

[84]See my discussion on pp. 52-53.

[85]See Karl Heim, *Christian Faith and Natural Science* (New York: Harper & Bros., 1953), pp. 151-249.

[86]For an appreciative commentary on Karl Heim's contribution to theology, see Carl Michalson, "Karl Heim," in *A Handbook of Christian Theologians,* ed. Dean G. Peerman and Martin E. Marty, enlarged ed. (Nashville: Abingdon, 1984), pp. 273-94.

[87]Also see Karl Heim, *The Transformation of the Scientific World View,* trans. W. A. Whitehouse (London: SCM Press, 1953).

[88]See Thomas F. Torrance, *Christian Theology and Scientific Culture* (New York: Oxford University Press, 1981); *Divine and Contingent Order* (New York: Oxford University Press, 1981); *Space, Time and Resurrection* (Grand Rapids: Eerdmans, 1976); and "Realism and Openness in Scientific Enquiry," *Zygon* 23, no. 2 (June 1988): 159-69. Torrance maintains that God is continually interacting with the world while always remaining transcendent over the world.

[89]See John Polkinghorne, *Science and Providence* (Boston: Shambhala Publications, 1989); *Science and Creation* (Boston: Shambhala Publications, 1989); *One World: The Interaction of Science and Theology* (Boston: Shambhala Publications, 1986); and *Reason and Reality* (Philadelphia: Trinity Press International, 1991). Polkinghorne is critical of process philosophy and theology for blurring the differences between God and creation. See *Science and Providence,* pp. 14-17, 80; *Science and Creation,* pp. 56-57; *Reason and Reality,* pp. 46-47. Polkinghorne also has difficulties with Pannenberg. See *Science and Creation,* pp. 63-64, 67.

[90]See Phillip E. Johnson, *Darwin on Trial,* 2d ed. (Downers Grove, Ill.: InterVarsity Press, 1993); and *Reason in the Balance: The Case Against Naturalism in Science, Law and Education* (Downers Grove, Ill.: InterVarsity Press, 1995).

[91]Richard Keyes, "The Idol Factory," in *No God but God,* ed. Os Guinness and John Seel (Chicago: Moody Press, 1992), p. 47. Richard Keyes is the founder and director of L'Abri Fellowship in Southborough, Massachusetts.

[92]Richard E. Creel is fairly convincing in his contention that we can enrich God's life extensively but not intensively. "What we affect is the 'texture' of God's happiness, not the intensity or purity of it." Creel tries to show the viability of classical theism in the face of the criticisms of process philosophy. Richard E.

Creel, *Divine Impassibility* (Cambridge: Cambridge University Press, 1986), p. 145.

[93]König, *Here Am I!* p. 214.

[94]Barth, *Church Dogmatics,* trans. G. W. Bromiley, ed. G. W. Bromiley and T. F. Torrance (Edinburgh: T. & T. Clark, 1956), 4(1):185.

[95]Barth, *Church Dogmatics,* 2:(1):550.

[96]Owen, *Concepts of Deity,* p. 150.

[97]Elsewhere in *Concepts of Deity* Owen acknowledges that God is infinite in love as well as in power, but God's love is definitely a minor theme in his overall discussion. In his more recent *Christian Theism* (1984) he gives God's love slightly more prominence. In accord with theological tradition Owen contends that God's act of love in Jesus Christ "adds nothing to his own perfection but is performed solely for the benefit of others" (p. 22).

[98]Gregory of Nyssa, *An Address on Religious Instruction* (chap. 24), ed. and trans. Cyril C. Richardson, in *Christology of the Later Fathers,* ed. Edward R. Hardy, Library of Christian Classics 3 (Philadelphia: Westminster Press, 1954), p. 301.

[99]George Foot Moore, *Judaism* (Cambridge: Harvard University Press, 1927), 1:357-400, 423.

[100]Ibid., p. 423.

Chapter 5: Power & Wisdom

[1]See Arthur O. Lovejoy, *The Great Chain of Being* (1936; reprint, Cambridge: Harvard University Press, 1976), pp. 40-54, 67-69.

[2]Ibid., pp. 49-50, 315.

[3]See Wilhelm Windelband, *A History of Philosophy,* trans. James H. Tufts (New York: Harper, 1958), 1:328-34.

[4]John Calvin, *Institutes of the Christian Religion,* ed. John T. McNeill, trans. Ford Lewis Battles, Library of Christian Classics 20-21 (Philadelphia: Westminster Press, 1960), 3.23.2, p. 950.

[5]Ibid.

[6]See Heinrich Heppe, *Reformed Dogmatics,* ed. Ernst Bizer, trans. G. T. Thomson (London: Allen & Unwin, 1950), p. 103.

[7]Ibid., p. 99.

[8]James Daane, *The Freedom of God* (Grand Rapids: Eerdmans, 1973), p. 7.

[9]Gordon H. Clark, *Predestination* (Phillipsburg, N.J.: Presbyterian & Reformed, 1987), p. 12.

[10]Karl Barth, *Church Dogmatics,* trans. T. H. L. Parker et al., ed. G. W. Bromiley and T. F. Torrance (Edinburgh: T. & T. Clark, 1957), 2(1):602. Barth does affirm God's "power over everything," but he cautions against treating this as an abstract concept; instead, it should be seen in the service of God's lordship over history.

[11]Ibid., p. 544.

[12]Ibid.

[13]Otto Weber, *Foundations of Dogmatics,* trans. Darrell L. Guder (Grand Rapids: Eerdmans, 1981), 1:444.

[14]Dietrich Bonhoeffer, *Letters and Papers from Prison,* trans. Reginald H. Fuller, ed. Eberhard Bethge (New York: Macmillan, 1953), pp. 219-20.

[15]Jürgen Moltmann, *The Crucified God,* trans. R. A. Wilson and John Bowden (San Francisco: Harper & Row, 1974), p. 223.

[16]Abraham Heschel makes a convincing case that for the Old Testament prophets God's love alone is enduring and his wrath and judgment are transient. See Abraham J. Heschel, *The Prophets* (New York: Harper & Row, 1962), pp. 279-98.

[17]W. Grundmann, "*dýnamai* etc.," *Theological Dictionary of the New Testament,* ed. Gerhard Kittel and Gerhard Friedrich, trans. and abridged by Geoffrey W. Bromiley (Grand Rapids: Eerdmans, 1985), p. 189.

[18]Ibid.

[19]Mary McDermott Shideler, *Consciousness of Battle* (Grand Rapids: Eerdmans, 1970), p. 135.

[20]Walter Brueggemann believes that Gen 1:2 presupposes an existing chaos before God's creative act. See his *Genesis,* Interpretation (Atlanta: John Knox Press, 1982), p. 29. Gerhard von Rad maintains that the idea of *creatio ex nihilo* is present in Genesis 1, but the focus is on creation out of chaos. Gerhard von Rad, *Genesis,* trans. John H. Marks, rev. ed., Old Testament Library (Philadelphia: Westminster Press, 1972), p. 51. Cuthbert A. Simpson holds that Genesis 1 implies the creation of the chaos by God as well as the creation of light. Simpson, "The Book of Genesis," in *Interpreter's Bible* (New York: Abingdon, 1952), 1:465-68.

[21]For my discussion on myth in the Bible, see Donald G. Bloesch, *Holy Scripture* (Downers Grove, Ill.: InterVarsity Press, 1994), pp. 255-77. I continue this discussion in my forthcoming volume four, chap. 4, of the Christian Foundations series.

[22]Brueggemann, *Genesis,* p. 18.

[23]For my further discussion, see pp. 130-32.

[24]Progressive creationism is set forth in Bernard Ramm, *The Christian View of Science and Scripture* (Grand Rapids: Eerdmans, 1954), pp. 112-17.

[25]Ted Peters, *God as Trinity: Relationality and Temporality in Divine Life* (Louisville: Westminster/John Knox Press, 1993), pp. 155-73. See esp. p. 166. For my further discussion of Peters, see pp. 182-83.

[26]Pierre Teilhard de Chardin, *Writings in Time of War,* trans. René Hague (New York: Harper & Row, 1968), p. 95.

[27]Bruce R. McConkie, *Mormon Doctrine,* 2d ed. (Salt Lake City: Bookcraft, 1966), p. 169.

28John A. Widtsoe, *A Rational Theology* (Salt Lake City: Deseret Book Co., 1952), p. 12.

29Note that theistic evolution (the view that God shapes the course of evolution) has been upheld not only by process thinkers but also by such stalwart defenders of orthodoxy as Benjamin Warfield. See B. B. Warfield, "The Antiquity and Unity of the Human Race," in *The Princeton Theology 1812-1921,* ed. Mark A. Noll (Grand Rapids: Baker, 1983), pp. 289-92; and Warfield, "Calvin's Doctrine of Creation," in *The Princeton Theology,* pp. 297-98.

30See Henry Nelson Wieman, *The Source of Human Good* (1946; reprint, Carbondale: Southern Illinois University Press, 1964), pp. 3-26, 287-93.

31See John N. Findlay, "The Impersonality of God," in *God: The Contemporary Discussion,* ed. Frederick Sontag and M. Darrol Bryant (New York: Rose of Sharon Press, 1982), p. 191.

32See Ioan P. Couliano, *The Tree of Gnosis,* trans. H. S. Wiesner (San Francisco: HarperCollins, 1992), pp. 73-74.

33See Kurt Rudolph, *Gnosis,* trans. Peter Coxon et al., ed. Robert McLachlan Wilson (San Francisco: Harper & Row, 1983), pp. 65-66.

34Paul Tillich, *Systematic Theology* (Chicago: University of Chicago Press, 1951), 1:252-56.

35Quoted in Shideler, *Consciousness of Battle,* p. 135.

36Raymond B. Blakney, ed. and trans., *Meister Eckhart: A Modern Translation* (New York: Harper & Bros., 1941), p. 85.

37See *Leibniz: Selections,* ed. Philip P. Wiener (New York: Charles Scribner's Sons, 1951), pp. 520-22, 528-30. Also see Frederick Copleston, *A History of Philosophy* (reprint, New York: Doubleday, 1985), 4:326.

38Simone Weil, *Gravity and Grace,* trans. Arthur Wills (New York: Farrar, Straus and Giroux, 1979), p. 130.

39See A. Dorner and St. George Stock, "Fate," *Encyclopaedia of Religion and Ethics,* ed. James Hastings (New York: Charles Scribner's Sons, 1914), 5:771-78, 786-90.

40See Donald Bloesch, "Fate, Fatalism," *Evangelical Dictionary of Theology,* ed. Walter A. Elwell (Grand Rapids: Baker, 1984), pp. 407-8.

41It should be noted that the Stoic philosopher Zeno identified fate with providence and nature. See Stock, "Fate," p. 789.

42For some of the ancient Greeks, fate included providence and fortune. Belief in fate can allow for a high measure of contingency in the universe. It was sometimes said that all things are included in fate but not all things are "done by and according to fate." See William Chase Greene, *Moira: Fate, Good and Evil in Greek Thought* (Cambridge: Harvard University Press, 1944), pp. 368-72. Interestingly, Tillich said that what makes fate a matter of anxiety is not "causal necessity" but "the lack of ultimate necessity, the irrationality, the impenetrable darkness of fate." In the fatalistic view the determining causes of our existence "cannot be logically derived." We are caught in "the whole web of causal relations. Contingently we are determined by them in every moment and thrown out by them in the last moment." Tillich, *The Courage to Be* (London: Nisbet, 1952), pp. 41–42. What we have in fatalism is a remorseless inevitability that defies rational norms and consequently empties life of meaning and purpose.

[43]Grundmann, "*dýnamai* etc.," p. 188.

[44]Karl Barth, *Church Dogmatics,* trans. G. W. Bromiley et al., ed. Bromiley and T. F. Torrance (Edinburgh: T. & T. Clark, 1957), 2(2):193.

[45]Cf. "The sovereignty of the Creator . . . is operative in the freedom of His creature without robbing it of freedom." Barth, *Church Dogmatics,* 2(1):596.

[46]Calvin cited with approval Augustine's *Enchiridion* (26.100-101): "In a wonderful and ineffable manner nothing is done without God's will, not even that which is against his will." *Institutes,* ed. McNeill, 1.18.3, p. 235.

[47]See Walter Harrelson, "Providence," *Encyclopedia of Religious Education,* ed. Iris V. Cully and Kendig Brubaker Cully (San Francisco: Harper & Row, 1990), pp. 515–16.

[48]See H. P. Owen, *Concepts of Deity* (New York: Herder & Herder, 1971), p. 31.

[49]Heppe, *Reformed Dogmatics,* p. 76.

[50]Ibid., p. 70. On Charnock's view on the timelessness of God's knowledge, see chap. 4, n. 45.

[51]Barth, *Church Dogmatics,* 2(1):558. The decisive thing for Barth is that God's knowledge of all things is "in eternal superiority to all things and eternal independence of all things" (pp. 558–59).

[52]I think it would be fair to say that Barth's overall position is that eternity is not the obverse of time but includes time within itself in the form of both fulfillment and negation. It is a fulfillment that "abrogates time as it is seen in the logic of the 'before' and 'after' of events." For Barth God's eminent temporality is at the same time God's dynamic eternity. See Richard H. Roberts, *A Theology on Its Way?* (Edinburgh: T. & T. Clark, 1991), p. 78. According to Colin Gunton interpreting Barth, "God's eternity is not non-temporality, but the eternity of the triune *life.*" Colin Gunton, "Barth, the Trinity and Human Freedom," *Theology Today* 43, no. 3 (1986):318.

[53]Colin E. Gunton, *Becoming and Being: The Doctrine of God in Charles Hartshorne and Karl Barth* (Oxford: Oxford University Press, 1978), p. 164.

[54]William J. Hill, *Search for the Absent God: Tradition and Modernity in Religious Understanding* (New York: Crossroad, 1992), p. 162.

[55]John B. Cobb Jr. and David Ray Griffin, *Process Theology: An Introductory Exposition* (Philadelphia: Westminster Press, 1976), p. 57.

[56]Daniel Day Williams, *The Spirit and the Forms of Love* (New York: Harper &

Row, 1968), p. 128.

57Anna Case-Winters, *God's Power: Traditional Understandings and Contemporary Challenges* (Louisville: Westminster/John Knox Press, 1990), p. 169. These are the words of Case-Winters.

58See Lewis Ford, "Divine Persuasion and the Triumph of Good," in *The Problem of Evil*, ed. Michael L. Peterson (Notre Dame, Ind.: University of Notre Dame Press, 1992), pp. 247-58.

59Tillich, *Systematic Theology*, 1:185.

60Ibid., p. 200.

61Ibid., p. 267.

62See J. Goetzmann, "Wisdom," *The New International Dictionary of New Testament Theology*, ed. Colin Brown (Grand Rapids: Zondervan, 1979), 3:1029.

63R. B. Y. Scott argues for "possess" in his *Proverbs, Ecclesiastes*, Anchor Bible 18 (New York: Doubleday, 1965), p. 72.

64Ibid., p. 69. "Monolatry" here means the unbalanced focus on the oneness of God as opposed to his threeness in oneness.

65Ibid.

66That Lady Wisdom is contrasted with Dame Folly in Proverbs 9 shows that we are dealing more with metaphors than with metaphysics.

67Crawford H. Toy, *A Critical and Exegetical Commentary on the Book of Proverbs*, International Critical Commentary (1899; reprint, Edinburgh: T. & T. Clark, 1977), p. 181.

68Interestingly, Luke associates wisdom with the Spirit in Acts 6:3, 10. See the discussion in James Leo Garrett Jr., *Systematic Theology* (Grand Rapids: Eerdmans, 1990), 1:219-21. It is well to note that Irenaeus differs from most of the church fathers by his identification of the Wisdom of Proverbs with the Spirit rather than with the Logos. See Philip Schaff, *History of the Christian Church* (1910; reprint, Grand Rapids: Eerdmans, 1994), 2:564.

69Isaac Watts, "Join All the Glorious Names," in *Praise! Our Songs and Hymns*, ed. Norman Johnson (Grand Rapids: Zondervan, 1982), no. 71.

70In the Wisdom of Solomon, Wisdom not only is present at creation but is herself creator as the "mother" of all good things and innumerable riches (Wisdom of Solomon 7:11-12).

71See Prov 7:4.

72It should be noted that providence derives from the Latin *providentia*, which is feminine.

73This does not mean that we as Christians may never address God as Wisdom, but this appellation must always be seen as an aspect of the self-revelation of God in Christ. Wisdom is not a proper name for God, but it may be an apt designation for the work of God in creation and redemption. The danger accrues when we begin addressing God as Mother, thereby implying that God has a distinctly female side, for this makes God bisexual (as in the gnostic view) rather than suprasexual (as in the biblical view).

[74]To be sure, the disciples could directly apprehend the figure of the risen Christ, but they would only come to recognize him as the divine Savior of the world through the outpouring of the Holy Spirit at Pentecost.

[75]One can discern striking parallels between this motto, mainly associated with Calvin, and Ignatius Loyola's *ad maiorem Dei gloriam* ("to the greater glory of God"). See René Fülöp-Miller, *The Power and Secret of the Jesuits,* trans. F. S. Flint and D. F. Tait (New York: Braziller, 1956), esp. pp. 10-13; and Hans Küng, *Christianity: Essence, History and Future,* trans. John Bowden (New York: Continuum, 1995), pp. 576-77.

[76]Barth, *Church Dogmatics,* 2(1):666-67.

[77]Ibid., p. 279.

[78]W. Norris Clarke is helpful when he denies that God can change in the sense of "moving to a *qualitatively higher* level of inner perfection," though granting that "God's inner being is *genuinely affected,* not in an ascending or descending way, but in a truly real, personal, conscious, relational way by His relations with us." W. Norris Clarke, *The Philosophical Approach to God: A Neo-Thomist Perspective,* ed. W. E. Ray (Winston-Salem, N.C.: Wake Forest University, 1979), p. 104. Also see p. 98.

[79]Petro Bilaniuk, "The Holiness of God in Eastern Orthodoxy," in *God: The Contemporary Discussion,* p. 60.

[80]Hans Jonas, *The Gnostic Religion,* rev. ed. (Boston: Beacon, 1963), p. 251.

[81]According to classical Buddhist teaching, behind craving or desire is ignorance. "When ignorance ceases, then all the following members of the chain will also cease and there will be no more birth, old age and death." K. K. S. Chen, "Buddhism," *Abingdon Dictionary of Living Religions,* ed. Keith Crim (Nashville: Abingdon, 1981), p. 128.

[82]See my discussion on pp. 211-13.

[83]See John Hick, *Evil and the God of Love* (New York: Harper & Row, 1966).

[84]Edwin Lewis sought to bring together Hellenistic and Hebraic understandings when he posited three external existents—the divine (the creator), the residue (the uncreative) and the demonic (the discreative). The trouble with this view is that God is no longer omnipotent but finite, though it is said that he will ultimately triumph in the end. See Lewis, *The Creator and the Adversary* (New York: Abingdon-Cokesbury, 1948).

[85]See James Muilenberg's comments in the *Interpreter's Bible,* ed. George Arthur Buttrick (Nashville: Abingdon, 1956) 5:524-25. Also see the discussion in the *Harper Study Bible,* ed. Harold Lindsell (Grand Rapids: Zondervan, 1977), p. 1070.

[86]Tillich, *Systematic Theology,* 1:186-92.

[87]Grace Jantzen, *God's World, God's Body* (Philadelphia: Westminster Press, 1984), pp. 136-37.

[88]*The Size of God: The Theology of Bernard Loomer in Context,* ed. William Dean and Larry Axel (Macon, Ga.: Mercer University Press, 1987). For an illuminating discussion of the views of Loomer and Bernard Meland, see William Dean, *History Making History: The New Historicism in American Religious Thought* (Albany: State University of New York Press, 1988), pp. 110-22.

[89]Joseph Campbell, *An Open Life,* ed. John M. Maher and Dennie Briggs (1988; reprint, New York: Harper & Row, 1990), pp. 28-29.

[90]See Barth, *Church Dogmatics,* trans. G. W. Bromiley and R. J. Ehrlich, ed. Bromiley and T. F. Torrance (Edinburgh: T. & T. Clark, 1961), 3(3):289-368.

[91]See my discussion in Donald G. Bloesch, *Essentials of Evangelical Theology* (San Francisco: Harper & Row, 1979), 2:131-32. For a penetrating analysis of Barth's position on the chaos and the demonic powers, see G. C. Berkouwer, *The Triumph of Grace in the Theology of Karl Barth,* trans. Harry R. Boer (Grand Rapids: Eerdmans, 1956), pp. 57-82, 219-23, 240-61, 370-81.

[92]That the Genesis story of the descent of the "sons of God" to the realm of humans (in 6:1-4) refers to a fall of angelic beings is given credence by Gerhard von Rad in his *Genesis,* pp. 113-16.

[93]John Calvin, *Concerning the Eternal Predestination of God,* trans. J. K. S. Reid (London: James Clarke, 1961), p. 169.

[94]See François Wendel, *Calvin,* trans. Philip Mairet (London: Collins, 1963), pp. 177-84. Also see discussion in Case-Winters, *God's Power,* pp. 39-93.

[95]See Ronald Goetz, "Jesus Loves Everybody," *Christian Century* 109, no. 9 (1992):274-77; "The Suffering God: The Rise of a New Orthodoxy," *Christian Century* 103, no. 13 (1986):385-89; "The Slaughter of Jesus Christ and the Culpability of God" (unpublished paper, 1992); and "In Pursuit of the Illusively Enigmatic: The Theology of Karl Barth" (unpublished paper, 1992).

[96]Goetz, "Jesus Loves Everybody," p. 277.

[97]Ibid., p. 276.

[98]Goetz, "Slaughter of Jesus Christ," p. 35.

[99]Barth was very firm that we cannot posit a dark side in God that is in conflict with his benevolence: "If there did not exist perfect, original and ultimate peace between the Father and the Son by the Holy Spirit, God would not be God. Any God in conflict with Himself is bound to be a false God." *Church Dogmatics,* 2(1):503.

[100]Wendy Farley, *Tragic Vision and Divine Compassion: A Contemporary Theodicy* (Louisville: Westminster/John Knox Press, 1990).

[101]Ibid., p. 107.

[102]Ibid., p. 124.

[103]Ibid.

[104]Ibid., p. 27.

[105]Ibid., p. 97.

[106]Ibid., p. 114.

[107]Ibid., p. 61.

[108]Like Calvin, Luther sometimes lapsed into determinism, but his view of the demons is richer and deeper. Calvin nonetheless shared with Luther (as well as with Augustine and Thomas Aquinas) a realistic view of a personal devil. While Barth believed in a real devil, he tended to make the devil a depersonalizing force.

[109]For a contemporary appreciation of Luther's (and also Tillich's) demonology, see Walter Sundberg, "A Primer on the Devil," *First Things* no. 29 (1993):15–21. Also see Heiko A. Oberman, *Luther: Man Between God and the Devil*, trans. Eileen Walliser-Schwarzbart (New York: Doubleday Image, 1992), esp. pp. 246–71.

[110]According to Jeffrey Burton Russell the devil is the personal embodiment of radical evil. See his enlightening *The Prince of Darkness: Radical Evil and the Power of Good in History* (Ithaca, N.Y.: Cornell University Press, 1988). This idea has been an embarrassment to liberalism, which has dismissed the idea of a personal devil as belonging to a mythological past (see pp. 215, 241–42, 257, 276).

Chapter 6: Holiness & Love

[1]See Rudolf Otto, *The Idea of the Holy*, trans. John W. Harvey (New York: Oxford University Press, 1958), pp. 50–59.

[2]Thomas C. Oden, *The Living God* (San Francisco: Harper & Row, 1987), p. 103.

[3]James Leo Garrett Jr., *Systematic Theology* (Grand Rapids: Eerdmans, 1990), 1:228.

[4]Henry Ward Beecher, *Sermons.* Cited in David Manning White, ed., *The Search for God* (New York: Macmillan, 1983), p. 201.

[5]Reinhold Niebuhr, "The Ethical Resources of the Christian Religion," in *Education Adequate for Modern Times*, ed. John Bennett (New York: Association Press, 1931), p. 65.

[6]See William J. Bouwsma, *John Calvin: A Sixteenth-Century Portrait* (New York: Oxford University Press, 1988), pp. 162–76.

[7]See William G. T. Shedd, *Dogmatic Theology,* 2d ed. (Nashville: Nelson, 1980), 1:362, 364, 385; 2:402–5. Shedd describes mercy as "an emanent, or transitive attribute, issuing forth from the Divine nature" (1:385). He can say: "The eternal Judge may or may not exercise mercy, but he must exercise justice" (2:436). For a helpful analysis of Shedd's position, see George Barker Stevens, *The Christian Doctrine of Salvation* (New York: Charles Scribner's Sons, 1911), pp. 174–79.

[8]Stevens, *Christian Doctrine of Salvation*, p. 178. Cf. Strong: "Love is a means to holiness, and holiness is therefore the supreme good and something higher than mere love." Augustus Hopkins Strong, *Systematic Theology* (Philadelphia: Judson, 1956), 1:271.

[9]P. T. Forsyth, *The Principle of Authority*, 2d ed. (London: Independent Press, 1952), p. 376.

[10]Forsyth, *The Preaching of Jesus and the Gospel of Christ* (Blackwood, South Australia: New Creation Publications, 1987), p. 74.

[11]David F. Wells, *God in the Wasteland* (Grand Rapids: Eerdmans, 1994), p. 136.

[12]Karl Barth, *Church Dogmatics*, trans. T. H. L. Parker et al., ed. G. W. Bromiley and T. F. Torrance (Edinburgh: T. & T. Clark, 1957), 2(1):363.

[13]Emil Brunner, *The Christian Doctrine of God*, trans. Olive Wyon (1950; reprint, Philadelphia: Westminster Press, 1974), p. 162.

[14]Ibid., p. 281.

[15]*The Book of Angelus Silesius*, trans. Frederick Franck (New York: Vintage, 1976), p. 87.

[16]I here agree with Barth in his *Epistle to the Romans*, trans. Edwyn C. Hoskyns (London: Oxford University Press, 1933), pp. 345–61.

[17]C. H. Dodd, *The Epistle of Paul to the Romans*, Moffatt's New Testament Commentary (1932; reprint, London: Hodder & Stoughton, 1954), p. 23.

[18]See Ernst Käsemann, *Commentary on Romans*, trans. and ed. Geoffrey W. Bromiley (Grand Rapids: Eerdmans, 1980), pp. 43, 138.

[19]Adrio König, *Here Am I!* (Grand Rapids: Eerdmans, 1982), p. 94.

[20]Wolfhart Pannenberg, *Systematic Theology*, trans. Geoffrey W. Bromiley (Grand Rapids: Eerdmans, 1991), 1:439.

[21]Paul K. Jewett, *God, Creation and Revelation: A Neo-evangelical Theology* (Grand Rapids: Eerdmans, 1991), p. 246.

[22]Paul Tillich, *Systematic Theology* (Chicago: University of Chicago Press, 1951), 1:283–84.

[23]Gustav Friedrich Oehler, *Theology of the Old Testament*, trans. Ellen D. Smith (Edinburgh: T. & T. Clark, 1880), 1:166.

[24]See A. A. Hodge, *The Atonement* (1867; reprint, Grand Rapids: Baker, 1974), p. 390.

[25]Larry Dixon, *The Other Side of the Good News* (Wheaton, Ill.: Victor, 1992), pp. 165–72. Also see Dixon, "Whatever Happened to Hell?" *Moody* 93, no. 10 (1993):25–29. This harsher view is also reflected in Jonathan Edwards: "If you cry to God to pity you, he will be so far from pitying you in your doleful case, or showing you the least regard or favor, that instead of that he will only tread you under foot." Harold P. Simonson, ed., *Selected Writings of Jonathan Edwards* (New York: Continuum, 1990), p. 110. These words are in accord with biblical truth so long as they are seen as reflecting God's penultimate, not

ultimate, judgment.

[26]For my earlier discussion, see Donald G. Bloesch, *Essentials of Evangelical Theology* (San Francisco: Harper & Row, 1979), 2:211-34. Stanley J. Grenz argues along similar lines in his *Theology for the Community of God* (Nashville: Broadman & Holman, 1994), pp. 835-39.

[27]G. Stählin, "Human and Divine Wrath in the NT," *Theological Dictionary of the New Testament,* ed. Gerhard Kittel and Gerhard Friedrich, trans. and abridged by Geoffrey W. Bromiley (Grand Rapids: Eerdmans, 1985), p. 725.

[28]Ibid., p. 723.

[29]One could say that in hell love appears in the form of wrath, and therefore wrath carries the balm of mercy.

[30]Hans Küng, *On Being a Christian,* trans. Edward Quinn (New York: Doubleday, 1976), p. 308.

[31]Ibid.

[32]See Anders Nygren, *Agape and Eros,* trans. Philip S. Watson (Philadelphia: Westminster Press, 1953), pp. 75-77.

[33]Eberhard Jüngel, *God as the Mystery of the World,* trans. Darrell L. Guder (Grand Rapids: Eerdmans, 1983), p. 325.

[34]Ibid.

[35]Reinhold Niebuhr, *An Interpretation of Christian Ethics* (1948; reprint, New York: Seabury/Crossroad, 1979), p. 32.

[36]Helmut Thielicke, *The Evangelical Faith,* trans. Geoffrey W. Bromiley (Grand Rapids: Eerdmans, 1977), 2:179.

[37]See Paul Tillich, *Systematic Theology,* 3 vols. (Chicago: University of Chicago Press, 1951-63), 1:279-83; 3:136-38.

[38]While the Old Testament concept of *ḥesed* ("loving-kindness") approaches agape, it falls short of agape because it is contingent on the people of God fulfilling their covenant obligations. This contingency is transcended, however, in a number of places (cf. Hos 11:8-9; 14:4-7; Jer 31:1-6; Mic 7:18-20). Yet even in these passages the reference is to God's love for his covenant people rather than for the whole world.

[39]*Meister Eckhart: A Modern Translation,* ed. and trans. Raymond B. Blakney (New York: Harper & Bros., 1941), p. 248.

[40]Charles Fillmore, *Jesus Christ Heals* (Kansas City, Mo.: Unity School of Christianity, 1944), p. 31.

[41]The compassion of liberationist theology must be sharply distinguished from the compassion of an attenuated liberalism—nonjudgmental acceptance. Liberationist compassion is active involvement in peace-justice issues, and this includes judgment and sometimes even violence. Compassion can also be understood in a biblical sense—pity for all who are lost and broken and willingness to come to their aid irrespective of their moral or spiritual status.

42Wendy Farley, *Tragic Vision and Divine Compassion: A Contemporary Theodicy* (Louisville: Westminster/John Knox Press, 1990), pp. 117, 116.

43Niebuhr, *Interpretation of Christian Ethics*, p. 33.

44Ibid., p. 137.

45Ibid., p. 139.

46Emil Brunner, *The Mediator*, trans. Olive Wyon (Philadelphia: Westminster Press, 1947), pp. 467ff. Also see Brunner, *Christian Doctrine of God*, pp. 157–74, 183–99.

47See Sallie McFague, *Models of God* (Philadelphia: Fortress, 1987), pp. 130–36. While making a firm place for eros as well as "motherly love," McFague sees special promise in *philia*, for the model of God as friend supports the vision of working with God "to save our beleaguered planet, our beautiful earth" (p. 180). See pp. 157–80.

48Jürgen Moltmann, *The Spirit of Life*, trans. Margaret Kohl (Minneapolis: Fortress, 1992), p. 261.

49Luther *Heidelberg Disputation* xxviii. See Nygren, *Agape and Eros*, pp. 725–26; and *Luther's Works*, ed. Harold J. Grimm (Philadelphia: Muhlenberg, 1957), 31:57.

50Niebuhr, *Interpretation of Christian Ethics*, p. 30.

51Augustine *On the Trinity* 8, in *Augustine of Hippo: Selected Writings*, trans. Mary T. Clark (New York: Paulist, 1984), p. 328.

52Moltmann, *Spirit of Life*, p. 187.

53Paul Tillich, *Political Expectation*, trans. and ed. James Luther Adams (Macon, Ga.: Mercer University Press, 1981), p. 118.

54For the rootage of the modern idea of justice in both classical philosophy and biblical faith, see Emil Brunner, *Justice and the Social Order*, trans. Mary Hottinger (New York: Harper & Bros., 1945), pp. 4–24.

55Cf. Wendy Farley's helpful discussion of justice in her *Tragic Vision and Divine Compassion*, pp. 81–83.

56See my discussion in Donald G. Bloesch, *Faith and Its Counterfeits* (Downers Grove, Ill.: InterVarsity Press, 1981), pp. 46–58.

57Niebuhr, *Interpretation of Christian Ethics*, p. 112.

58Dietrich Bonhoeffer, *A Testament to Freedom: The Essential Writings of Dietrich Bonhoeffer*, ed. Geffrey B. Kelly and F. Burton Nelson (San Francisco: HarperCollins, 1990), p. 260.

59Reinhold Niebuhr, "The Christian Religion in Modern Civilization," in *Education Adequate for Modern Times*, p. 37.

60Reinhold Niebuhr, "The Montgomery Savagery," *Christianity and Crisis* 21, no. 10 (1961):103.

61Reinhold Niebuhr, *Christianity and Power Politics* (New York: Charles Scribner's Sons, 1940), p. 104.

[62]Emil Brunner, *The Divine Imperative,* trans. Olive Wyon (Philadelphia: West-minster Press, 1947), pp. 272-73.

[63]See particularly Jacques Ellul, *The Political Illusion,* trans. Konrad Kellen (New York: Knopf, 1967), esp. p. 186.

[64]Jacques Ellul, *The Presence of the Kingdom,* trans. Olive Wyon (Philadelphia: Westminster Press, 1951), p. 47.

[65]See Karl Barth, *Against the Stream,* trans. E. M. Delacour and Stanley Godman (London: SCM Press, 1954), pp. 42-43; and *The Christian Life,* trans. Geoffrey W. Bromiley (Grand Rapids: Eerdmans, 1981), pp. 260-71.

[66]See my discussion in Donald G. Bloesch, *Freedom for Obedience* (San Francisco: Harper & Row, 1987), pp. 126-49.

[67]See Susan Thistlethwaite, ed., *A Just Peace Church* (New York: United Church Press, 1986); and *Presbyterians and Human Sexuality* (Louisville: Office of the General Assembly, Presbyterian Church U.S.A., 1991).

[68]See Bloesch, *Freedom for Obedience,* pp. 64-66, 189-93.

[69]Reinhold Niebuhr, *The Children of Light and the Children of Darkness* (New York: Charles Scribner's Sons, 1944), p. 189.

[70]For Niebuhr pure love negates as well as fulfills the demands of justice, but an immoral society can only rise to the level of mutual love, which falls short of the suffering love of the cross. Pure love transcends love as law, but there is always an element of pure, sacrificial love in mutual love.

[71]Niebuhr said: "The Kingdom of God is always at hand in the sense that the impossibilities are really possible, and lead to new actualities in given moments of history. Nevertheless every actuality of history reveals itself, after the event, as only an approximation of the ideal; and the Kingdom of God is therefore not here. It is in fact always coming but never here." Niebuhr, *Interpretation of Christian Ethics,* p. 36. The question can be raised whether Niebuhr missed another important note in the New Testament, namely, that the kingdom as a fellowship of outgoing love is already and ineradicably present in the world of sin and death, and this fellowship is now molding a new society as a leaven in the lump (cf. Mt 13:33; Lk 13:21). His provisional pessimism is complemented by an ultimate optimism, which becomes more apparent in his later writings.

[72]See Dietrich Bonhoeffer, *The Cost of Discipleship,* trans. R. H. Fuller (London: SCM Press, 1959).

[73]Bonhoeffer, *Testament to Freedom,* p. 261.

[74]Bonhoeffer, *Ethics,* ed. Eberhard Bethge, trans. Neville Horton Smith (New York: Macmillan, 1965), p. 137.

[75]Niebuhr in his maturity believed in both partial redemptions within history and the final redemption of history itself, though these salvific events can be described only in symbolic, poetic language. See Reinhold Niebuhr, *Faith and*

History (New York: Charles Scribner's Sons, 1949), pp. 214–43.

76See John Calvin, *Institutes of the Christian Religion,* ed. John McNeill, trans. Ford Lewis Battles, Library of Christian Classics 20–21 (Philadelphia: Westminster Press, 1960), 1.2.1–2, pp. 39–43. See notes on p. 40. See also Calvin, *Instruction in Faith (1537),* trans. Paul T. Fuhrmann (Philadelphia: Westminster Press, 1949), pp. 18–19.

77Quoted in Walther von Loewenich, *Martin Luther: The Man and His Work,* trans. Lawrence W. Denef (Minneapolis: Augsburg, 1986), p. 153.

78See *Praise! Our Songs and Hymns,* ed. Norman Johnson (Grand Rapids: Zondervan, 1982), no. 203.

79Brunner, *Divine Imperative,* p. 189.

80Barth, *Romans,* p. 382.

81Ibid., p. 131.

82See Arthur C. Cochrane, ed., *Reformed Confessions of the 16th Century* (Philadelphia: Westminster Press, 1966), p. 322.

83Samuel Bolton, *The True Bounds of Christian Freedom* (1645; reprint, London: Banner of Truth Trust, 1964), p. 155.

84*Meister Eckhart: A Modern Translation,* ed. and trans. Blakney, p. 6.

Chapter 7: The Mystery of the Trinity

1See pp. 37, 40, 43, 77.

2"Their formulae were not meant to make the incomprehensible comprehensible or to define it in formulae. They were designed to show that we cannot take any of the ways that try to make the incomprehensible comprehensible and are ready to sacrifice essential elements of the faith in order to attain this comprehensibility." Helmut Thielicke, *The Evangelical Faith,* trans. and ed. Geoffrey W. Bromiley (Grand Rapids: Eerdmans, 1977), 2:157.

3Leo Scheffczyk, "God: The Divine," *Encyclopedia of Theology: The Concise "Sacramentum Mundi,"* ed. Karl Rahner (New York: Seabury, 1975), p. 564.

4For a helpful discussion of the plural of majesty with regard to *Elohim,* see B. W. Anderson, "God, Names of," *Interpreter's Dictionary of the Bible,* ed. G. A. Buttrick (New York: Abingdon, 1962), 2:413.

5With Robert Lightner, among many others, I find the basis of the Trinity in the Bible. The difference is that Lightner maintains that the doctrine of the Trinity is revealed in the New Testament and not merely hinted at. Robert P. Lightner, *The First Fundamental: God* (Nashville: Nelson, 1973), p. 73.

6For Barth's discussion of the biblical roots of the doctrine of the Trinity, see *Church Dogmatics,* trans. G. W. Bromiley, ed. Bromiley and T. F. Torrance, 2d ed. (Edinburgh: T. & T. Clark, 1975), 1(1):304–33.

7Cited in Jaroslav Pelikan, *The Christian Tradition* (Chicago: University of Chicago Press, 1971), 1:196.

[8]Ibid., p. 198.

[9]"The Nicaeno–Constantinopolitan Creed," in Philip Schaff, *The Creeds of Christendom* (New York: Harper & Bros., 1919), 2:58.

[10]See Bonhoeffer's critique of subordinationism and modalism in *Christ the Center,* trans. John Bowden (New York: Harper & Row, 1966), pp. 102-4.

[11]See Ioan P. Couliano, *The Tree of Gnosis,* trans. H. S. Wiesner (San Francisco: HarperCollins, 1992); Giovanni Filoramo, *A History of Gnosticism* (Cambridge, Mass.: Blackwell, 1990); and Elaine Pagels, *The Gnostic Gospels* (New York: Random House, 1979).

[12]R. P. C. Hanson, *The Attractiveness of God* (Richmond, Va.: John Knox Press, 1973), p. 83.

[13]See Otto W. Heick, *A History of Christian Thought* (Philadelphia: Fortress, 1965), 1:117-18.

[14]See H. R. Mackintosh, *The Doctrine of the Person of Jesus Christ* (1913; reprint, Edinburgh: T. & T. Clark, 1962), p. 166.

[15]J. F. Bethune-Baker, *An Introduction to the Early History of Christian Doctrine* (London: Methuen, 1903), p. 107.

[16]The Athanasian Creed, no. 25. Schaff, *Creeds of Christendom,* 2:68.

[17]G. L. Bray. "Trinity," *New Dictionary of Theology,* ed. Sinclair B. Ferguson, David F. Wright and J. I. Packer (Downers Grove, Ill.: InterVarsity Press, 1988), p. 693.

[18]Paul Tillich, *A History of Christian Thought,* ed. Carl E. Braaten (New York: Harper & Row, 1968), p. 93. According to Pelikan, for Dionysius the true God is above all names, above being, above the incarnation and even above the Trinity. Pelikan, *Christian Tradition,* 1:347-48.

[19]Quoted in Aldous Huxley, *The Perennial Philosophy* (New York: Harper & Bros., 1945), p. 31.

[20]On the ladder of mysticism, see Anders Nygren, *Agape and Eros,* trans. Philip S. Watson (Philadelphia: Westminster Press, 1953), pp. 512-18, 633-37, 700-709.

[21]For a reformulation of the doctrine of the Trinity along Neoplatonic lines, see James P. Mackey, *The Christian Experience of God as Trinity* (London: SCM Press, 1983).

[22]John S. Whale, *Christian Doctrine* (Cambridge: Cambridge University Press, 1950), pp. 112-13.

[23]See Emil Brunner, *The Christian Doctrine of God,* trans. Olive Wyon (1950; reprint, Philadelphia: Westminster Press, 1974), pp. 205-40.

[24]Thielicke, *Evangelical Faith,* 2:170.

[25]Cyril C. Richardson, *The Doctrine of the Trinity* (New York: Abingdon, 1958), p. 113.

[26]Paul Tillich, *Systematic Theology* (Chicago: University of Chicago Press, 1963), 3:291-94.

[27]Ibid., p. 290.

[28]Tillich, *Systematic Theology* (1951), 1:228.

[29]G. W. H. Lampe, *God as Spirit* (Oxford: Clarendon, 1977).

[30]See the review of Lampe by Ray S. Anderson, *TSF News and Reviews,* January 1979, pp. 12–14.

[31]For his discussion, see *Church Dogmatics,* 2d ed., 1(1):348–83.

[32]Barth, *Church Dogmatics,* trans. T. H. L. Parker et al., ed. G. W. Bromiley and T. F. Torrance (Edinburgh: T. & T. Clark, 1957), 2(1):463.

[33]Barth, *Church Dogmatics,* trans. G. T. Thomson (Edinburgh: T. & T. Clark, 1936), 1(1):157.

[34]For a helpful discussion, see William J. Hill, *The Three-Personed God: The Trinity as a Mystery of Salvation* (Washington, D.C.: Catholic University of America Press, 1982), pp. 130–45.

[35]Cf. Karl Rahner, *Theological Investigations,* trans. Kevin Smyth (Baltimore: Helicon, 1966), 4:84, 91, 102.

[36]Walter Kasper, *The God of Jesus Christ,* trans. Matthew J. O'Connell (New York: Crossroad, 1984), p. 288.

[37]Rahner, *Theological Investigations,* 4:113.

[38]See Christopher B. Kaiser, "From Leuenberg to Minsk and Kappel: Trinitarian Theology in Orthodox-Reformed Dialogue," *Perspectives* 7, no. 4 (1992):11–12. Also see Thomas F. Torrance, *The Trinitarian Faith* (Edinburgh: T. & T. Clark, 1988), pp. 302–40.

[39]See Robert W. Jenson, *The Triune Identity* (Philadelphia: Fortress, 1982), esp. pp. 161ff.

[40]Jürgen Moltmann, *The Crucified God,* trans. R. A. Wilson and John Bowden (San Francisco: Harper & Row, 1974), p. 249.

[41]Ibid., pp. 246–48.

[42]Moltmann, *The Trinity and the Kingdom,* trans. Margaret Kohl (San Francisco: Harper & Row, 1981), p. 173.

[43]Paul D. Molnar, "The Function of the Immanent Trinity in the Theology of Karl Barth: Implications for Today," *Scottish Journal of Theology* 42, no. 3 (1990):384.

[44]See Leonard Hodgson, *The Doctrine of the Trinity* (New York: Charles Scribner's Sons, 1944), pp. 95–96, 183–87, 190–92.

[45]Schoonenberg speaks of "God becoming triune by a historical decision of himself." He calls his position "a christological humanism." See Piet Schoonenberg, *The Christ* (New York: Herder & Herder, 1971), pp. 86, 91; and his "Process or History in God?" *Theology Digest* 23, no. 1 (1975):38–44.

[46]Wolfhart Pannenberg, *Systematic Theology,* trans. Geoffrey W. Bromiley (Grand Rapids: Eerdmans, 1991), 1:324.

[47]Ibid., pp. 324–25, 334.

[48]See Ted Peters, *God as Trinity: Relationality and Temporality in Divine Life* (Louisville: Westminster/John Knox Press, 1993), p. 138.

[49]See ibid., p. 140.

[50]Ibid.

[51]Roger Olson, "Wolfhart Pannenberg's Doctrine of the Trinity," *Scottish Journal of Theology* 43, no. 2 (1990):203.

[52]See Peters, *God as Trinity*, pp. 146-87.

[53]Ibid., p. 147.

[54]Ibid., p. 179.

[55]Ibid., p. 186.

[56]See Catherine Mowry LaCugna, *God for Us: The Trinity and Christian Life* (San Francisco: HarperCollins, 1993).

[57]Peters, *God as Trinity*, p. 73.

[58]See Hill, *Three-Personed God.* Hill goes beyond Thomas Aquinas in allowing for genuine novelty in human history. See Mary Catherine Hilkert, "*Sacra Doctrina* in the Twentieth Century: The Theological Project of William J. Hill," in Hill, *Search for the Absent God* (New York: Crossroad, 1992), pp. 1-13.

[59]Hill, *Three-Personed God,* p. 281.

[60]Ibid., p. 277.

[61]Ibid., p. 272.

[62]Ibid.

[63]Ibid.

[64]Against the process view Hill contends that "the mark of divine love is not its sharing in suffering but its saving and rescuing from such evil." Hill, *Search for the Absent God,* p. 138.

[65]See Jenson's defense of "person" in the modern sense in his *Triune Identity,* pp. 144-48.

[66]Ron Rhodes comes dangerously close to tritheism when he speaks of three "personalities" or "personal self-distinctions" or "self-consciousnesses" within the Trinity. He contends, however, that these do not act independently. Rhodes, *Christ Before the Manger* (Grand Rapids: Baker, 1992), pp. 265-66.

[67]See Brunner, *Christian Doctrine of God,* p. 227.

[68]In its stress on the unity of God, Islam also underlines his incomprehensibility so that we never really know God in himself but only his will and work. The Islamic scholar Josef van Ess says that when a human being surrenders to God "it is to God's will, not to God as a person." The Islamic God is a God of power more than of love, whereas the trinitarian God not only *has* love but *is* love. See the discussion in Hans Küng et al., *Christianity and the World Religions: Paths of Dialogue with Islam, Hinduism and Buddhism* (New York: Doubleday, 1986), pp. 70-96; and Karen Armstrong, *A History of God: The 4000-Year Quest of Judaism, Christianity and Islam* (New York: Knopf, 1993), pp. 132-69.

[69]This illustration is open to misinterpretation. It could be used to support a covert unitarianism in which God appears first as Father, then as Son and finally as Spirit. Trinitarianism asserts that God is Father, Son and Spirit not successively but simultaneously.

[70]See further discussion on p. 201.

[71]Claude Welch, *In This Name* (New York: Charles Scribner's Sons, 1952), p. 284.

[72]Ibid.

[73]See Pelikan, *Christian Tradition,* 1:222-23.

[74]Jenson, *Triune Identity,* pp. 138-43.

[75]For important works in feminist theology, see Rosemary Radford Ruether, *Sexism and God-Talk: Toward a Feminist Theology* (Boston: Beacon, 1983); Elisabeth Schüssler Fiorenza, *In Memory of Her* (New York: Crossroad, 1983), and *Jesus, Miriam's Child, Sophia's Prophet: Critical Issues in Feminist Christology* (New York: Continuum, 1994); and Elizabeth A. Johnson, *She Who Is* (New York: Crossroad, 1992).

[76]Geoffrey Wainwright, *Doxology: The Praise of God in Worship, Doctrine and Life* (New York: Oxford University Press, 1980), p. 59.

[77]See Donald G. Bloesch, *The Struggle of Prayer* (1978; reprint, Colorado Springs: Helmers & Howard, 1988).

[78]See Johnson, *She Who Is,* pp. 129-30.

[79]See H. R. Mackintosh, *Types of Modern Theology* (London: Nisbet, 1937), p. 78. See Friedrich Schleiermacher, *The Christian Faith,* ed. H. R. Mackintosh and J. S. Stewart (New York: Harper & Row, 1963), p. 738.

[80]See Thomas J. J. Altizer, "William Blake and the Role of Myth in the Radical Christian Vision," in Thomas J. J. Altizer and William Hamilton, *Radical Theology and the Death of God* (Indianapolis: Bobbs-Merrill, 1966), pp. 171-91; Altizer, *The New Apocalypse: The Radical Christian Vision of William Blake* (East Lansing: Michigan State University Press, 1967).

[81]Mackintosh, *Types of Modern Theology,* p. 105.

[82]Gerald Heard, *A Preface to Prayer,* 4th ed. (New York: Harper, 1944), p. 126. He also spoke of God as "Absolute Reality beside which all the physical universe is only a significant dream." Heard, "My Discoveries in Vedanta," in *Vedanta for the Western World,* ed. Christopher Isherwood (New York: Viking, 1945), p. 62.

[83]For the discussion, see F. Ernest Stoeffler, *German Pietism During the Eighteenth Century* (Leiden: Brill, 1973), pp. 140-67, esp. 147-49.

[84]In the present Unitarian-Universalist Association God is an immanent force in humanity rather than a personal being above the world of space and time. See "Deleted Deity," *Time* 121, no. 26 (1983):62-63.

[85]Emanuel Swedenborg, *The True Christian Religion* (London: J. M. Dent & Sons, 1933), p. 37. The liturgy of the General Convention of the New Jerusalem in

the USA affirmed among its primary doctrines: "That there is one God, in whom there is a Divine Trinity; and that He is the Lord Jesus Christ." In Arthur Carl Piepkorn, *Profiles in Belief* (San Francisco: Harper & Row, 1978), 2:658. It is Jesus whom Swedenborgians address in prayer.

[86]See George Woodcock and Ivan Avakumovic, *The Doukhobors* (New York: Oxford University Press, 1968); Aylmer Maude, *A Peculiar People: The Doukhobors* (New York: AMS Press, 1970); Harry B. Hawthorn, ed., *The Doukhobors of British Columbia* (Vancouver: University of British Columbia Press, 1955); Marcus Bach, *Strange Sects and Curious Cults* (New York: Dodd, Mead, 1961), pp. 182–201; and Charles W. Ferguson, *The New Books of Revelations* (New York: Doubleday, Doran, 1931), pp. 110–32.

[87]See Robley E. Whitson, ed., *The Shakers: Two Centuries of Spiritual Reflection* (New York: Paulist, 1983); Robert S. Ellwood Jr., *Alternative Altars* (Chicago: University of Chicago Press, 1979), pp. 74–84; and Everett Webber, *Escape to Utopia* (New York: Hastings House, 1959), pp. 31–73.

[88]James E. Talmage, *A Study of the Articles of Faith* (reprint, Salt Lake City: Church of Jesus Christ of Latter-Day Saints, 1957), p. 42. See also B. H. Roberts, *The Mormon Doctrine of Deity* (Bountiful, Utah: Horizon, 1903).

[89]Mary Baker Eddy, *Science and Health, with Key to the Scriptures* (Boston: 1934), p. 588.

[90]Cf. Robert Jenson's model of later Western Trinitarianism, which is somewhat less subordinationist than mine:

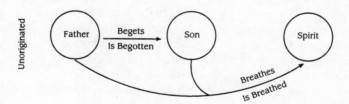

See his *Triune Identity,* p. 122. For the model that he proposes as a substitute, see p. 147.

[91]See Hubert Cunliffe-Jones and Benjamin Drewery, eds., *A History of Christian Doctrine* (Philadelphia: Fortress, 1980), pp. 93–94, 112–13.

[92]David N. Bell, *A Cloud of Witnesses* (Kalamazoo, Mich.: Cistercian Publications, 1989), pp. 87–89.

[93]According to Torrance the Augustinian view seems "to fall short of the biblical approach of Greek Patristic theology in which the Holy Spirit" is depicted "as a distinct and fully hypostatic or personal Mode of God's *self*-giving, parallel with but interpenetrating that of the Son, and as God of God in the same way

in which the Son is God of God." Thomas F. Torrance, *Reality and Scientific Theology* (Edinburgh: Scottish Academic Press, 1985), p. 191.

[94]I believe my model is consonant with early church tradition, which depicts the Spirit as proceeding from the Father *through* the Son, but it also leaves room for the idea that the Son is an active participant in this process. It resonates with Torrance's interpretation of Nicene theology: "There is, then, only one divine activity, that of God the Father through the Son and in the Spirit," though this one activity is manifested "in the distinctive operations of the three divine Persons" (*Trinitarian Faith*, pp. 233-36). I am at one with Jenson in his intention to underscore the reciprocity in the Trinity. One should note that neither Jenson's own model (see his *Triune Identity*, p. 147) nor mine contradicts the traditional notion of the Father as begetting, the Son as begotten and the Spirit as breathed. But they go beyond this notion in that they see an active or creative role for both Son and Spirit—not just in relation to the world but in relation to the Godhead.

[95]Gregory of Nazianzus had reservations about viewing the Father as the principle of the Trinity. "I am alarmed at the word 'principle,' lest I make him the Principle of inferiors, and insult him through the idea of precedence in honour." Still he could call the Father "greater" than the Son and Spirit because their equality derives from him. See Torrance, *Trinitarian Faith*, p. 239.

[96]God's essence can also be described as holy love or lordly freedom. God is the Holy One who loves, but in a threefold way—as Father, Son and Spirit. He is the one Lord who rules, but again in a threefold manner. This is why God can be envisioned as both one person and three persons—but never as three separate persons or three distinct personalities, for this would be tritheism.

[97]One should add that the Father too is dependent for his identity on the Son and Spirit, since he is always the Father *of* the Son and *in* the Spirit. The glory of the Father can only be the glory of the triune God.

[98]On other persons and movements that make the Spirit the all-inclusive category of divinity, see my discussion on pp. 178, 196, 198.

Chapter 8: The Biblical-Classical Synthesis

[1]For my earlier discussion, see Donald G. Bloesch, *A Theology of Word and Spirit* (Downers Grove, Ill.: InterVarsity Press, 1992), pp. 212-20.

[2]Vladimir Lossky, *The Vision of God,* trans. Asheleigh Moorhouse (Crestwood, N.Y.: St. Vladimir's Seminary Press, 1983), p. 67.

[3]See Reinhold Niebuhr, *The Nature and Destiny of Man,* 2 vols. (New York: Charles Scribner's Sons, 1951), esp. 1:4-25.

[4]See Reinhold Niebuhr, "Biblical Thought and Ontological Speculation in Tillich's Theology," in *The Theology of Paul Tillich,* ed. Charles W. Kegley and Robert W. Bretall (New York: Macmillan, 1952), pp. 216-17.

[5]Abraham Joshua Heschel, "The Concept of Man in Jewish Thought," in *The Concept of Man,* ed. S. Radhakrishnan and P. T. Raju (Lincoln, Nebr.: Johnsen, 1960), p. 124–25.

[6]For my earlier critique of Tillich, see Bloesch, *Theology of Word and Spirit,* pp. 149–52, 260–61.

[7]See chap. 1, n. 22.

[8]Samuel M. Zwemer, *The Glory of the Cross* (London: Marshall, Morgan & Scott, n.d.), p. 97.

[9]Ted Peters, *God as Trinity* (Louisville: Westminster/John Knox Press, 1993), p. 168.

[10]Ibid.

[11]R. P. C. Hanson, *The Attractiveness of God* (Richmond, Va.: John Knox Press, 1973), p. 77.

[12]Paul Tillich, *A History of Christian Thought,* ed. Carl E. Braaten (New York: Harper & Row, 1968), p. 29.

[13]David Ray Griffin, "Augustine and the Denial of Genuine Evil," in *The Problem of Evil,* ed. Michael L. Peterson (Notre Dame, Ind.: University of Notre Dame Press, 1992), p. 202.

[14]See Colin Gunton, "Augustine, the Trinity and the Theological Crisis of the West," *Scottish Journal of Theology* 43, no. 1 (1990):47.

[15]See John N. Findlay, "The Impersonality of God," in *God: The Contemporary Discussion,* ed. Frederick Sontag and M. Darrol Bryant (New York: Rose of Sharon Press, 1982), p. 191.

[16]Wolfhart Pannenberg, *Basic Questions in Theology,* trans. George H. Kehm (1971; reprint, Philadelphia: Westminster Press, 1983), 2:138.

[17]Anselm, *Cur Deus Homo,* in *St. Anselm: Basic Writings,* trans. S. W. Deane (LaSalle, Ill.: Open Court, 1962), p. 190.

[18]*Meister Eckhart: A Modern Translation,* ed. and trans. Raymond B. Blakney (New York: Harper & Bros., 1941), p. 65.

[19]Ibid., p. 85.

[20]Frederick W. Robertson, *Sermons Preached at Brighton* (New York: Harper & Bros., n.d.), p. 312. Cf.: God is "enthroned in His everlasting calmness, with no agitation of emotions in Him. To approach this state is to be like God. The more serene a man be—the more incapable of being ruffled and agitated by outward circumstances . . . the more nearly does he resemble God." Robertson, *"The Human Race" and Other Sermons* (New York: Harper & Bros., n.d.), pp. 41–42; cf. p. 126.

[21]A. A. Hodge, *The Atonement* (1867; Grand Rapids: Baker, 1974), p. 187.

[22]See pp. 91–96, 105–8.

[23]Cf. Gerald Heard: "Silence and darkness are almost essential conditions for a practical man's deepest worship. For his knowledge of himself, which is not

slight but intuitional, teaches him where his reason must stop and he with it wait, while the metareason does its work." Heard, *Is God in History?* (New York: Harper & Bros., 1950), p. 188.

[24]Carl F. H. Henry, *God, Revelation and Authority* (Waco, Tex.: Word, 1982), 5:304.

[25]James Oliver Buswell Jr., *A Systematic Theology of the Christian Religion* (Grand Rapids: Zondervan, 1962), 1:56–57. For an illuminating examination of the biblical-classical synthesis in modern conservative evangelicalism, see John Sanders, "Historical Considerations," in Clark Pinnock et al., *The Openness of God* (Downers Grove, Ill.: InterVarsity Press, 1994), pp. 94–96.

[26]For my earlier discussion, see pp. 113–14.

[27]G. Faggin, "Fate and Fatalism," *New Catholic Encyclopedia* (New York: McGraw-Hill, 1967), 5:850.

[28]Michael Maher, "Fatalism," *The Catholic Encyclopedia* (New York: Gilmary Society, 1913), 5:791–92.

[29]St. George Stock, "Fate (Greek & Roman)," *Encyclopaedia of Religion and Ethics,* ed. James Hastings (New York: Charles Scribner's Sons, 1914), 5:790.

[30]Cf. Aeschylus, *The Libation Bearers,* lines 105–6; *Prometheus Bound,* lines 104–6.

[31]See my discussion on pp. 113–16.

[32]Pannenberg, *Basic Questions in Theology,* 2:165.

[33]For the reappearance of fatalistic thought in deism, see Isaak August Dorner, *Divine Immutability,* trans. Robert R. Williams and Claude Welch (Minneapolis: Fortress, 1994), pp. 110–12. Also see pp. 83–85.

[34]See p. 118.

[35]Paul Tillich, *Systematic Theology* (Chicago: University of Chicago Press, 1951), 1:201.

[36]Reinhold Niebuhr, "Biblical Thought and Ontological Speculation in Tillich's Theology," in *Theology of Paul Tillich,* ed. Kegley and Bretall, pp. 216–27.

[37]Tillich questions the prayer that expects God to interfere in the conditions of human existence (*Systematic Theology,* 1:267). For him it is the faith that undergirds our prayer that transforms the existential situation rather than God's active response to our supplications.

[38]See Donald G. Bloesch, *Holy Scripture* (Downers Grove, Ill.: InterVarsity Press, 1994), pp. 278–302.

[39]Cf. Augustine *Of True Religion* 66. In *Augustine: Earlier Writings,* ed. John H. S. Burleigh (Philadelphia: Westminster Press, 1953), pp. 258–59.

[40]For a helpful discussion, see Hendrik M. Vroom, *Religions and the Truth,* trans. J. W. Rebel (Grand Rapids: Eerdmans, 1989), pp. 238–40.

[41]Niebuhr, *Christian Realism and Political Problems* (New York: Charles Scribner's Sons, 1953), p. 189.

[42]Niebuhr, *Nature and Destiny of Man,* 2:216.

⁴³Ibid., 2:217.

⁴⁴Niebuhr, *Christian Realism,* p. 188.

⁴⁵Ibid., p. 198.

⁴⁶Ibid., pp. 198–99.

⁴⁷For my critique of Niebuhr's doctrine of the Fall, see Donald G. Bloesch, *Essentials of Evangelical Theology* (San Francisco: Harper, 1978), 1:100–101, 104–5.

⁴⁸John Scotus Erigena, *Periphyseon: On the Division of Nature,* trans. Myra L. Uhlfelder (Indianapolis: Bobbs-Merrill, 1976), 1.69, p. 91.

⁴⁹Bonaventure, *The Mind's Road to God,* trans. George Boas (New York: Liberal Arts Press, 1953), p. 8.

⁵⁰Niels Thulstrup, "Commentator's Introduction," in Kierkegaard's *Philosophical Fragments,* trans. David F. Swenson and Howard V. Hong, 2d ed. (Princeton: Princeton University Press, 1962), p. lvi.

⁵¹*Selected Shorter Writings of Benjamin B. Warfield,* ed. John E. Meeter (Nutley, N.J.: Presbyterian & Reformed, 1973), 2:99–100. Theodore P. Letis sees Warfield as closer to the Enlightenment than to Protestant orthodoxy. See Letis, "B. B. Warfield, Common-Sense Philosophy and Biblical Criticism," *American Presbyterians* 69, no. 3 (1991):175–90, esp. 186–87.

⁵²Athanasius, *The Life of Antony and the Letter to Marcellinus,* ed. and trans. Robert C. Gregg (New York: Paulist, 1980), p. 88.

⁵³Reinhold Niebuhr, *Discerning the Signs of the Times* (New York: Charles Scribner's Sons, 1946), p. 172.

⁵⁴Ibid.

⁵⁵Reinhold Niebuhr, *Faith and History* (New York: Charles Scribner's Sons, 1949), p. 165.

⁵⁶Ibid.

⁵⁷See pp. 145–52.

⁵⁸Quoted in Eberhard Jüngel, *God as the Mystery of the World,* trans. Darrell L. Guder (Grand Rapids: Eerdmans, 1983), p. 322.

⁵⁹See Jürgen Moltmann, *The Spirit of Life,* trans. Margaret Kohl (Minneapolis: Fortress, 1992), p. 340.

⁶⁰Thomas à Kempis, *The Imitation of Christ,* trans. E. M. Blaiklock (Nashville: Nelson, 1981), pp. 97–98.

⁶¹Jaroslav Pelikan, *The Christian Tradition* (Chicago: University of Chicago Press, 1978), 3:102.

⁶²Cited in Wilhelm Pauck, *From Luther to Tillich,* ed. Marion Pauck (San Francisco: Harper & Row, 1984), p. 138.

⁶³Friedrich Schleiermacher, *On Religion,* trans. Terrence N. Tice (Richmond, Va.: John Knox Press, 1969), p. 121.

⁶⁴William J. Hill, *Search for the Absent God* (New York: Crossroad, 1992), pp.

128–41.

65Ibid., pp. 131–32.

66Ibid., p. 132.

67Ibid.

68Tillich, *Systematic Theology,* 1:281.

69On the nuances of meaning in the two Greek words for "blessed" that are used in these passages *(eulogētos* and *makarios),* see Luci Shaw, "Yes to Shame and Glory," *Christianity Today* 30, no. 18 (December 12, 1986): 22–24. For a more extended discussion, see Joseph A. Fitzmyer, *The Gospel According to Luke* (New York: Doubleday, 1979), pp. 364–65; 632–34.

70See Richard A. Muller, *Dictionary of Latin and Greek Theological Terms* (Grand Rapids: Baker, 1985), p. 57.

71Peter Kreeft, *Making Choices* (Ann Arbor: Servant, 1990), pp. 78–91.

72*Catechism of the Council of Trent for Parish Priests,* trans. and ed. John A. McHugh and Charles J. Callan (New York: Joseph F. Wagner, 1934), p. 138.

73Cited in David Manning White, ed., *The Affirmation of God* (New York: Macmillan, 1984), p. 195.

74Evelyn Underhill, *The Life of the Spirit and the Life of Today* (1922; reprint, San Francisco: Harper & Row, 1986), p. 73.

75Apocryphal texts like Tobit 12:9, Ecclus 3:30 and 2 Esdras 8:33 all teach that good works bring merit.

76In Craufurd Tait Ramage, *Great Thoughts from Classic Authors* (New York: John B. Alden, 1891), p. 445.

77Thomas F. Torrance, *The Doctrine of Grace in the Apostolic Fathers* (Edinburgh: Oliver & Boyd, 1948), p. 1.

78Ibid., p. 54.

79Ibid., p. 124.

80Athanasius, *The Life of Antony,* p. 46.

81John Cassian, *Third Conference of Abbot Chaeremon,* chap. 13 in *A Select Library of Nicene and Post-Nicene Fathers of the Christian Church* (2d series), ed. Philip Schaff and Henry Wace (New York: Christian Literature Co., 1894), 11:430.

82In Patrick Grant, *A Dazzling Darkness: An Anthology of Western Mysticism* (Grand Rapids: Eerdmans, 1985), pp. 244–45.

83Isaac of Nineveh, *Directions on Spiritual Training* in *Early Fathers from the Philokalia Together with Some Writings of . . . St. Isaac of Syria,* trans. and ed. E. Kadloubovsky and G. E. H. Palmer (London: Faber & Faber, 1954), p. 210.

84Bonaventure, "The Triple Way," in *The Works of Bonaventure,* trans. José de Vinck (Paterson, N.J.: St. Anthony Guild Press, 1960), 1:63.

85J. P. de Caussade, *Abandonment to Divine Providence,* ed. J. Ramière (St. Louis: B. Herder, 1921), pp. 134–35.

[86]See the discussion in Alister E. McGrath, *Iustitia Dei: A History of the Christian Doctrine of Justification* (Cambridge: Cambridge University Press, 1986), 1:85–87.

[87]McGrath maintains that for Thomas neither merit *de condigno* nor merit *de congruo* represents "a just claim on man's part before God," since justice in the strict sense "can only exist among equals." Ibid., p. 114.

[88]Texts that the Reformers often appealed to were Jn 1:16; Rom 3:23-24; 4:16; 1 Cor 15:10; Gal 2:16; Eph 2:8-10; and Tit 3:7.

[89]*Luther's Works,* ed. Hilton C. Oswald (St. Louis: Concordia, 1972), 25:90.

[90]One should note that the word "worthy" *(axios)* is used seven times in the New Testament. Its meaning is never "to make worthy" but ordinarily "to deem worthy." In 2 Thess 1:11-12 "Paul prays that God may deem them worthy because of that purpose and faith which he sees in them." John W. Bailey, "1 & 2 Thessalonians," in *Interpreter's Bible* (New York and Nashville: Abingdon, 1955), 11:324.

[91]Henry Ward Beecher, *Plymouth Pulpit: Sermons* (Boston: Pilgrim, 1875), 1:47.

[92]See my earlier discussion, pp. 128-36.

[93]Quoted in Niebuhr, *Nature and Destiny of Man,* 1:173. See Augustine, *Against Two Letters of the Pelagians,* chap. 7.

[94]Gregory of Nyssa, *The Lord's Prayer; The Beatitudes,* trans. and ed. Hilda C. Graef (Westminster, Md.: Newman, 1954), p. 31.

[95]Clement of Alexandria *On Spiritual Perfection, Miscellanies* 7 in *Alexandrian Christianity,* ed. John E. L. Oulton and Henry Chadwick (Philadelphia: Westminster Press, 1954), p. 102.

[96]Bengt Hoffman, trans. and ed., *The Theologia Germanica of Martin Luther* (New York: Paulist, 1980), p. 61.

[97]See Albrecht Ritschl, *The Christian Doctrine of Justification and Reconciliation,* trans. H. R. Mackintosh and A. B. Macaulay (Clifton, N.J.: Reference Book Publishers, 1966), pp. 376-84. For my earlier discussion, see Donald G. Bloesch, *Freedom for Obedience* (New York: Harper & Row, 1987), pp. 120-21.

[98]Niebuhr, *Nature and Destiny of Man,* 1:17.

[99]See Jacques Ellul's discussion in *To Will and to Do,* trans. C. Edward Hopkin (Philadelphia: Pilgrim, 1969), pp. 5-58, esp. 40.

[100]In David Manning White, ed., *The Search for God* (New York: Macmillan, 1983), p. 128.

[101]Ibid., p. 122.

[102]Kallistos Ware, "Hesychasm," *A Dictionary of Christian Spirituality,* ed. Gordon S. Wakefield (London: SCM Press, 1983), p. 190.

[103]Cited in Thomas Merton, *Contemplative Prayer* (New York: Doubleday Image, 1971), p. 30.

[104]Ibid., p. 90.

[105]See G. D. Dragas, "Hesychasm," *New Dictionary of Theology,* ed. Sinclair Ferguson, David F. Wright and J. I. Packer (Downers Grove, Ill.: InterVarsity Press, 1988), p. 298; Ware, "Hesychasm," *Dictionary of Christian Spirituality,* pp. 189-90; *On the Invocation of the Name of Jesus* (London: Fellowship of St. Alban & St. Sergius, 1949); and *The Way of a Pilgrim,* trans. Helen Bacovcin (New York: Doubleday Image, 1992).

[106]*The Sermons and Conferences of John Tauler,* trans. Walter Elliott (Washington, D.C.: Apostolic Mission House, 1910), p. 320.

[107]*The Way of a Pilgrim,* p. 146.

[108]Paul Tillich, *The Eternal Now* (New York: Charles Scribner's Sons, 1963), p. 86.

[109]Tillich espouses a much more this-worldly mysticism where God is found in the passions of the flesh rather than beyond materiality.

[110]See P. T. Forsyth, *The Soul of Prayer,* 2d ed. (London: Independent Press, 1951), esp. pp. 57-70, 81-92.

[111]See Friedrich Heiler, *Prayer,* trans. and ed. Samuel McComb and J. Edgar Park (New York: Oxford University Press, 1958), pp. 353-63.

[112]See Richard J. Bauckham, *Jude, 2 Peter,* Word Biblical Commentary 50 (Waco, Tex.: Word, 1983), p. 180.

[113]William A. Clebsch, preface, in Athanasius, *Life of Antony,* p. xvi.

[114]Ibid.

[115]Cf. *Maximus Confessor: Selected Writings,* trans. George C. Berthold (New York: Paulist, 1985), pp. 167, 210-11.

[116]*Catechism of Council of Trent,* p. 136.

[117]Ibid.

[118]Irving Singer, *The Nature of Love,* 2d ed. (Chicago: University of Chicago Press, 1984), 1:338-39. Not surprisingly Nygren disputes the association of the Greek idea of deification with Luther's understanding. Anders Nygren, *Agape and Eros,* trans. Philip S. Watson (Philadelphia: Westminster Press, 1953), p. 734.

[119]The church fathers often appealed to 2 Pet 1:4 in support of their doctrine of the deification of redeemed humanity. One should note that this verse attributes the ills of humanity to sin rather than to finitude or mortality (as in the Platonic view). Other texts cited but not always in context were Ps 82:6, Ps 116:11 and Jn 10:33-36. See the helpful discussion by G. W. H. Lampe in *A History of Christian Doctrine,* ed. Hubert Cunliffe-Jones with Benjamin Drewery (Philadelphia: Fortress, 1980), pp. 149-55.

[120]Kurt Rudolph, *Gnosis,* trans. Peter Coxon et al., ed. Robert McLachlan Wilson (San Francisco: Harper & Row, 1983), p. 192.

[121]Augustine, *The Confessions of St. Augustine,* trans. and ed. E. M. Blaiklock (Nashville: Nelson, 1983), 4.16, p. 98.

[122]*John of Ruysbroeck: The Adornment of the Spiritual Marriage,* trans. C. A. Wynschenk Dom, ed. Evelyn Underhill (London: John M. Watkins, 1951), chap.

57, p. 127.

[123]Hans Denck, *On the Law of God*, cited in White, ed., *Search for God*, p. 114.

[124]*Angelus Silesius: The Cherubinic Wanderer*, trans. Maria Shrady (New York: Paulist, 1986), p. 94.

[125]Madame Guyon, *A Method of Prayer*, trans. Dugald Macfadyen (London: James Clarke, 1902), p. 103.

[126]See the discussion in Frederick Copleston, *A History of Philosophy* (reprint, New York: Doubleday, 1985), 7:126–35.

[127]See pp. 178, 233.

[128]Reinhold Niebuhr, *The Self and the Dramas of History* (New York: Charles Scribner's Sons, 1955), pp. 98–99.

[129]See, for example, Robertson, *"The Human Race" and Other Sermons*, p. 111. Note that Robertson began as an evangelical and moved gradually toward a Broad Church Anglicanism. In Barth's view God is already reconciled to humanity by his inner decision of love, but fallen humanity still needs to be reconciled to God. Barth bases his position on God's all-loving nature rather than on God's unchangeableness.

[130]Cf. Nicephorus the Solitary: "We cannot be reconciled with God and be intimate with Him if we will not first return to ourselves and enter into the depths of ourselves." See "Directives of the Fathers on Prayer of the Heart," in *The Way of a Pilgrim*, p. 181.

[131]Whether Origen explicitly taught reincarnation is an open question, but it is implied in some of his ideas. See D. F. Wright, "Metempsychosis," *New Dictionary of Theology*, p. 424; and Geddes MacGregor, *Dictionary of Religion and Philosophy* (New York: Paragon House, 1989), pp. 531–32; and MacGregor, *Reincarnation in Christianity* (Wheaton, Ill.: Quest, 1978), pp. 48–62.

[132]R. E. O. White, "Resurrection of the Dead," *Evangelical Dictionary of Theology*, ed. Walter A. Elwell (Grand Rapids: Baker, 1984), p. 943.

[133]Basil of Caesarea, *Ascetical Works*, trans. M. Monica Wagner (New York: Fathers of the Church Inc., 1950), p. 435.

[134]See Heinrich Quistorp, *Calvin's Doctrine of the Last Things*, trans. Harold Knight (Richmond, Va.: John Knox Press, 1955), pp. 55–107.

[135]Oscar Cullmann, *Immortality of the Soul or Resurrection of the Dead?* (London: Epworth, 1958), p. 60.

Chapter 9: The Biblical-Modern Synthesis

[1]See my earlier discussion on pp. 13, 264.

[2]Garrett E. Paul, "Why Troeltsch? Why Today? Theology for the 21st Century," *Christian Century* 110, no. 20 (1993):679.

[3]Teilhard de Chardin gives cogent expression to the new worldview: "All that exists is matter becoming spirit." Pierre Teilhard de Chardin, *Human Energy*,

trans. J. M. Cohen (London: Collins, 1969), p. 57.

[4]See Nicolas Berdyaev, *Truth and Revelation,* trans. R. M. French (New York: Collier Books, 1962).

[5]Roland E. Murphy, "The Theological Legacy of Karl Rahner," *Books & Religion* 16, no. 1 (Winter 1989): 10.

[6]Plato is still important in modern spirituality. Philosophers like Whitehead, who speaks of eternal objects, reflect Plato's emphasis on transcendental ideals.

[7]See Sallie McFague, *The Body of God: An Ecological Theology* (Minneapolis: Fortress, 1993).

[8]McFague describes God as "the spirit that is the breath, the life, of the universe" (p. 144). She also says that God is not primarily "the orderer and controller of the universe but its source and empowerment, the breath that enlivens and energizes it" (p. 145).

[9]Frederick Copleston, *A History of Philosophy* (reprint, New York: Doubleday, 1985), 7:86. See I. H. von Fichte, *On the Nature of the Scholar,* 2.5.

[10]See *The Empirical Theology of Henry Nelson Wieman,* ed. Robert W. Bretall (New York: Macmillan, 1963), p. 281.

[11]Tillich, *Systematic Theology* (Chicago: University of Chicago Press, 1951), 1:110, 186–92.

[12]Alan Watts, *Behold the Spirit* (New York: Vintage, 1971), p. xviii.

[13]Nikos Kazantzakis, *The Saviors of God: Spiritual Exercises,* trans. Kimon Friar (New York: Simon and Schuster, 1960), p. 103.

[14]Friedrich Schleiermacher, *On Religion: Speeches to Its Cultured Despisers,* trans. John Oman (New York: Harper & Row, 1958), pp. 36, 237.

[15]See Alfred North Whitehead, *Process and Reality* (New York: Macmillan, 1929), p. 528.

[16]See Paul D. Molnar, "The Function of the Immanent Trinity in the Theology of Karl Barth: Implications for Today," *Scottish Journal of Theology* 42, no. 3 (1990):387. Molnar here compares Barth with Moltmann.

[17]See Julian Roberts, *German Philosophy* (Atlantic Highlands, N.J.: Humanities Press International, 1988), p. 214.

[18]See Donald G. Bloesch, *Holy Scripture* (Downers Grove, Ill.: InterVarsity Press, 1994), pp. 240–44.

[19]Peter C. Hodgson, *God in History* (Nashville: Abingdon, 1989), p. 239.

[20]See Louis J. Shein, *The Philosophy of Lev Shestov* (Queenston, Ontario: Edwin Mellen, 1991), pp. 21, 63.

[21]Lev Shestov, *Kierkegaard and the Existential Philosophy,* trans. Elinor Hewitt (Athens, Ohio: Ohio University Press, 1969), p. 95. While these words come from Kierkegaard, they apply even more to Shestov, who is here giving his full endorsement. Kierkegaard is a transitional figure who incorporates elements of all three spiritualities in question.

[22]John Baillie, *The Roots of Religion in the Human Soul* (1926; reprint, London: James Clarke, 1937), p. 75.

[23]See Sheila Greeve Davaney, *Divine Power: A Study of Karl Barth and Charles Hartshorne* (Philadelphia: Fortress, 1986), p. 225.

[24]Charles Hartshorne, "The Dipolar Conception of Deity," *Review of Metaphysics* 21, no. 2 (1967):285.

[25]Ideological multiculturalism, according to one definition, promotes the virulent notion that "race is the determinant of a human being's mind, that the mind cannot, and should not, try to wrest itself from its biological or sociological origins. . . . 'Multiculturalism' holds that the traditional idea of free thought is an illusion propagated by the spoilers of freedom, by the relations of power that obtain in any given society. It holds, more specifically, that the old liberal notion of freedom is only a sentimental mask of a power structure that is definitionally oppressive of those who are not white Western males." "The Derisory Tower," *The New Republic* 204, no. 7 (1991):5-6.

[26]See Schleiermacher, *On Religion,* trans. Oman, pp. 210-53.

[27]For my discussion of providence, see pp. 113-16, 211-13.

[28]Charles Hartshorne, *Beyond Humanism* (Chicago: Willett, Clark, 1937), p. 131.

[29]Theodore Roszak, *Unfinished Animal: The Aquarian Frontier and the Evolution of Consciousness* (New York: Harper & Row, 1975), p. 102.

[30]*The Philosophy of Nietzsche,* introduction by Willard Huntington Wright (New York: Modern Library, 1927), p. 183.

[31]See Reinhold Niebuhr, *Faith and History* (New York: Charles Scribner's Sons, 1949), pp. 1-101.

[32]See Donald Bloesch, *Freedom for Obedience* (San Francisco: Harper & Row, 1987).

[33]P. T. Forsyth, *The Cruciality of the Cross,* 2d ed. (London: Independent Press, 1948), p. 33.

[34]Peter Kreeft, "Gender and the Will of God," *Crisis* 11, no. 8 (1993):23.

[35]Ted Peters, *God as Trinity* (Louisville: Westminster/John Knox Press, 1993), p. 149.

[36]Ibid., p. 175.

[37]Norman Pittenger, *God's Way with Men* (Valley Forge, Penn.: Judson, 1971), p. 154.

[38]Norman L. Geisler, "Process Theology," in *Tensions in Contemporary Theology,* ed. Stanley N. Gundry and Alan F. Johnson (Chicago: Moody Press, 1976), p. 276. God does indeed acquire new relationships and activities, yet these do not add to God's perfection but reveal and confirm it.

[39]See my earlier discussion in chap. 5, p. 127.

[40]This perfection is to be understood, however, not in the Greek sense of benign imperturbability but in the biblical sense of unfailing love. See chap. 4, n. 92.

[41]Unlike the river of the water of life, the rivers of this passing world are not inviolable but ever changing. This is why the river metaphor finds ready acceptance in the new spirituality. See William R. Taylor's exegesis of Ps 46:1-8 in *Interpreter's Bible*, ed. George A. Buttrick (New York: Abingdon, 1955), 4:242-43. Scripture also describes the transcendent power as a mighty wind that blows as it wills but ever remains what it eternally is—the breath of the living God (cf. Gen 1:2; Ezek 37:1-14; Jn 3:5-8; Acts 2:2). See Wolfhart Pannenberg's helpful discussion on the linking of "wind" and "Spirit" in *Systematic Theology*, trans. Geoffrey W. Bromiley (Grand Rapids: Eerdmans, 1994), 2:77-79.

[42]William J. Hill, *Search for the Absent God* (New York: Crossroad, 1992), p. 161. On Hill's divergences from Thomas Aquinas, see Mary Catherine Hilkert, "*Sacra Doctrina* in the Twentieth Century," in Hill, *Search for the Absent God*, pp. 1-13.

[43]Hill, *Search for the Absent God*, p. 161.

[44]Ibid., p. 160. This is close to Barth, who argued that God suffers not *in* God but *as* God in Jesus Christ. In Barth's theology, however, God's suffering in humanity reflects the self-abasement and self-emptying that characterize the inner life of the Trinity. See Karl Barth, *Church Dogmatics*, trans. G. W. Bromiley, ed. G. W. Bromiley and T. F. Torrance (Edinburgh: T. & T. Clark, 1958), 4(2):357-58. Also see John Thompson, *Modern Trinitarian Perspectives* (New York: Oxford University Press, 1994), pp. 55-58.

[45]One could also say that God's glory is enhanced by his condescension to our level in Jesus Christ, but this is to the eye of the human creature. From a deeper perspective we can only assume that the event of the incarnation does not increase the glory God already possesses but rather extends it to the created order.

[46]See Georgia Harkness, *The Recovery of Ideals* (New York: Charles Scribner's Sons, 1937), pp. 156-58; and Whitehead, *Process and Reality*, pp. 524-26. In its depiction of God as the molder of chaos into order and beauty, modern idealism shows its rootage in classical philosophy. For the evangelical Christian the world is more than the product of artistry and craftsmanship: it is the arena of redemption from sin and lostness.

Like Whitehead, with whom she acknowledged an affinity, Georgia Harkness was both an idealist and a naturalist. As an idealist she believed in God as organizing mind and in the reality of eternal forms or ideals. But she also saw God as the "Power within the universe" that directs us toward the eternal ideals (p. 156). God did not create the world ex nihilo, but the created universe is "an eternal process—the never-beginning and never-ceasing activity of an immanent yet transcendent deity" (p. 169). In this perspective God is limited both by the inertia of nature and by chance, which he "struggles to overcome"

(p. 180). It should be noted that Harkness was a respected Methodist theologian as well as a keen philosopher of religion. She described her position as "creative idealism" (pp. 29-31, 185).

[47]Henry Nelson Wieman and Walter Marshall Horton, *The Growth of Religion* (Chicago: Willett, Clark, 1938), p. 363.

[48]See Clark Pinnock, Richard Rice, John Sanders, William Hasker and David Basinger, *The Openness of God* (Downers Grove, Ill.: InterVarsity Press, 1994). The title suggests an affinity with the view of process theologians, since their God is open to the world by necessity. For open-view theists God's openness is an act of his freedom.

[49]Open-view theists as well as process theists would be prone to attribute the Holocaust to the shameful failure of human beings to harness the forces of human good rather than to the secret will of an all-powerful God who remains hidden even in his revelation. From my perspective the Holocaust and other acts of genocide testify both to the abysmal depths of human depravity and to the implacable reality of a superhuman antigod power in the world (the devil) that is unwittingly made to serve the ultimate purposes of a God who is laying the groundwork for a new world where sin and death will no longer exist. Barthian theology would say that the Holocaust is not what God expressly wills but what God negates, rejects and condemns and yet allows to happen for reasons that presently elude human comprehension. For an illuminating discussion of the Holocaust and its theological implications, see Richard L. Rubenstein and John K. Roth, *Approaches to Auschwitz: The Holocaust and Its Legacy* (Atlanta: John Knox Press, 1987).

[50]Pinnock et al., *Openness of God*, p. 114.

[51]Ibid., p. 159.

[52]Ibid., p. 163.

[53]Ibid., p. 119.

[54]Ibid.

[55]Ibid., p. 122.

[56]Ibid., p. 32.

[57]Ibid., p. 124.

[58]Ibid., p. 116.

[59]One should note that the God of process theology is free to choose some other world than this one. But he must choose *some* world if he is to exist as deity.

[60]Ibid., p. 133.

[61]Ibid., p. 194.

[62]Ibid., p. 161.

[63]Ibid., p. 173.

[64]My position is neither compatibilism nor incompatibilism. I do not believe that divine determination and human freedom can ever be made fully compatible

with human reason, but neither do I think that they are necessarily incompatible. Freedom in the Christian sense is indeed incompatible with a God of unrestrained power in which the distinction between good and evil is eclipsed. Both compatibilists and incompatibilists build their case mainly on the logic of analytic reasoning, and such reasoning is indeed to be held in high respect. The problem is that the mystery of God's self-revelation in Jesus Christ cannot be captured in either analytic or synthetic reasoning. The mystery of the incarnation and the mystery of God's foreordination through human self-determination baffle human reason, but they do not negate reason. The mystery of faith is suprarational, but it is not irrational. We can gain some light from these mysteries but must not presume to comprehend them. I subscribe to what Frederick Ferré calls "the logic of obedience": we begin to understand only when we bow and submit to the mystery in faith and resolve to walk the pathway that this mystery reveals to us. See Frederick Ferré, *Language, Logic and God* (New York: Harper, 1969), pp. 78-93. (Note that Ferré makes clear that this is not his own position.) For a contemporary defense of compatibilism, see Mark Shaw, *Doing Theology with Huck and Jim* (Downers Grove, Ill.: InterVarsity Press, 1993), pp. 121-35. Other current works on this subject that merit serious consideration are D. A. Carson, *Divine Sovereignty and Human Responsibility: Biblical Perspectives in Tension* (Grand Rapids: Baker, 1994); and I. John Hesselink, *Sovereign Grace and Human Freedom: How They Coalesce* (Grand Rapids: Eerdmans, 1996).

[65] I am here close to James I. Packer, who regards divine sovereignty and human responsibility as an antinomy that defies rational resolution but throws much light on human experience. See Packer, *Evangelism and the Sovereignty of God* (Chicago: InterVarsity Press, 1961), pp. 18-36.

[66] Genuine freedom is not a freedom to go in two directions, to evil as well as to good, but it is a freedom for God. It is not Hercules standing at the crossroads but Mary submitting to the directives of the angel of God.

[67] God is not subject to any contingency external to himself, but contingency is included in his being, so that he acts freely, often surprisingly and unexpectedly, but never capriciously. As Barth poignantly declares, "There is in God both supreme necessity and supreme contingency. This supreme contingency in the essence of God which is not limited by any necessity, the inscrutable concrete element in His essence, inscrutable because it never ceases or is exhausted—is His will." *Church Dogmatics,* trans. T. H. L. Parker et al., ed. G. W. Bromiley and T. F. Torrance (Edinburgh: T. & T. Clark, 1957), 2(1):548.

[68] See Donald G. Bloesch, *Essentials of Evangelical Theology* (San Francisco: Harper, 1978), 1:181-222.

[69] Pinnock et al., *Openness of God,* p. 175.

[70] Ibid.

71While Barth sees evil as inexplicable and irrational, he does not regard it as outside the sovereign rule of God. It is allowed only in order to be overthrown and dispelled from God's good creation. It is forced to serve the kingdom of God even though it contradicts this kingdom. See *Church Dogmatics,* trans. G. W. Bromiley and R. J. Ehrlich, ed. Bromiley and T. F. Torrance (Edinburgh: T. & T. Clark, 1961) 3(3):349–68; *Church Dogmatics,* trans. G. W. Bromiley, ed. Bromiley and T. F. Torrance (Edinburgh: T. & T. Clark, 1961), 4(3a):185–93.

72I here appear to be close to Clark Pinnock, whose position reflects that of the other authors in this study: "God's openness to the world is freely chosen, not compelled" (*Openness of God,* p. 112). Pinnock says nothing, however, of God being free to take back his openness to the world. My principal difference with Pinnock and his colleagues is that I find it supremely difficult to reconcile a God who continues to learn and grow with the sovereign, eternal God of the Bible.

73Pinnock et al., *Openness of God,* p. 176. Basinger makes clear that he personally finds the open view the most plausible and rationally appealing, though other views may also make a justifiable claim to self-consistency and comprehensiveness. One should note that in this concluding section much is said of logical consistency but little of biblical fidelity.

74Other Christian scholars who give a measure of support to open-view theism, also sometimes called the moral government theory, are Keith Ward, Anthony Kenny, Gregory Boyd, Stephen Davis, Axel D. Steuer and James William McClendon Jr. See Steuer and McClendon, eds., *Is God God?* (Nashville: Abingdon, 1981). A conservative critique of this position is found in Robert A. Morey, *Battle of the Gods: The Gathering Storm in Modern Evangelicalism* (Southbridge, Mass.: Crown, 1989). This book is marred by its wholesale condemnation of authors who raise any question whatever about the credibility and sufficiency of classical theism. We must be charitable and gracious in our theological criticisms even while resolutely adhering to the truth as we see it. Such charity is possible, however, only when we recognize the element of relativity and sinful bias in our own position, only when we confess that our thoughts too lie under the judgment of a holy God.

75While I prefer to envisage the future as partly open, I do not mean that any part of the future is outside the compass of God's design and direction (as in indeterminacy) but that the future is partly dependent on human determination. My principal criticism of open-view theism is that it assumes that God surrenders control when he gives humans freedom. But God is simply choosing to exercise his control in a different way—indirectly rather than directly.

Name Index

Achtemeier, Elizabeth, *76*
Adams, James Luther, *270, 292*
Aeschylus, *212, 302*
Alexander, Samuel, *242*
Althaus, Paul, *279*
Altizer, Thomas J. J., *195, 298*
Ames, Edward Scribner, *54, 271*
Anderson, B. W., *294*
Anderson, Ray, *178, 296*
Anselm, *66, 91, 186, 209, 301*
Aquinas, Thomas, *9, 15, 34, 35, 39, 45,
 51, 66, 67, 82, 83, 91, 116, 183, 206,
 214, 216, 217, 226, 268, 269, 273, 289,
 297, 305, 310*
Aristotle, *33, 36, 39, 47, 128, 191, 216,
 221, 224, 243, 270*
Arius, *121, 171, 178, 191, 197*
Arminius, Jacobus, *273*
Armstrong, Karen, *297*
Athanasius, *16, 171, 174, 203, 218, 225,
 235, 303, 304, 306*
Augustine, *15, 16, 40, 65, 75, 81, 82, 91,
 115, 152, 167, 174, 175, 186, 192, 202,
 203, 206, 209, 214, 219, 225, 226, 227,
 229, 231, 235, 236, 237, 258, 269, 273,
 276, 285, 289, 292, 302, 306*
Aurobindo, Sri, *17, 264*
Avakumovic, Ivan, *299*

Bach, Marcus, *299*
Baillie, John, *246, 309*
Baily, John W., *305*
Barth, Karl, *1, 9, 14, 16, 23, 33, 35, 37, 41,
 48, 49, 52, 56, 58, 59, 63, 77, 79, 84, 85,
 86, 90, 93, 94, 98, 100, 103, 105, 115,
 116, 117, 126, 130, 131, 132, 133, 135,
 141, 163, 164, 167, 168, 169, 178, 179,
 180, 181, 182, 185, 203, 251, 258, 268,*
 *269, 270, 271, 272, 274, 277, 278, 279,
 280, 282, 285, 287, 288, 290, 293, 296,
 307, 308, 309, 310, 312, 313*
Basil of Caesarea, *180, 240, 307*
Basinger, David, *255, 256, 311, 313*
Battles, Ford Lewis, *282, 294*
Bauckham, Richard J., *306*
Beecher, Henry Ward, *17, 72, 83, 140,
 228, 274, 277, 289, 305*
Bell, David N., *202, 299*
Bennett, John, *289*
Berdyaev, Nicolas, *242, 308*
Bergson, Henri, *18, 242, 264*
Berkouwer, G. C., *279, 288*
Bethge, Eberhard, *283*
Bethune-Baker, J. F., *174, 295*
Bilaniuk, Petro, *287*
Bizer, Ernst, *277, 282*
Blake, William, *195, 298*
Blakney, Raymond B., *284, 291, 301*
Blumhardt, Christoph, *1*
Boehme, Jakob, *38, 130, 133, 195, 244,
 266*
Boethius, *86*
Bolton, Samuel, *165, 294*
Bonaventure, *217, 225, 303, 304*
Bonhoeffer, Dietrich, *105, 154, 157, 158,
 264, 283, 292*
Booth, William, *152, 162*
Bouwsma, William J., *289*
Bowden, John, *271, 279, 283, 287, 295,
 296*
Boyd, Gregory, *313*
Braaten, Carl E., *265, 274, 295, 301*
Braden, Charles S., *266*
Bray, Gerald, *266, 279, 295*
Bretall, Robert W., *265, 308*
Bromiley, Geoffrey W., *75, 268, 272, 273,*

Subject Index

Scripture Index